The Thin Blue Lifeline

Ellis Amdur, M.A., N.C.C., C.M.H.S.
Chief John Hutchings, M.A.

Verbal De-escalation of Mentally Ill
and Emotionally Disturbed People

A Comprehensive Guidebook for

Law Enforcement Officers

An Edgework Book
www.edgework.info

Notes and Notices

The Thin Blue Lifeline: Verbal De-escalation of Mentally Ill and Emotionally Disturbed People

By Ellis Amdur, M.A., N.C.C., C.M.H.S and Chief John Hutchings, M.A. © 2011

ISBN: 978-0-9823762-8-7

A Message to Our Readers

Edgework is committed to offering the best of our years of experience and study in the interest of professional and public safety. We ask that you express your respect for these intentions and honor our work by adhering strictly to the copyright protection notice you'll find below. By choosing NOT to reproduce these materials, you're supporting our work and making it possible for us to continue to develop materials that will enhance the safety of both the professionals for whom this book is written and the public. We thank you sincerely for your vigilance in respecting our rights!

Credits

Photographs by: Dreamstime.com
Illustrations by: Shoko Zama
Design: Soundview Design Studio

Contents

Books by the Author (and Co-Author) vi

In Gratitude For Expert Critique vii

Introduction ix

Preface: It's About Safety xi

Language in the Text xiii

Historical Note xvii

Section I   Core Requirements for De-escalation and Control of
**   Agitated, Aggressive or Mentally Ill Individuals** 1

Chapter 1   The Essentials 3

Chapter 2   Threat Assessment 9

Chapter 3   Honing Intuition 15

Section I   Centering—Standing with Strength and Grace in Crisis Situations 19

Chapter 4   Introduction to Centering 21

Chapter 5   Stillness in Motion 23

Chapter 6   Peer Support Is a Survival Tactic 25

Chapter 7   It's Not Personal Unless You Make It So 27

Chapter 8   Circular Breathing: Be the Eye in the Center of the Hurricane 31

Chapter 9   The Intoxication and Joy of Righteous Anger 37

Section III   Dealing With Unusual, Intense, and Eccentric Communication Styles 39

Chapter 10   Overview 41

Chapter 11   Rigid Personality 43

Chapter 12   Tell It Like it Is: Communication With Concrete Thinkers 47

Chapter 13   Information Processing and Retention: Consolidating Gains 49

Chapter 14   Coping With Stubborn Refusals 51

Chapter 15   Stuck: Coping with Repetitive Demands, Questions, and Obsessions 53

Chapter 16   The Need for Reassurance 55

Chapter 17   Dealing With Mood Swings 57

Chapter 18   They Aren't Moving: What to do? 59

Chapter 19   Should a Police Officer Ever Apologize? 61

Chapter 20   Useful Tactics for Dealing With Symptoms of Paranoia and Persecution 63

Section IV   **Recognizing the Strategies of Manipulative and Opportunistic Individuals**......67

Chapter 21   Divide and Confuse: Borderline Personality Disorder and Splitting...........................69

Chapter 22   Bad Intentions: Recognizing the Strategies of Manipulative and Opportunistic Individuals 73

Chapter 23   The Psychopath 77

Section V   **Communication With Those With Severe Mental Illness or Other Conditions That Cause Severe Disability** 83

Chapter 24   Overview..85

Chapter 25   Struggling in a Fog: Dealing With Symptoms of Disorganization..........................89

Chapter 26   Dropping Stones in a Well: Latency 93

Chapter 27   Withdrawal From Intoxicating Substances...95

Chapter 28   Psychosis: Delusions and Hallucinations 97

Chapter 29   Communication With Someone Who Is Experiencing Delusions or Hallucinations....101

Chapter 30   Tactics for Dealing With Symptoms of Mania...111

Chapter 31   Communication With Elderly Demented People 117

Section VI   **Suicidal Individuals**..121

Chapter 32   Why Is Suicide a Concern of Law Enforcement? 123

Chapter 33   The Basics of Intervention With Someone You Believe Might Be Suicidal 125

Chapter 34   Essential Questions 129

Chapter 35   The Art of Communication With the Suicidal Person 133

Chapter 36   Suicide as Self-murder: A Taxonomy 137

Chapter 37   Suicide-by-Cop 141

Chapter 38   Self-mutilation and Para-suicidal Behavior 145

Chapter 39   Crying Wolf: Identifying and Helping Para-suicidal Individuals.............147

Section VII   **Recognition of Patterns of Aggression** 149

Chapter 40   The Nature of Aggression 151

Chapter 41   Why Would Someone Become Aggressive?...157

Chapter 42   What Does Escalation Look Like? 161

Section VIII   **De-escalation of Angry Individuals** 167

Chapter 43   Core Principles of Intervention With Angry People................................171

Chapter 44   Physical Organization in the Face of Aggression 173

Chapter 45   The Tone and Quality of Your Voice for De-escalation 177

Chapter 46   Dealing With People Across the Spectrum of Anger 179

Chapter 47   Diamonds in the Rough: Essential Strategies for De-escalation of Anger 183

Chapter 48   Tactical Paraphrasing: The Gold Standard With Angry People..........................189

Chapter 49   Some Guidelines on Limit Setting..197

Chapter 50   Techniques That Don't Work: The Big Mistakes That Seemed Like Such Good Ideas 199

Section IX   **A Consideration of Communication With Mentally Ill, Emotionally Disturbed, and Drug Affected Youth** 203
Chapter 51   Working With Potentially Aggressive Youth 205
Chapter 52   No Brake Pads: A Consideration of the Impulsive Youth 209
Chapter 53   Contact Disorder: Fierce Youth 211
Chapter 54   Dynamite Under a Rock: Explosive Kids 213
Chapter 55   Opposition-Defiant Kids: "Even if You Make Me, I'll Still Make You Miserable" 215
Chapter 56   Post Traumatic Stress Disorder in Youth 217
Chapter 57   Pseudo-Nihilism 219

Section X   **Managing Rage and Violence** 221
Chapter 58   Preface to Rage 223
Chapter 59   Chaotic Rage: A Consideration of Rage Emerging From Various Disorganized States 225
Chapter 60   Terrified Rage 235
Chapter 61   Hot Rage 239
Chapter 62   Predatory or Cool Rage 253
Chapter 63   Feeding Frenzy—Mob Rage 257
Chapter 64   Deceptive Rage 261
Chapter 65   The Aftermath: What Happens Within the Mind, Individual After an Aggressive Incident? 263
Chapter 66   Managing Threats to Your Family 265
Chapter 67   Conclusion 267

Recommended Reading List 269

Appendices 271
Appendix A   Setting Up a Crisis Intervention Training (CIT) Program 273
Appendix B   Example of a Plan Developed to Assist a Chronically Para-suicidal Individual 275
Appendix C   Support Staff: Managing Aggressive Individuals in the Lobby and on the Phone 277
Appendix D   Concerning Military Personnel, Both Active Duty and Veterans 285
Appendix E   The Question of Positional and Compression Asphyxia – by Dr. Gary M. Vilke 287
Appendix F   Suggested Response Protocol for Police Concerning Suspected Excited Delirium Incidents – by Lieutenant Michael Paulus 291

Endnotes 305
About the Authors 309

Books by the Author (and Co-Author)

Published by Edgework www.edgework.info

On the De-escalation of Aggression

EVERYTHING ON THE LINE: Calming and De-escalation of Aggressive and Mentally Ill Individuals on the Phone
A Comprehensive Guidebook for Emergency Dispatch (9-1-1) Centers
Ellis Amdur

FROM CHAOS TO COMPLIANCE: Communication, Control, and De-escalation of Mentally Ill, Emotionally Disturbed and Aggressive Offenders
A Comprehensive Guidebook for Parole and Probation Officers
Ellis Amdur & Alan Pelton

GRACE UNDER FIRE: Skills to Calm and De-escalate Aggressive and Mentally Ill Individuals in Outpatient Settings: 2nd Edition
A Comprehensive Guidebook for Health and Social Services Agencies, and Individual Practitioners
Ellis Amdur

GUARDING THE GATES: Calming, Control and De-escalation of Mentally Ill, Emotionally Disturbed and Aggressive Individuals
A Comprehensive Guidebook for Security Guards
Ellis Amdur & William Cooper

IN THE EYE OF THE HURRICANE: Skills to Calm and De-escalate Aggressive and Mentally Ill Family Members: 2nd Edition
Ellis Amdur

SAFE BEHIND BARS: Communication, Control, and De-escalation of Mentally Ill and Aggressive Inmates
A Comprehensive Guidebook for Correctional Officers in Jail Settings
Ellis Amdur, Chris De Villeneuve & Michael Maxey

SAFE BEHIND THE WALLS: Communication, Control, and De-escalation of Mentally Ill and Aggressive Inmates
A Comprehensive Guidebook for Correctional Officers in Prison Settings
Ellis Amdur & Notable Consultants in the Field of Corrections

SAFE HAVEN: Skills to Calm and De-escalate Aggressive and Mentally Ill Individuals: 2nd Edition
A Comprehensive Guidebook for Personnel Working in Hospital and Residential Settings
Ellis Amdur

SAFETY AT WORK: Skills to Calm and De-escalate Aggressive and Mentally Ill Individuals
A Comprehensive Guidebook for Corporate Security Managers, Human Resources Staff, Loss Prevention Specialists, Executive Protection, and others involved in Threat Management Professions
Ellis Amdur & William Cooper

THE THIN BLUE LIFELINE: Verbal De-escalation of Mentally Ill and Emotionally Disturbed People
A Comprehensive Guidebook for Law Enforcement Officers
Ellis Amdur & John Hutchings

On Martial Arts

DUELING WITH OSENSEI: Grappling with the Myth of the Warrior Sage
Ellis Amdur

HIDDEN IN PLAIN SIGHT: Tracing the Roots of Ueshiba Morihei's Power
Ellis Amdur

OLD SCHOOL: Essays on Japanese Martial Traditions
Ellis Amdur

In Gratitude for Expert Critique

The following professionals have closely reviewed this book. With each draft, we corrected errors of fact, added new information, and fine-tuned the manuscript. One of the qualities of a good law enforcement officer is the understanding that the task supersedes protecting someone's feelings: therefore, we have appreciated all the direct criticism.

In the interests of making a book that is applicable to law enforcement agencies throughout the Western world, we have had this book vetted, among others, by senior law enforcement professionals from Great Britain, Northern Ireland, and Canada.

All responsibility for this book, however, must lie in our hands. Any errors, in particular, are ours alone. Given that lives are on the line in work such as this, please do not hesitate to contact us if you believe that any part of this book is inaccurate or needs additional material. We will revise the book, as needed, in future editions. Our thanks to:

Sergeant Ashley Beattie has 20 years service in the RUC/PSNI, the majority of which has been spent in a Tactical Support Group dealing with public disorder, terrorism and crime. He is currently working in the Northern Ireland Police College, delivering courses on custody-related matters. He has an Honors Degree in Economics from Queens University, Belfast and a Masters Degree in Public Policy and Management from the University of Ulster.

Sergeant Rick Bowen Rick Bowen has worked for the King County Sheriff's Office for 21 years. His past assignments include reactive patrol, Field Training Officer, community policing storefront officer, vice/narcotics detective, robbery/homicide detective, and training deputy in the sheriff's office Advanced Training Unit. He has earned credentials as a firearms instructor, Emergency Vehicle Operations (EVOC) instructor, Taser instructor and in-custody death prevention instructor.

Detective Kendra Conley began her law enforcement career with the City of Snohomish, Washington State in 2002. She has served as a Patrol Officer, a Field Training Officer, and most recently major crime Detective. In 2009 she helped establish the first ever CIT training in Snohomish County. Since 2010, along with continuing the full CIT program training, she is responsible for assisting with training every Deputy and Officer in Snohomish County on a shortened CIT curriculum.

Sherwin Cotler, Ph.D. is a clinical psychologist who, among his other specialties, is known for his work with people having Post Traumatic Stress Disorder. He was part of the original CIT program in Olympia, Washington. In 2010, he, along with Dr. Steve Macuk, received an award from the National Advocates for the Mentally Ill as one of the outstanding psychologists in the country for work they have been doing at the Mental Health Access Program.

Chris de Villeneuve is a Mental Health Professional who lives and works in Yakima County Washington. He is a director for Central Washington Comprehensive Mental Health and a Coordinator for the Yakima County CIT program, as well as a hostage negotiator for the Yakima Police Department.

Sergeant Lisabeth J. Eddy is a 31-year veteran of the Seattle Police Department (SPD). She has worked 29 years as a crisis negotiator with 18 years as the team leader. Sergeant Eddy helped plan and coordinate the Seattle Police Department's Crisis Intervention Training (CIT), and has spent 10 years as the supervisor/coordinator. Eddy also spent 6 years as a volunteer phone worker for the King County Crisis Clinic.

Staff Sergeant Joel A. Johnston is a 25-year police veteran with a background in patrol, foot patrol, traffic enforcement, as well as specializing in Use of Force training & program development, and Emergency Response (ERT) with the Vancouver Police Department. He is currently on secondment as a Staff Sergeant with the British Columbia Ministry of Public Safety and Solicitor General as the Provincial Use of Force and Municipal Emergency Response Teams Coordinator. Recognized as a Use of Force Subject Matter expert witness by the Courts across Canada, he is a published author, presenter to numerous national and international conferences, consultant, and certified instructor in numerous defensive tactics systems, less lethal weapons and firearms systems. He is a Force Response Options Instructor-Trainer for the Province of British Columbia and has instructed use of force-related subject matter internationally.

Constable Rob King is a 23-year Police Officer serving with Cleveland Police, in the North East of England, and has over 14 years experience as a Mental Health Liaison Officer. Rob currently works in partnership with the Forensic Mental Health Services as the Joint Lead for Offender Health, and sits on a number of National Working Groups.

Sergeant Paul Lower has been a police officer for 12 years with Olympia Police Department, seven of those years as a detective. He has a B.A. from St. Martin's College in Criminal Justice and a M.A. from Seattle University in Psychology. Paul is the administrator of the Crisis Intervention Training program for the Olympia Police Department and the greater Thurston and Mason Counties, Washington.

Sergeant Cherie Smith has been a police officer with Wenatchee Police Department for 25 years. She has a B.S. in Psychology from Eastern Washington University and an M.S. in Organization Development from Central Washington University. She was instrumental in bringing CIT training to North Central Washington.

Introduction

This book focuses on encounters between law enforcement officers and people undergoing emotional or behavioral crises, whatever the cause. It addresses both face-to-face encounters as well as larger systemic issues.

It is also for trainees entering the field of law enforcement. You're given an overwhelming amount of information in basic training. Then you hit the street, and the abstract information in books, computer training modules, and role-play becomes real, sometimes terrifyingly so. This book, which encompasses over 50 years of experience of encounters with mentally ill and emotionally disturbed individuals, will be invaluable in readying you for such encounters. The authors have a tremendous amount of practical experience dealing with mentally ill persons, both non-threatening and violent. They share both their academic and their face-to-face, sometimes life-threatening experiences with the hope it will serve others in a positive way.

A frequent observation among our critical readers was that they found some sections to be less relevant to their professional concerns. Significantly, each reader cited different sections of the book. We have striven to ensure that, whatever your specialty, you will find the information you need regarding communication with the people about whom you're most concerned. That said, we strongly urge you to read the entire book the first time around. Dealing with mentally ill individuals is a system-wide issue: it is rare that you will be able to solve a problem on your own. Furthermore, although you may be able to cherry pick chapters of a book, but you can't cherry pick what you will encounter on the street. "Less relevant" is not irrelevant. A homicide detective may have to deal with a mentally ill witness who is 15 years old, a school resources officer may encounter a psychotic grandparent of a child, and anyone can encounter a suicidal subject in the course of one's job.

You may want more information after reading this book. In varying capacities, the authors offer direct instruction, traveling to your location to provide not only basic de-escalation training, but also advanced training in such areas as strategic communication with individuals with character disorders or anti-social traits, and assistance in setting up a CIT program. We also offer consultation where we take difficult cases, and discuss options as well as formulate the best strategies to ensure safety for everyone, based on the presenting behaviors of the people of concern. Please refer to the website www.edgework.info for more information.

PREFACE

It's About Safety

You want to do exemplary work as law enforcement officers. You wish to protect the public, but you also wish to go home, unscathed at the end of your shift.[1] The job, however, keeps changing. Not only are there new types of offenses, such as cyber-crime, but also due to changes in the law, activities either previously accepted in society or things that we could do nothing about are newly classified as crimes. Some of these have significant psychological ramifications. An example of the latter would be stalking. Although a terrifying, often-violent activity throughout human history, the first anti-stalking law was only passed in 1990.

Enhancing public safety now requires police officers to intervene in medical or psychiatric issues. You must deal with mentally ill citizens who may do anything from breaking laws and presenting extreme danger, to simply causing other people concern and fear due to their sometimes-bizarre actions.

If law enforcement is going to play a proper role in protecting society, which can include both protecting ordinary citizens *from* mentally ill people as well as protecting the often-victimized mentally ill citizens from those who mean to harm them, we need to understand whom we're dealing with. If we find the behaviors of mentally ill individuals to be incomprehensible and their actions unpredictable, someone may be hurt, perhaps unnecessarily. This should cause any rational officer to ask a number of questions every time they're dispatched on a call involving an allegedly mentally ill individual:

- Many mentally ill people look just like anyone else. How can we recognize them?
- There is not just one "type" of mentally ill person. Furthermore, people with the same diagnosis can be very different. How can I tell what to expect from a specific person even when I know something about mental illness in general?
- How can I tell if I'm going to be safe? This person seems to be acting so strangely. Is what they're doing an indicator of hostility or potential violence?
- Can I handle this call by myself? I don't want to appear weak or not able to handle a simple call like a mentally ill person just needing a ride to the hospital. When should I call for a back-up officer?

The problems police face in dealing with mentally ill citizens can't be made to disappear. Our jails fill with them, mostly due to arrests for various nuisance crimes: trespass, drinking or urinating in public, dine and dash, pedestrian interference, assault, etc.

Even with grey areas, such as disorderly conduct, what are cops to do when relatively minor problems concerning mentally ill citizens, perhaps one individual, obstruct their shift? After the second, third, or fourth encounter, we put them away for the night and let the next shift (or corrections officer) deal with them.

Statement of a Veteran Officer

What makes things even harder for police is that there isn't a good place to take the mentally ill in most jurisdictions. Hospital emergency rooms become a revolving door. Even a mental health detention can turn around within six to twelve hours, and the officer may see the same person they detained back on the street before the end of their shift. If we can't count on them being detained by mental health, they *will* end up in jail, where at least they will be temporarily safe.

Housing the mentally ill in jails may solve the immediate issue by getting the individuals off the street, but it affects other systems. We start with the responding officer, and possibly back-up officers. In many cases, emergency medical services (EMS) and/or specialized mental health professionals (MHP) are called. Even with the involvement of EMS and MHPs, an individual will often be taken to jail. Then, your supervisor needs to approve the report, which is processed by records personnel. Corrections have their own issues to deal with, including trying to provide safety and treatment, with often abysmally inadequate resources, as well as liability issues when housing a mentally ill individual. Finally, the clerk in the prosecutor's office and the prosecutor must consider the case. If charges are to be filed, then the court becomes involved (clerk and judge). A defense attorney may be assigned, and short of a dismissal, probation gets involved.

We can't begin to estimate how much one nuisance-crime can cost the city, county, or state, but it very easily can run in the thousands of dollars. We aren't advocating letting anyone, whether they are mentally ill or not, get away with a crime. Nonetheless, as money is the lifeblood of our society, we're draining all too scarce funds in very unproductive ways. **And on a human level, we're responding to our most vulnerable citizens in a woefully inadequate manner.** The bottom line is these folks did not ask to be born with a mental illness, and they may be doing the best they can do to survive.

To establish safety, you must have an ability to assess danger and deal with it. Through the information in this book, you will learn to respond to agitated mentally ill people with calm strength, to be very tactical without appearing tactical at all. Rather than being concerned about "what if" situations that you concoct in your own imagination, you will become more skilled in assessing if someone truly is dangerous. In many situations, you will have the ability to calm them as well. You will find your presence alone often quiets a situation, through a different kind of "command presence" than you were taught in the academy. You will then embody a trait that can be termed "grace under fire," that ability to become the center of gravity within a situation so that it coalesces into an ordered system around you.

Language in the Text

Different words are used to describe mentally ill people, based on the professional encountering them and the particular context in which that occurs. Some appellations are considered pejorative; there is often debate, however, both among professionals and within advocacy groups for the mentally ill, about which terms are stigmatizing. In this text, we will refer to people by "descriptors:" the "mentally ill person," the "drug affected person," for example. At other points, we will refer to people as "subjects," "aggressors," "people," "citizens," "individuals," or "folks," depending on the context of the discussion.

The Stigma of Mental Illness (John Hutchings)

Having compassion and a sense of humor is a good thing. They sometimes conflict. At the beginning of my career, I was driving through town with one of my sergeant friends. We saw an individual walking along the sidewalk, obviously suffering from some type of mental illness. I immediately came out with a very humorous line that would reduce any cop to either laughter or comical retort. Instead, my friend said in the most non-judgmental voice, "I don't make fun of somebody who did not ask to be that way. I save it for people who make the choice." We talked about that for a mile or so and it sunk in. That was nearly 25 years ago. To this day, I don't make fun of individuals that had no choice in their disability or mental illness.

When it comes to someone's personal choices leading to their own damaged brain, substance abuse for example, you may find it harder to summon up compassion in the same way. One thing that both of the writers do is the following: We have both been to terrible homes, where people lead degenerate, violent, and/or degraded lives. Sometimes we see small children—tender babies, toddlers or kids—all with the brightness and innocence of childhood. Already, however, we can see signs of damage in these children, and we have thought, "That child is already lost." We both remind ourselves of this, because the obnoxious, mentally ill, or substance abusing adult was probably once one of those kids. As both of our careers have lasted a long time, we may have seen that stumbling meth addict 20 years before as a baby, and imagined for a moment, stealing him/her from the physically or possibly sexually abusive place that was their "home."

This doesn't change how one of us enforces the laws, and how the other approaches treatment, but it reminds us not to let ourselves become contemptuous, when such an attitude is such an easy way to go. We can understand how drugs can seem a comfort compared to the chaos inside both their head and their surroundings.

There are so many disparaging terms and words for those with mental illness; too many to count, so let us get this out of the way. We refer to the mentally ill as: mentals, E.D's, whack-jobs, fruit cakes, window lickers (UK term), nut jobs, freaks, loons, loony-toons, and a host of others. Here are some phrases used to describe the developmentally disabled: a brick shy, an unaddressed envelope, the porch light's not on, etc. If you have more, yell them out now if you need get them out of your system. The only purposes these terms serve is to 1) make fun of someone, 2) immediately describe the person so another cop will know, supposedly, what you're talking about, or 3) de-sensitize oneself so that one doesn't have to be impacted by the painful lives such people live.

If your objective is **not** to make fun at someone else's expense, then terms like: mentally ill, consumer, patient, person, mentally disordered or sufferer (UK term) may be more applicable, and get the same point across. The problem with demeaning language is that words become a self-fulfilling prophecy. When you call someone a demeaning name, or describe him or her by some pejorative term, it is a short step to seeing them as merely that.

Please recall how my friend set me straight 25 years ago. I, and my often very politically incorrect co-author, aren't suggesting that you, our readers, should be policing other officers' way of speaking. Nonetheless, we're suggesting that you watch your own. Words shape reality and it is a very different call when one is going to see a nut-case or whack-job, as opposed to a mentally ill man or woman, someone's son or daughter, husband or wife.

And yes, there *are* times when one should speak out. In a recent command staff meeting, our discussion began surrounding a chronic caller of 9-1-1. She has been making para-suicidal calls for over 25 years, using police and fire services far past the point of abuse. Typical of cops (at all levels of the administration); the jokes came to the surface, as did the inappropriate terms used to describe her. They all took away all references to an actual human being. Beyond human disrespect, it actually impeded a resolution to the issue. Correcting those using less than sensitive labels brought some ridicule down on my head, but it brought us back to task, so that we returned to focusing on how to deal with a very aggravating, but clearly suffering human being. The issue of this very problematic woman did not get resolved that day. It is possible that it never will. If there is any hope that we can eventually manage her behavior better, however, it must begin with human respect. As my co-author has written, "People either rise to our hopes or sink to our expectations."

Examples of the Mentally Ill People that Law Enforcement Officers Frequently Contact

- Victims of crimes
- Victims of exploitation and abuse by caregivers
- Subjects whom you have contact with for disorderly conduct, suspicious person calls, or welfare checks
- Witnesses to crimes
- People who, though mentally ill, commit crimes themselves. The majority of these crimes are misdemeanors. They're often repeat offenders.
- People who, though mentally ill, commit severe felonies. Some of these crimes are inarguably connected to their mental illness, whereas others are voluntary and conscious criminal acts committed by someone who happens also to be mentally ill.

Remember this: You will need to know how to communicate with mentally ill individuals in far broader circumstances than de-escalation of aggression or controlling violence. Communication with mentally ill individuals encompasses the spectrum of police work.

Historical Note

President John F. Kennedy signed the "Community Mental Health and Construction Act" on October 31, 1963, and America has been in a state of crisis with regard to mentally ill people ever since. Kennedy called for a two-prong approach: the deinstitutionalization of the mentally ill and local community mental health treatment centers. Better medications, treatment therapies, and the sometimes misdiagnosis of mental illness made this a needed mandate. Two thousand community mental health treatment centers were to be built by 1980 to assist with the integration of the mentally ill back into neighborhoods, and provide them with ongoing support. By 1984, however, less than five hundred treatment centers had been built across the country.

Without the support of community treatment centers, those hundreds of thousands of people with varying diagnoses and varying degrees of mental illness had to care for themselves. They also were released right into the maelstrom of drugs sweeping the country in the 1980s. Even those who refused to drink or take illicit drugs continued to decompensate along with those that did.

The failure of de-institutionalization has led to a kind of re-institutionalization, except that the mentally ill are now, ever increasingly, involved in an imperfect amalgam of the criminal justice system and the emergency medical system. We have moved from the de-institutionalization of the mentally ill to their criminalization. The seriously mentally ill are far too often not the concern of any community mental health services: rather, they're the concern of 9-1-1 dispatchers, law enforcement officers, paramedics and EMS, local hospital emergency rooms, or most commonly, local jails and State or Federal prisons. Research estimates there are about 70,000 inmates in United States prisons that are psychotic. Overall, an estimated 200,000 to 300,000 male and female inmates suffer from some form of mental illness. (Note the incredible disparity of numbers in the latter estimate. We don't even know with any degree of reliability exactly how mentally ill inmates we have!).

This is a near flip-flop of what it was in the 1960s and 1970s, where these were the numbers of people in inpatient psychiatric facilities. The most basic human and medical needs of this disenfranchised segment of our population have been unmet. That so many persons with mental illness are not in hospitals or institutions or in outpatient mental health services has caused many unnecessary and premature deaths from overdose, exposure, suicide, and physical illness. Those who survive are "institutionalized" in jails and prisons, rather than hospitals. It is hard to consider this progress.

With such limited options available, the police officer is expected to recognize, protect, and defend the mentally ill whether they're suspect or victim—or both. Whether you like it or not, you're tasked with *doing the right thing each time* it comes to dealing with the mentally ill or more frightening, the *violent* mentally ill when, all too often, you have nowhere to house them or get them help, even when they ask for it.

Even under these circumstances, your interaction with the mentally ill or drug-affected individual may serve both public safety and the well being of that person, or it may do just the opposite. The phrase "knowledge is power" was never more true than for a law enforcement officer attempting to deal with an emotionally or mentally ill individual. That is what we offer here.

SECTION I

Core Requirements for De-escalation and
Control of Agitated, Aggressive,
or Mentally Ill Individuals

CHAPTER 1

The Essentials

Training

The responsibilities of a law enforcement officer can be divided in three major categories: service delivery, law enforcement, and the maintenance of order. When dealing with mentally ill individuals, we need to quickly decide in which category we're functioning, even though we sometimes jump from one to another. Often it is just service delivery: we call for an ambulance or transport the individual to a local hospital. Other times, our main function is to stop a crime, or make an arrest. Order maintenance can be the most complex: the United States Constitution enshrines numerous rights, which apply equally to mentally ill and drug abusing citizens who may be acting in very disorderly, but possibly legally permissible ways. To fulfill these three functions, every law-enforcement officer must maintain on-going training, an understanding of the political and social environment, and, above all else, an overarching ethic that promotes integrity and professionalism.

It is our professional and moral responsibility to be skilled in communication and de-escalation methods. This certainly requires an effort on the part of the individual officer, but even more so, it must be agency policy that good training is made available, and that times are set aside on a *regular* basis to practice these skills. Given that the BEST training should mirror the actualities of the profession, optimum training on verbal de-escalation should be integrated within higher use of force training. In each training exercise, officers must make a choice what is the most effective tactic to deal with what they're presented: from verbal de-escalation to come-alongs and restraints through pepper spray, electronic control devices and other less-lethal weaponry, and finally deadly force.

High standards apply to both physical and verbal defensive tactics. If you're not physically fit *and* strong enough (two distinct things) to execute proper defensive tactics and restraint techniques against a struggling subject, you're a danger to citizens, to fellow officers and to yourself. The same goes if you don't have the skills necessary to execute proper techniques, within the full range of force response options. If you don't know how to calm and de-escalate an agitated or angry subject, when it is practicable, then all you have is physical skills and you're definitely a danger to citizens, however skilled you are. An untrained or unfit police officer, responsible for the physical well-being of citizens whom they must calm and restrain as well as arrest and sometimes engage in combat, is not functioning as a professional. So is any agency that puts them in that position of responsibility, yet doesn't hold officers to high standards or provide them with effective training.

Information Sharing

Information must be shared among all those concerned with a dangerous or at-risk mentally ill subject. This should include everyone from hospital staff, a mental health or substance-abuse treatment agency, parole or probation officers. All information that is associated with potential danger must be shared, not only for ethical reasons, but also because it is the best way for everyone to remain safe. You will get feedback that you hadn't thought of, and furthermore, people will be prepared to help you.

Figure 1.1 Concerning Confidentiality

In most states, there are rules governing confidentiality as well as other rules stipulating when collaboration and sharing of information between mental health workers and law enforcement is a **requirement**. Check with legal advisors in your locale to find out your legal requirements and rights in your jurisdiction.

NOTE: There are sometimes conflicts between Federal HIPAA laws (Health Insurance Portability and Accountability), and individual state and local laws and ordinances governing confidentiality. Consult with your legal advisor to ensure that you're fully in compliance with the laws governing confidentiality – and that you're also able to hold others to those same statutes.

Information sharing is not only an interagency question. Make sure all relevant officers within your department are aware of changes in behavior or verbalizations by any person of concern. All too often, someone is left out of the loop. The permutations are endless, but the consequences are dire. If all members of an organization aren't aware of dangerous elements within their perimeter, someone is very likely going to be hurt. For those reasons, use all available media to ensure that everyone has all necessary information.

Figure 1.2 One Author's Experience

Several decades ago, I made a referral to an office responsible for the welfare of elderly citizens regarding a woman who was probably demented. She was reported as trying to heat her room with a hot plate. I emphasized, of course, that this was a very dangerous situation. One month later, she burned to death in the hotel fire that resulted from her actions. The social services agency never went out to see her. They claimed, in a newspaper interview, that the referral from "the mental health professional" had been vague and didn't underscore the danger. The only thing that saved my career was *a three-line chart note* that clearly stated the concerns I had, and that I had so explained things to the agency for the follow-up they never carried out. **From that day forward, I never made a referral to a social services agency without sending a fax summarizing our phone – or even email – conversation.** Phone calls can be denied, emails are lost in spam filters, deleted deliberately or accidentally, or snatched into the ozone by aliens, but a faxed document not only has to be place in the subject's file, but you have a record on your end that it was sent.

While you're en route to a call involving a mentally ill individual, you need as much information as you can get, including: history at the specific address or on the person (if you're lucky enough to have their name), dispositions of the previous event, history of violence, weapons, previous threats (those threats can be both suicidal and homicidal), have they been drinking, or do they take some type of medication? Much of this can be given to dispatch to be placed in Computer Aided Dispatch (CAD) notes, depending on jurisdictional protocols and laws. For example, consider an individual who makes numerous allusions suggesting that they're going to force a cop to shoot them. This must be documented as it shows intent and highlights risk. Years later, should an officer be on the way to deal with this individual, such forewarning may save his/her life. Furthermore, if they actually confront the person who is bent of self-destruction, and be forced to used deadly force, such a documented history will prove invaluable to the involved officer, the coroner, the family, the officer's agency (for any future lawsuit), for the shooting review board, the District Attorney or Prosecuting Attorney, any insurance company, the public, and the media, to name a few.

Such history may be essential in the mentally ill person getting access to services as well. If you have ever called a mental health professional to discuss a person you're dealing with in hope of them detaining him/her, you always get, "What is their history," or "Are they escalating in their behavior," because this establishes a previous pattern that enables them to predict, to some degree, future behavior. Mental health professionals need facts, documentation, and a report of both the recent and distant past, not just an anecdote on "right now." Beyond what they need to do effective crisis intervention, they need it for the judge conducting the detention hearing.

It may take only 5-10 minutes to bang out a *suspicious circs* report or something similar. Having that report is insurance, forever. If the individual moves to another jurisdiction, your agency will have vital information to pass on, because it is a matter of record.

Figure 1.3 Concerning Written Reports

In 31 years in law enforcement, I have never seen an officer get into trouble for actually writing a report. The old adage remains: if it is not documented in a report, it never happened, or worse, no one else knows the dangers.

Past History Is Data—Not a Prediction

Don't expect your encounter with a mentally ill person to be the same each time, just because you've dealt with them before in an effective way, or because the previous reports describe a pattern. This doesn't mean previous success can't be repeated; however, persons suffering with mental illness can be extremely unpredictable. Treat each call as a brand new event. We have had several tragic incidents over the last decade where seasoned officers were killed by a mentally ill individual, someone with whom the respective officers had each had successful contact in the past.

Respect Is a Matter of Safety

Some of the mentally ill have numerous contacts with law enforcement, sometimes many times a week. Keep in mind they weren't always repeat customers. They all started somewhere, and with some cop. Their first encounter with law enforcement can often establish future encounters.

I've been sent to the scene of many a mental disturbance call with certain officers, and I think, "Oh, this is going to go badly." There are, unfortunately, officers on your force who will make fun of someone or jack them up to the point that you will have to go hands on with them. It doesn't have to be that way. Too many times, I have heard a mentally ill subject ask if a certain officer is on duty. Sometimes, their voice has hope in it. Sometimes it has fear or anger. They recall when they were treated with respect and understanding, and when they weren't. The next time you're dealing with someone with mental illness either on the street, or on the way to or in jail, ask them this question, "What can the police do to help when you're in crisis?" You will hear, as I have many times, "Treat us with respect. We aren't stupid. We know when you're making fun of us."

Respect could be termed, "banking for the future." If an individual believes they're being demeaned or abused, they may remember and seek revenge in the future. This may be against the person they perceive as abusive or, all too frequently, they target all those whom they perceive associated with the abuser. Therefore, if Officer A makes fun of or otherwise demeans an individual, it may be Officer B, much later, and utterly unaware of the previous incident, who suffers the consequences.

Figure 1.4 One Author's Experience

I once worked with a young man who had severe bipolar disorder. When on his medications, he was, for all intents and purposes, normal: a friendly, bright, and articulate guy. During the six months I saw him, we simply had very friendly conversations and enjoyed each other's company. Approximately one year later, I was asked by another mental health agency to do a welfare check on him. I went to his apartment alone, and spoke with him a few minutes. Off his meds, he was irrational and psychotic. Sensing danger, I quickly left. He subsequently was detained for involuntary treatment, assaulting a number of officers in the process. He was hospitalized over half a year. Sometime after his release, I ran into him in the street, once again on his medications and apparently doing well. He was overjoyed to see me, far more so than I thought the situation warranted. When I asked him why, he said, "I was afraid that you were dead. I remember you coming to my apartment, and I decided to kill you. I was just about to make my move when a voice went off in my head and said, 'You can't kill him, he's your friend.' I was arguing with the voice, because I couldn't remember what a friend was, but the voice said it was against the rules to kill friends. Then, you were gone. For nine months, I've been hoping you left my apartment, but I couldn't remember. I've been afraid that I actually killed you, cut you up and buried you some place. I'm so glad to see you!!!"

Remember: respect saves lives.

Crisis Intervention Teams (CIT)

One of the most exciting innovations in law enforcement in both America and Great Britain is the Crisis Intervention Training/Team (CIT) model, in which law enforcement officers receive 40 hours of training on dealing with mentally ill individuals in crisis. In many law enforcement agencies, somewhere between 20-40 percent of the officers are CIT trained. It has been researched internationally and is now considered evidenced based in the Northwest of America. On the increase, nationally, is the multi-jurisdictional CIT course. Officers from several agencies, sometimes including 1st responders, corrections, dispatch, parole/probation and even mental health practitioners coming together for this training fosters a networking seldom seen.[2]

CHAPTER 2

Threat Assessment

Figure 2.1 Any Call-out Can Become an Emergency

Many of your calls-outs aren't full emergencies, but you may be contacting someone who could easily shift into violence or a mental health crisis, now or at another time. If you can acquire any portion of the following information, it can provide you, other officers, and non-law-enforcement professionals with vital information relevant to any risk they may present, now or later.

The information in this section is not a mere checklist that you should tick off, item by item, with each call. All information has a context. For example, you may become aware that a man owns several knives. That, in itself, tells you little. You need to know why he owns them: for cooking, for a collection, or as part of his rape kit. You need to know if he has ever used them and in what context, and what the weapons mean to him. Consider another example. A woman is depressed. Because this can be a risk factor in physical child abuse, any information about her own personal history of victimization, suicidal behavior, or violence may prove vital in helping to determine if her children are in danger.

Standard threat assessment information isn't an absolute predictor of aggression or violence. Nonetheless, such information can give you a better idea who and what to watch out for. When available, such information can be gathered and entered in a computer assisted dispatch system to serve as an "alert" for you or any officer when you're sent to contact that person.

Among the most important items to consider:

1. **A past history of violence**. This is one of the most important factors. A capacity for violence is both innate and learned; a behavior that becomes easier to use as a problem-solving strategy the more it is enacted. Furthermore, it is rewarding for many people; power over others may be the best experience of their lives.

2. **History of bullying, threats or intimidation.** This is the psychological counterpart to physical violence.

3. **Prior arrest**. Any arrest is a heightened risk factor, even if the arrest was for a non-violent crime. They may be terrified or outraged at the idea of being arrested again, or even at having more contact with law enforcement. Furthermore, with the prevalence of physical and sexual assault within corrections institutions, the non-violent arrestee may have come out a very different person than they went in.[3]

4. **Possession of weapons, fascination with weapons, and/or past history of using weapons.** Of greatest concern is a history of brandishing or using the weapon, talking about the weapon in

menacing terms, or fantasizing in a pathological manner. Having moved the weapons recently to make them more accessible, or sleeping with a weapon next to the bed, under a pillow or the like may also be an important sign. Weapons paraphernalia and gun magazines can indicate weapon possession, even when none is immediately apparent. Here, too, this can range from a quite reasonable hobby or concern for accurate information about weaponry to a morbid obsession.

5. **History of physical abuse or the witnessing of physical abuse and violence.** Beyond a history of victimization, it is particularly traumatic to have witnessed abuse of a family member. The victim of abuse often hates his own weakness, and begins hating weakness in others as well. Once this occurs, it is a natural move for some people to begin victimizing what they hate: the weak.[4]

6. **Head injuries.** Many of our young soldiers are coming home from twenty-first century combat with closed head injuries. However, war zones and the damage they cause do not only exist in foreign lands. All too often, they are right next-door. All too many people have suffered severe physical violence, with trauma similar to combat injuries, within their own home. Traumatic brain injuries (TBI) are associated with impulse control problems. Some such injured people may have hair-trigger tempers and difficulty controlling negative emotions.

7. **Dementia.** Elderly people with Alzheimer's or other degenerative brain illnesses can show some of the same impulse control problems as those with traumatic brain injuries.

8. **Low frustration tolerance.** Inability or unwillingness to tolerate limit setting. "I want what I want and I want it now, and you'd better not keep me from it." This is something that the subject will often verbalize.

9. **Recent stressors and losses.** Bereavement, separation, divorce, and loss of job, can make one more willing to become violent. One also feels that one has nothing left to lose. Given the current financial crisis in the Western world, we will see increasing levels of aggression and violence due to these causes.

10. **A feeling of victimization and grievance.** When presented with a problem or complaint, such people believe that it is ALWAYS someone else's fault. If nothing else, this is very typical thinking of most career criminals.

11. **Fear of attack or invasion of personal space.** Fearful people lash out in defensive violence. If you're properly "tracking" the subjects of your attention, you should be aware when they become increasingly stressed due to the pressure they experience from close physical proximity to you

12. **Almost all intoxicating substances can be disinhibiting.** An intoxicant acts like a solvent; it tends to dissolve the internal barriers that hold an individual back from base desires, among them aggression.

13. **Physical pain or discomfort (particularly chronic).** This also includes medication side-effects or withdrawal from drugs. Unfortunately, many medications that help mentally ill people can have very nasty side-effects, particularly when the patient is inadequately monitored, something that happens both in corrections settings and in the community.

14. **The individual has already "given up."** Expecting the interaction to be difficult or absolutely negative, their response can be, "What the hell. Nothing will help. If I'm aggressive, at least I can make my mark on the world—or on you."

15. **Severe psychopathological symptoms**
    - Rapid mood swings. Such a person is unpredictable, and can suddenly flare into rage just when the responder thinks he/she has solved the problem.
    - Hallucinations, particularly command hallucinations. Auditory hallucinations may be telling the person to do something terrible. If you think someone is hearing voices, ask what they're hearing.
    - Mania. This is a state of excitement, typified by rapid speech, grandiose thinking, very poor judgment, and impulsive behavior. It is a behavior we see in people with bipolar disorder (manic-depression) or intoxication on stimulants such as methamphetamine or cocaine, and not infrequently, alcohol.
    - History of predatory or manipulative behaviors.

16. **Interactional factors between the aggressor and victim.** Particularly in domestic violence situations, the aggressor views the victim as having power over them, as being inflexible or controlling, or denying the aggressor his/her due. In short, the aggressor usually believes himself/herself to be the victim. This also is true regarding interactions—past and present—between the subject and law enforcement officers.

17. **Religious and cultural clashes**. Culture is any set of rules and customs that orders the relationships between people. Some cultures sanction violence with different cultural rules from those of our own mainstream culture.

A Review of the Past Aggressive Encounters With Mentally Ill Individuals

Take some time to reflect on the aggressive and/or violent incidents in which you have been involved. Try to learn more about the patterns of behavior that might have preceded their aggression, as well as any actions on the part of law enforcement that were either unhelpful or contributory towards the individual becoming violent.

- What were the circumstances that led to the aggressive encounter?
- What was the *first* sign that indicated that the situation was getting volatile or dangerous?
- Remember what they said and what they did just before the aggressive incident.
- People are generally able to control their verbal signals better than their non-verbal signals, so recall the subject's body language prior to the incident. Tension can also create a change in the quality of the voice such as rate of speech, pitch, and/or volume.
- Consider what you physically felt at each stage of the encounter. This may be the most important data you can recover. The sensations evoked within the context of an encounter with another person are physical expression of intuition. When you next experience that same sensation, it is an early warning sign that a similar situation is developing.
- What do you believe you should have done differently?
- What were the results of the after-action review of the incident? What did you learn?

Figure 2.2 One Author's Experience

In 1980, while still a rookie, I received a call regarding a suspicious person. The dispatcher informed me this man had been walking around a 24-hour gas station for about 45 minutes. The attendant called 9-1-1, thinking he was being cased for yet another armed robbery.

Upon my arrival, I spotted a heavily-built man standing in a nearby vacant lot. He was wearing a puffy down jacket, on what was a hot summer night. I approached him, holding my handgun at my side. When I got about 30 feet away, he suddenly turned toward me. I pointed my gun at him, and demanded he keep his hands in open view. Staring right through me, he quietly and calmly said, "I'm going to cut out your heart." He had a weird smile, like it was painted on his face, and I realized that it was very likely that he was severely mentally ill.

I tried to engage him in a short non-threatening conversation, with my gun still positioned at low ready. He didn't respond, but at least he wasn't attacking. I think my voice, particularly my tone, had something to do with it. It bought enough time for back-up officers to arrive and surround the man.

He ignored all commands, and it took all three of us to jump on him and wrestle him to the ground for handcuffing and transport to the local psychiatric ward. He *could* have cut out my heart, too. He has a three-inch bladed knife in his coat pocket. All the way to the hospital, he sang the Coke jingle, "I want to teach the world to sing in perfect harmony...."

I started my after-action review from that day. I realized that a review of what I felt, what I perceived, what I said and what I did, even my mood driving up to the scene, might save my life in the future. Whatever I did right, I wanted to do again, and I'd only be able to do that if I was fully aware of these things.

The Core Questions Regarding Potential Violence

Mentally ill individuals are sometimes too decompensated or overwhelmed to undertake a comprehensive questioning. However, there are times when you should include direct questions about their previous history of assaults and their potential for violence. You have to make it clear that you're asking for the information to ground your understanding, not because you're afraid. You're also trying to convey that you're able to handle anything they might mention, even angry or threatening statements. Therefore, be sure to hold yourself in a calm, relaxed manner, offering a direct gaze. Reminder: The quality of their answer—tone of voice, body language, and facial expression is as important, or more so, than the specific answer they give. Questions can include (Note: This isn't a complete list. These are examples to help you understand the scope and nature of the questions you need to ask.):

- "Have you hit anyone within the last six months?" "How about the last year"? "Have you ever been arrested for assault?" "How about for fighting with someone?" Notice the nuanced levels of the questions. This way you can assess their familiarity with the legal system, (What if they deny assault, but endorse an arrest for "fighting?). By asking "six months," you may get a more manipulative person, who otherwise might lie, to say, "Not in six months," because they think that is all you care about.

- "Tell me what happened?" "Why do you think this situation occurred?" "Was there anything you could have done to avoid such a confrontation?" The context of why they were assaultive, what it meant to them, why they thought they had no other options, or why they might have chosen violence first, not last, is all vital information to the investigating officer.
- "What do you do when someone really makes you angry?" "What kind of thing might someone say that would make you mad?" Among other things, this gives you advanced warning of what the individual's triggers are. Predatory intimidators sometimes seize this opportunity to try to say something vaguely menacing, like, "Oh, you don't want to know."
- "If you got mad at someone here, what would you do? How would you handle it?"
- "Is there any situation where you might get so mad that you might want to hit someone?" "Are there any situations where you would want to hit a police officer?"
- "If you did get mad, how could I help you calm down?"
- "Do you take any medication?" "Does it help you with anger?" "Does it help in any other way?"

Looking for Patterns

Review a person of interest's history of aggression. Through this, you will sometimes be able to discern patterns that help in predicting future incidents. Often, it is *only* when all the incidents are placed together that one is able to see such a pattern. Here are some examples of the type of patterns you might discover, through either a record search or investigation with either the subject or collateral contacts.

Figure 2.3 Examples of Patterns

Let us imagine two individuals, both of whom served time in prison for a life-threatening assault on another person. The first smirks and describes how he fractured the skull of a rival drug dealer. He casually says that he'd never do anything like that again, "because I'm not in the game anymore." The second describes, in a tone of outrage, how he went to a club with his wife, and while he went to pick up their drinks, returned to find a man mauling her sexually. He broke a glass and slashed the man's face, blinding him. Which man is more dangerous? We don't know. We do know, however, that the contexts of their aggression are poles apart. Furthermore, they tell their stories in very different ways. One obviously savors the opportunity to recount his violence, and probably savored the act as well. The other is horrified by what he did, but still feels justified in doing it. Not only are their triggers different, but also it suggests that they will need different tactical interventions (on a verbal level), were either of them to become enraged.

Figure 2.4 What Patterns Reveal

A teenager with six assaults on school staff. Every attack occurs on about the tenth day of the month. His mother gets disability payments that she spends on crack cocaine. She runs out of money somewhere after the first week and begins prostituting to get more for her drugs. Her son feels bitter shame and rage, but he would never hit his mother, and her customers are too dangerous. He displaces his rage on his teachers.

A mentally ill woman who has aggressive outbursts to her case managers. Police keep getting called to assist at a group home. A review of critical incidents reveals that all her outbursts are at the staff with whom she has, otherwise, the best rapport. She reveals that her husband physically abuses her son, and she is reminded of her father abusing her brother, while her mother did nothing to stop it. She is enraged at her case managers who "should" be stopping the current abuse, something that, in fact, they couldn't do as she hadn't disclosed it.

A small child becomes explosively violent to her mother when she tries to take her to a mental health center, which also has a drug-treatment support program. One of the men has flirted with the mother, and because he is such a likable guy, she usually sits next to him. He's a pedophile, has been surreptitiously sexually abusing the child, when her mother gets up for water, or to check on something with the receptionist. The child only discloses when the police officer notices that her angry outbursts are always associated with plans to go to the treatment center.

Don't Let the Abnormal Become Normal

We can't underscore how important it is to check out your concerns and intuitions with fellow officers, and sometimes with professionals outside the law enforcement arena. Not only should you be consulting when you're concerned about an individual, but also consult when you *should* be concerned and aren't. Some cops become so familiar with pathology that the abnormal becomes normal. The officer no longer reacts in a natural way, tolerating or not even noticing covert aggression, or precursors to assault. Beat officers or walking patrol officers can easily become complacent when dealing with those people they have nicknamed because they deal with them so often. We have witnessed officers allow such people to get too close to them, abandoning their tactical advantage. Remember the adage, "There is nothing routine in police work." Don't get so focused on accomplishing a task that you ignore or discount signs of danger.

CHAPTER 3

___

Honing Intuition

There must be free communication of and respect for each other's intuitions. Such gut feelings are sometimes vague, but they're often the *first* signs that you're in a dangerous situation.

- Officers shouldn't minimize their gut feelings and intuitions when exchanging information. Don't begin by stating "I know it's nothing, but…." In doing so, the officer may lead others to minimize the situation as well.
- Officers shouldn't be hesitant because they don't have "hard evidence" to support their concern.
- Veteran officers or senior staff members must not belittle other officers' or support staffs' intuitions of danger. Even the most senior officer hasn't experienced every possible contingency.

Figure 3.1 Example of Lifesaving Intuition
Very early in my career as a police officer, I was dispatched to a domestic dispute. My back-up officer and I separated the two combatants, and I directed the male to sit in the nearby rocking chair and tell me what had happened. He began to walk toward the couch next to him. I redirected him to the rocker. He became adamant he was going to sit on his couch! With the hair on my neck raised, I shoved him down into the rocker where he remained until it was time to arrest him. After he was seated in my patrol car, I went back inside, went directly to the sofa. Under the cushions was a loaded 4 inch .357 revolver. Was it intuition, my Guardian Angel, or my basic training? Whatever it was, trusting it may have saved my life.

Communicating with mentally ill people is most difficult when they're becoming agitated. Agitated people experience words, particularly a lot of them, as confusing, aggravating, and/or threatening; for this reason, whatever you say, keep it simple. Realize that the agitated subject is paying more attention to other aspects of communication: muscular tension, the amount of physical space between you, the positioning of your hands, and the quality of your voice. These become more important to the aggressive individual than what you're saying. As you evaluate the other person's potential for violence, the same should apply to you.

Although the **basic** emotions are expressed in definitive ways, irrespective of culture,[5] non-verbal behaviors can be idiosyncratic: not only do people often have their own ways of physically expressing their emotions, but they also have their own ways of interpreting (or misinterpreting) yours. A cookbook approach won't allow you to be as effective as you need to be.

We must develop our intuition to pick up the subtle warning signs that a dangerous situation is developing. This ability, seemingly so rare, is actually something you can practice and improve, making it an activity under your control rather than wild magic.

The best way to improve your intuitive ability is the study of interpersonal space. This is not just a matter of feet and inches. Simply asserting that you keep an arms length and a half, or two arms length apart between you and a potentially dangerous is not enough. How much space would you want if the person has a blade, or is twice your size, and half your age?

Our attitude towards others as well as our mood can affect our sense of space. For example, the more relaxed you're in the company of someone you trust, the less personal space you require, something that manipulative aggressors try to take advantage of. When you're uncertain or suspicious of someone, you instinctively move to get more distance from them. If you're having a bad day, you need more space to tolerate others' proximity. Spacing defines, in a physical sense, the nature of relationship.

Figure 3.2 Two Cautions Concerning Personal Space
1. DON'T knowingly step inside someone's personal space, unless doing so helps you establish a clear tactical advantage.
2. DON'T accommodate anyone by allowing them to stand too close to you.

You MUST be aware of the physical sensations of someone in your "zone." When you set such a limit as "Sir, I very much wish to hear what you have to say, but you are standing too close. Move back four feet and then we will continue to talk."

The reply you get will be great threat assessment information. You are dealing with very different individuals when one, told to step back, responds with profuse apologies opposed to someone who smirks and says, "What's the matter, officer, are you nervous around men?"

The Brain Wants to Survive

There are parts of the brain that are solely concerned with survival. These parts of the brain don't care about being polite, politically correct, or intellectualizing why someone is the way they are. These parts of the brain don't use words. They perceive by recognizing significant patterns, and signal their recognition through physical reactions. These sections of the brain is fast, about half a second faster than the thinking brain. About to step on a squiggly shape on the ground, the adrenaline hits and you jerk back your foot even before the rest of your brain thinks, "SNAKE!"

It's not just about what you see. The space between human beings has a kind of "texture," that we perceive through both physical and emotional reactions. One way, therefore, to develop your intuition is to become more aware of the signals our bodies send us. Being aware of the space between you and others can give you an early warning system that a situation is becoming potentially explosive.

Thus, if someone is aggressive, psychotic, excited, depressed, menacing, hateful, is trying to con you—any "strong" interaction—the survival brain recognizes a pattern in what they're doing, and reacts. For example, when in proximity to the scared person, perhaps you feel warmth in your chest, but with the con-man, your lips compress and neck tightens. With psychotic people, you feel a sensation of cold in your stomach and your hands and jaw clench with aggressive people. There are no rules to these physical reactions: they are individual to you.

Some of your physical reactions may be unpleasant or unflattering to your own self-image. For example, let us imagine that you get somewhat sick to your stomach when facing an aggressive person, or experience a subtle, but real sense of revulsion when dealing with someone who is depressed. You don't need to change this reaction because, if you're a person of integrity, you don't live by feelings or your emotions. Your feelings and emotions *convey information*, but they don't *demand* that you act.

If you continue to hone your awareness in this matter, you will develop a specialized form of intuition called **MINDFULNESS**. Mindfulness is the ability to be **consciously** aware of what is going on in your interactions with another person.

Figure 3.3 Honing Intuition

It is very easy to train yourself to become more intuitive. Simply carry a small notebook in your pocket. If you encounter an individual who interacts with you in a significant way (aggressive, manipulative, depressed, etc.), note down (later) how your body reacts. After some time, you will see the patterns emerge. Once you've accomplished this, it becomes a kind of auto-pilot. Another part of your brain actively scans people for certain patterns, and you, now trained, are aware of and *understand* your physical reaction, and react as necessary.

Where these reactions really come in handy is when someone is trying to hide their intentions, smiling, for example, while trying to get close to you to stab you. Let's say, in this case, it is a woman who you helped when her baby choked on food. Your "thinking mind" tells you, "She wouldn't want to hurt me! I saved her baby's life!" But your eyes are tightening and you're getting the same tension in your lower back that you have had on every occasion when someone has assaulted you in the past. Don't talk yourself out of it! Danger and a blade are about to hit you right in the gut. **By taking notes on sensations, you're training yourself to recognize the patterns, consciously, that your survival brain notices subconsciously.** Instead of concluding "I was having a lucky day. Something told me not to knock on that door," you say, "I had that feeling in my hands I always get right before a fight. I knew something was going to happen, so I went around the back and saw him standing behind the door with a piece of rebar."

Figure 3.4 One Author's Experience

An individual once thanked me profusely at the end of my encounter with him. Instead of the warm pride I get when I've helped someone (and I HAD helped him), I had the same reaction that I always have when someone overtly threatens me. I mentally brushed it aside, thinking, "You're being an idiot; the man just complimented me." Sometime later, he poisoned me. I'm only alive today because he chose to degrade me by contaminating my food rather than putting something lethal in it. I learned in the most ugly way possible to always pay attention to what my body "tells" me. Our bodies are linked to the most primitive areas of the brain, structures that serve to protect us from danger through pattern recognition rather than verbal cognitions. To treat our bodily reactions with disrespect is to disavow that which has kept humanity alive for eons.

SECTION II

Centering: Standing with Strength
and Grace in Crisis Situations

CHAPTER 4

Introduction to Centering

Dealing with individuals who are mentally ill, drug dependent, victims of traumatic events, struggling with developmental disabilities, brain injuries, or personality disorders is an essential part of twenty-first century police work.

It can also be terribly demanding. Being confused, distracted, or intimidated by a mentally ill individual can easily lead to poor decision-making. Even more troubling is to realize that your reactions to such people sometimes make things worse. Internalizing feelings of frustration can lead to burnout, a state of being which could be summed up in the phrase, "I don't want to see any more of this." Burnout can cause you to not pay attention at moments when awareness is most necessary

The strategies in the chapters of this section revolve around maintaining self-control. This is also about mentoring other cops. Mastering methods of self-control is a way for you to role model proper behavior to others. This is the ability to adapt to circumstances in a powerful, fluid, and purposeful way. Not only will this make you more able to roll with the seemingly never-ending problems that the mentally ill present, on both a personal and systems level, but also it will make you more effective in crisis situations.

Figure 4 Centering: It's All About Tactics

We had a small dilemma with this section. Given its subject, which includes tactical breathing methods, and an awareness of triggers that an aggressor could use to set you off-balance, we were concerned that some readers might interpret this as "touchy-feely" stuff. It's not. Consider an example we include of a sniper, who uses breathing methods to stay absolutely calm so that he can accomplish his mission. Or another method of breathing used to coordinate any entry team before going through a door.

What it comes down to is this: many of the tactics in this book are dependent on being centered. You can say all the right things, but if you aren't "lined up right," they will be of no use.

The more control you have over "you," the more certain you will do the right thing if they are mentally ill, and, in any case facing an aggressor, mentally ill or not, the more certain your victory in the event that the situation becomes physical. So we'll keep it here.

CHAPTER 5

Stillness in Motion

When people are in crisis, they believe that they have no time to solve the problem. If you agree with them, then you're in crisis too. You must have an attitude that, no matter what, you have all the time you need. Whether the other person agrees or not is not the question. Whether or not they're mentally ill, demented, intoxicated, or deranged is not the question, either. The answer must start within you. Command presence is often "stillness in motion." One of the authors recently had the opportunity to watch a master firearms instructor during an "active-shooter" drill. What was startling was how slowly he *seemed* to be moving. In fact, he made every movement count. Each shot was a "kill." He looked like a tiger taking a stroll through a pack of hyenas.

This attitude equally applies to situations where verbal de-escalation and control is required with a mentally ill person. It is as if we're standing on the bank of a flooding river, and there is a person struggling in the water. If we dive in to save them, they will try to climb on top of us to reach just a little more air, and we will both drown. Instead, we throw them a rope, point to it, and encourage them to take hold. Were we to throw too fast, we'd miss them, or end up with a tangle of cord. Instead, "hurrying slowly," we cast the rope in the right place with the right speed. If they take hold, we can pull them in. If they refuse, there is, sadly, nothing we can do. The greatest likelihood that they *will* take hold is if we convey a sense of confidence. We pass to the other person that we *both* have all the time we need.

CHAPTER 6

Peer Support Is a Survival Tactic

There may be nothing worse than feeling helpless or shamed after experiencing a physical or emotional attack. When placed in fear of losing one's life or well-being, we can feel profoundly isolated. Often, our mind replays the incident over and over again, in an incessant loop. This sense of isolation and helplessness gets far worse if there is no one with whom we can discuss what happened to us. Some of the things that most powerfully affect officers are so ugly or appalling that they are reluctant to discuss them in detail with their spouses or other family members. To do so would be inviting violence or obscenity into their home, and police officers don't wish to pass the burden of grief or horror on to a loved-one.

In such circumstances, you need fair witnesses, often fellow officers, who know you, who respect you, and who are willing to hear you out. Such peer support can include strategizing sessions, (debriefings) or tactical review, but we must underscore that there are times that this is the last thing you need. Unlike participants in an after action review, a fair witness informs you, often simply by being there, that you're still a part of the human family, a valued member of the organization, despite the negative emotions that may have been engendered by the traumatic event you just went through. **To some of our readers, this chapter may seem far from a discussion on safety, but when we talk about someone "getting our back," it doesn't only mean that they're with us while going through the door. If we don't have an assurance that someone will be there when we return it's a lot harder to go through the doorway in the first place.**

Many agencies have incorporated a formal system of peer support, referred to by such terms as Critical Incident Response Teams (CIRT), Critical Emergency Response Teams (CERT), Critical Incident Stress Management (CISM), or Critical Incident Stress Debriefing (CISD). A critical incident is an extraordinary event that forces an officer to face vulnerability and mortality during the course of their official duties. These incidents typically occur without warning and jeopardize one's physical safety or emotional well-being. Incidents such as being victimized in an assault or engaging an individual in a lethal force encounter can overwhelm the officer's stress capacity. A prompt and structured response can reduce the negative consequences of such incidents and help restore the affected officer's physical and mental health.

CISM members are fellow officers who are trained to respond to critical events within the agency, and provide the affected officer with emotional support and assistance. In the event of an emergency, CISM officers will report to the scene as soon as possible where they will assess the officer's physical and mental condition, request that emergency medical services be dispatched to the scene if necessary, or serve as a liaison to other first responders already present. CISM members will also accompany the affected officer to the hospital, if necessary, and attend to any number of related duties, such as contacting the officer's family, and assuming control of their personal property.

Following the incident CISM members can also consult with the affected officer's immediate supervisor and recommend services (counseling, for example) as deemed necessary and appropriate. CISM members can also assist with any necessary paperwork that must be completed by the affected officer. Typically, the CISM member will contact the affected officer once a week for at least one month following the incident, and remain in contact with them until they're confident that the affected officer's physical and emotional needs have been addressed.

Figure 6 The Debate Concerning Documentation

CISM is used for a variety of professions besides law enforcement, including fire fighters, EMS, corrections officers, and parole/probation officers. Some CISM protocols recommend submitting a critical incident report to the administrative unit for the purpose of collecting information necessary to provide short-term and long-term assistance to the affected officer and to document activities, services, and progress.

The problem is that, although this report is not to be used as an investigative tool, it can be. As an official record, it may also be subpoenaed in a lawsuit or other legal proceeding. Therefore, many CISM protocols recommend that nothing should be put in writing. This helps the affected officer feel like he/she can talk more freely. For law enforcement officers, the authors recommend that CISM teams take no notes. Written records should be confined to formal after-action reviews.

CHAPTER 7

It's Not Personal
Unless You Make It So

Law enforcement officers must take care to not personalize any disagreements or altercations with individuals, no matter what the provocation. Responding to an aggressive individual, perhaps mentally ill, on a personal or emotional level will cloud an officer's judgment, while distracting him/her from legitimate safety concerns.

Although their attacks on you might *seem* personal, that is only true if you make them so. If the attack is false, why react as if it is true? On the other hand, if what the aggressor said is valid, then you're reacting in anger when someone tells you the truth. You knew it anyway, so what are you upset about?

- They call you fat? Well, you knew that already, didn't you?
- They called you a Nazi? You aren't, so why are you taking it personally?

Law enforcement officers must remember that any attempt to "get even," is unacceptable to the true professional. Your actions must be the result of unbiased decision-making based on the facts at hand. A move towards revenge is a manifestation of an attempt to assert dominance over the other as opposed to an attempt at establishing either safety or conflict resolution. When mentally ill individuals hurt your feelings because of what they say or do, *it is an act of valor not to respond in kind.* This is not about *"contempt of cop."*

Some aggressors use obscenity and other verbal violation as a distraction to get you focused on what they're saying rather than what they're doing. Others are just spewing nasty verbalizations and suddenly realize that you, upset at what they just said, have lost focus and are open to attack. Still others suddenly perceive in your response to what they said that *you* have "lost it," and they "attack you back first," because they believe you're about to react. Others challenge you by trying to offend you or through trying to make you explain yourself. Provocative challenges are for the purpose of getting leverage on you.

No One will Own Me

The verbal aggressor is trying to "push your buttons," often in an attempt to elicit an unprofessional or off-centered reaction. As previously described, the brain is organized to respond to danger through pattern-recognition that engenders a rapid reaction by the more primitive areas of the brain. A large object moving rapidly towards us, a sudden pain, or a violent grab initiates a cascade of responses—fight/flight/freeze/faint/flinch—that are geared to keep us alive in the worst of circumstances. At lower levels of danger, particularly that presented by another human being, we're provoked into posturing—dominance/submission displays—that serve to maintain or enhance our position in a social structure.

The curse of being human, however, is that these survival responses are precipitated by any noxious stimuli, particularly those that shock or surprise us. When someone unexpectedly violates our sense of right and wrong or verbally assaults us, because of our physical reaction to the offense, we often respond by automatically shifting into those primitive responses, even when survival is not truly an issue. **When our buttons are pushed, we react as if we're threatened with bodily harm.** This reaction, in most cases, ill-serves us in establishing peace or controlling the other person.

Anything that puts you off-balance puts you at risk. Therefore, it is important that you're **aware** of what your buttons are. Beyond that, use a technique called **bracketing** to make it harder, if not impossible for others to even get to your buttons. Bracketing requires you to face your vulnerabilities head on, so that no one can use them against you. It takes guts to examine yourself closely and say, "These are my weak spots." Doing so will give you greater strength. Not doing so will make you more vulnerable to attack.

You might think that a fair witness could be of great assistance here. However, talking about such difficult issues with another person often results in them trying to reassure or comfort you, reframing the "bad" as "not so bad," or helping you find excuses to explain why you're the way you are. To really identify your vulnerabilities, you must face the worst without the refuge of a comforting friend or witness.

Here's a worksheet that can help you name and bracket your own hot buttons. (You can make a photocopy to work on it separate from the book). Some example statements may include:

1. I can't stand it when someone attacks or demeans <   >, because that's something I love and treasure.
2. I feel outraged when someone demeans <   > because it is something I believe to be unquestionably right and good.
3. People get me defensive when they say or point out <   >, because, to tell the truth, I hate it in myself or, it is a flaw....
4. When people say or do <   >, I lose it because it's as if they're taking control of me, or disrespecting me.
5. They better not say <   >. That's the one word I won't take from anyone.

Statement	Why Does this Get to Me?
EXAMPLE: When people say or do < >, I lose it because it's as if they are taking control of me, or disrespecting me.	

Taking Inventory

Not surprisingly, we're most likely to lose our temper (our flexibility and strength) when we're blind-sided. Sudden emotional shock elicits the same responses in the nervous system as a physical attack. For example, if someone you trust suddenly insulted your race, religion, or gender, it is very likely that you will shift into a response using those parts of your brain, the limbic system and the midbrain, that express raw emotions. These primitive areas of the brain are not concerned about the truth, about negotiation, or how to make peace. Instead, they view the world as one at war, with the other person trying to destroy one's position of strength.

To avoid this, you do the equivalent of checking your kit before going out into the field. **Every morning, upon waking, and maybe even a few times during the day, you simply run an inventory, as if flipping through a set of cards, and call to mind each of your emotional triggers.** By bringing them to consciousness, you prepare yourself for the possibility that someone may try to set you off that day. Some people might believe this sort of inventory is either depressing or unnecessary, but these responses are no more realistic than regarding the requirement to check your mirrors before backing out of your driveway as an unfair burden. When (not "if"), someone tries to push one of your buttons, you aren't caught off guard. You expected it without being anxious about it. If you take inventory, you center yourself for another day, ready for the worst without it tearing you down.

When one's safety is on the line, it's not a burden: it's the intelligent thing to do. It is not self-therapy with the aim of fixing those flaws. The purpose is for you to become aware enough of your triggers that when people launch any verbal attacks, you're prepared to deal with them, already balanced. The only thing that you will take personally is your own dignity. So what if someone calls you a <Fill in your own obscenity>! The longer you're in this business the less and less name-calling gets to you.

If you have taken emotional inventory on a regular basis, you will greatly reduce the possibility of being blindsided. We don't mean that you're at hair-trigger readiness: that is closer to paranoia. Rather, you develop a sense of spaciousness so that you can see the attack coming, "brush it aside," and maintain your focus on the most important task: the establishment of safety and public order.

CHAPTER 8

Circular Breathing: Be the Eye in the Center of the Hurricane

Aggression and violence can smash through a previously peaceful day with the suddenness and force of a hurricane. Chaos doesn't only take over the day, but it may also overtake you. However, when you can respond by stepping coolly into the worst of situations, you embody the eye of the hurricane, with all the chaos coalescing and revolving around you. The root of this skill lies in breath control. Using a method called "circular breathing," you regain control of your physical self. When you control your body, you control your life. Then you're in a position to take control of the crisis as well as the person causing it.

Figure 8.1 Clarification: One Author's Experience

This is NOT a "time-out" where you take a few deep breaths and then return to the subject, refreshed. That is ridiculous. You can be moving very fast while breathing very slowly. You are training your body and mind to go into this breathing as a response to danger and stress. It is a trained response that should be instantaneous.

As someone who has practiced the following technique for over 30 years, I can assert that it has become automatic. Unlike my younger days when the adrenalin would hit and I'd start breathing fast and high in the chest, my breathing usually slows down in emergency situations. You are practicing to develop a "pseudo-instinct: a trained response so bone-deep that you don't even have to think about it, anymore than you have to tell yourself to yank your hand from a hot stove.

Two Variations

Circular breathing is derived from East Asian martial traditions and was used to keep warriors calm on the battlefield. There are two variations. Try both, alternating between them, until you know which one works best for you. From that point on, exclusively practice the one you prefer. *If you train regularly, it will kick in automatically, rather than being something you must think about.* In essence, your breath itself becomes your center, not your body posture, not the situation in which you find yourself, or whatever is going on between you and the aggressor.

Circular Breathing Method #1 – Initial Practice Method

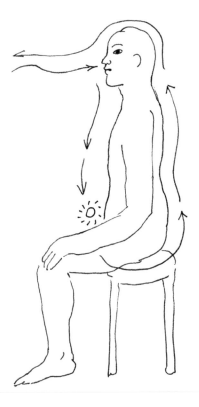

- Sit comfortably, feet on the floor, hands in your lap.
- Sit relaxed, but upright. Don't slump or twist your posture.
- Keep your eyes open. (**As you practice, so you will do.** If you practice with your eyes closed, your newly trained nervous system will send an impulse to close your eyes in emergency situations. If you want to use a breathing method for closed-eye guided imagery or relaxation, to get *away* from your problems, so to speak, use another method altogether.)
- Breathe in through the nose.
- Imagine the air traveling in a line down the front of your body to a point 2 inches below the navel.
- Momentarily pause, letting the breath remain in a dynamic equilibrium.
- As you exhale, imagine the air looping around your lower body, between your legs and up through the base of your spine.
- Continue to exhale, imagine the air going up your spine and around your head and then out of your nose.

Circular Breathing Method #2 – Initial Practice Method

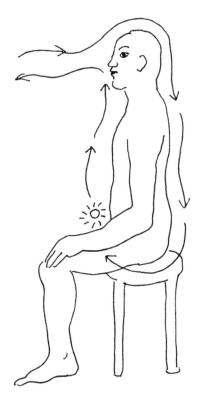

- Sit comfortably, feet on the floor, hands in your lap.
- Sit relaxed, but upright. Don't slump or twist your posture
- Keep your eyes open. (**As you practice, so you will do.** If you practice with your eyes closed, your newly trained nervous system will send an impulse to close your eyes in emergency situations. If you want to use a breathing method for closed-eye guided imagery or relaxation, to get *away* from your problems, so to speak, use another method altogether.)
- Breathe in through the nose.
- Imagine the air going up around your head, looping down the back, falling down each vertebra, continuing down past the base of the spine to the perineum, and looping again, this time up the front of the body to a point 2 inches below the navel.
- Momentarily pause, letting the breath remain in a dynamic equilibrium.
- As you exhale, imagine the air ascending up the centerline of your body and out your nose.

How to Practice Circular Breathing

Some people find that imagining their breath has light or color is helpful. Others take a finger or object to trace a line down and around the centerline of the body to help focus their attention. Choose what works better for you.

When you first practice, do so while seated and balanced. Once you develop some skill, try circular breathing standing, leaning, or even while driving. Most people find that after a short period of time they don't need to visualize the circulation of the breath. You literally will feel it, a ring of energy running through your body. You begin to feel balanced and ready for anything.

Once you're comfortable with your chosen pattern of breathing, experiment with it in slightly stressful circumstances, like being stuck in a line at the post office, issuing a traffic ticket to an arrogant or complaining citizen, or sitting through a meeting as a supervisor drones on about new paperwork requirements. When you can better manage yourself in these slightly aggravating or anxiety-provoking situations, you're ready to use it in an emergency situation. If you have practiced enough, you will naturally shift into this mode of breathing when the crisis hits. There will no longer be a need to tell yourself to "do" circular breathing. It will become reflexive, automatic, replacing old patterns of breathing that actually increased anxiety or anger within you.

Remember, this is a skill to be used during emergencies, not for relaxation or meditative purposes. Instead, you're trying to enhance that ability to do whatever is needed to fight, to dodge, to leave, to think gracefully and intelligently: whatever is required for the situation at hand.

When Should You Use Circular Breathing

The way you organize physically affects your thinking. For example, if you assumed the posture and breathing of a depressed person (slumped body, shallow breathing, sighing), and maintained it awhile, you would actually start to feel depressed. Similarly, if you clenched your fists, and start glaring around you with a lot of tension in your body, you'll start to feel angry. (You have probably observed a number of individuals working themselves up from anger through rage into an attack in just this way.) Similarly, circular breathing creates a specialized mindset; one adaptable and ready for anything, equally prepared for an easy conversation and for a fight, yet fixed on neither.

This method of breathing is very helpful when you're anticipating a potentially dangerous situation, anything from driving towards someone's residence to serve a warrant, to seeing potential danger down the street and moving in that direction. This breathing activates the entire nervous system in a way that enhances both creativity and the ability to survive.

This breathing can have a very powerful effect even in the middle of a confrontation. Not only do we get more stressed or upset in the presence of an agitated person, we become more peaceful in the presence of a calm one. Human beings tend to template their mood to the most powerful individual close by. We're sure that you know officers who, when they walk onto a scene, often calm it down before they have said a word. You have probably seen the opposite as well. Using this breathing method is a vital tool in making you the former type, a man/woman of quiet power.

Use this method of breathing after the crisis as well. You will need to regroup to go on with the rest of your shift. Circular breathing will bring you back to a calm and relaxed state, prepared to handle the next crisis, should one occur.

If you bring feelings from a crisis situation back home, you carry violence back to your family. Therefore, before entering your home, sit quietly in your car or even in the yard, and practice this breathing for a moment or two. The only thing that should come home is "you," not the crises you weathered.

Figure 8.2 One Author's Experience

Our breathing can either leave an opening for the crisis to take us over or it can enhance our ability to take it over. Despite all my years practicing this breathing, one can easily forget when the crisis hits full force. For example, I was the supervisor on an extremely intense call with a paranoid schizophrenic, armed with a knife. All of us thought that the situation was inevitably going south. Cliff, one of my best CIT trained officers arrived, and came up to me so I could brief him. He looked at me and instantly told me, "Hey, Sarge, circular breathing! You look so damn intense." I looked at him, took a deep breath, and it kicked right in. I had to control myself before I could control the scene.

Circular Breathing to Ward Off or Even Heal from Trauma

Figure 8.3 Concerning Circular Breathing

Although the material in this section may seem a little to "therapy" oriented to some, it is invaluable if you ever find yourself having difficulty dealing with a traumatic reaction and help is either not available, or you can't or shouldn't avail yourself of the help that is offered. Keep this in reserve for when you need it.

Post-Traumatic Stress Disorder (PTSD) isn't defined by how horrible the event sounds in description. It is defined by the victim's response to the event. PTSD isn't exactly a problem of memory, it is a problem because the event has not fully *become* a memory, and the event is still primarily experienced as if it is happening right now. When an event is fully a memory, it is experienced as something in the past, over and done with. Another way to think of it is a scar: it may not be pretty, and it certainly is a signpost that something significant happened to the person, but it no longer hurts. A trauma, on the other hand, is an open-wound. It is an *experience*. It isn't in the past, and in fact, may be affecting every moment of the person's life, or emerge suddenly, when evoked by something that elicits a sense that the event is happening again.

In PTSD, the person's nervous system is set to react as if there is an emergency whenever the trauma is recalled. This can be anything from an explicit memory to a small reminder; for example, although he doesn't consciously know why, an officer gets anxious every time someone coughs. This is because one of his squad coughed right before they found the dead child or the guns went off and a fellow officer was shot. Because trauma affects the brain at the deepest levels associated with survival, logical interventions (anything from reassurance to cognitive therapy) offer only equivocal success in helping people emerge from trauma. On the other hand, image-associated breathing techniques, which affect the brain as a whole, can assist people in realizing that the event is over and no longer a part of present experience. The following should be helpful in handing PTSD:

- Let us imagine that something very upsetting has happened to you. Perhaps you even recall an old trauma that still plagues your mind.
- Whenever you think about it (or it forcibly intrudes into your consciousness), your body tenses or twists in various ways. Your breathing pattern often changes.
- If this is your situation, go someplace where you won't be disturbed for a while. Make the mental image of that trauma as vivid as you can tolerate. This takes some courage, because most of us simultaneously avoid-as-we-remember. Rather, if only for a moment or two, meet it head on and re-experience it. If you physically organize *as if* something is happening, the brain believes that it truly is. Notice, in fine detail, how you physically and emotionally react to the traumatic memory. As difficult as this may be, it is important to establish for yourself what your baseline response is to the trauma. You must clearly experience what it "does" to you.
- Now take a couple of deep sighs. Sighing breaks up patterns of muscular tension and respiration. This is like rebooting your computer when the program is corrupt.
- Mentally say to the ugly experience: "Hush. Move over there to the right (or left). I'll get to you in a minute." For some people, it is even helpful to make a physical gesture, "guiding" or "pushing" the experience off to the side. We can't *force* ourselves to stop thinking about an experience if it has psychological power. Instead, we move it aside, as if we're guiding a wounded comrade to a seat in a hospital waiting room.
- Now initiate your preferred method of circular breathing.
- As the memory creeps back in (and it will), just breathe and center yourself, again placing the memory off to the side." Once again say, "Hush, I'll get to you in a minute." You can't fight it, so don't try. Just ease it aside until you're ready.
- When your breathing is smooth and your body is centered, you will be relaxed like an athlete, ready to move but with no wasted effort.
- Now, deliberately bring that ugly memory or trauma into your thoughts and imagination. Now, as you find yourself reacting, continue circular breathing, trying to bring yourself back to physical balance as you focus on the traumatic memory.

- Bit by bit, in either one session or a few, you will notice that you're increasingly able to hold the image with a relaxed body and a balanced posture. You're now able to re-experience the memory without the same painful, tense, or distorted response you used in the past. You're, metaphorically speaking, turning the open wound into scar tissue.

- You aren't wiping the slate of memory clean. Rather, you're placing it in a proper context—something that happened to you, but doesn't define you.

Figure 8.4 A Particular Value of Circular Breathing Imagery: Doing for Yourself

What is particularly valuable to many officers is that it allows one to take power back on one's own. There is no doubt that sometimes counseling is invaluable. However, it is sometimes hard to find a good counselor who understands a police officer's situation, that, for example, a trauma could be created because you were not successful in shooting someone, rather than be traumatized *because* you shot them. (Of course, the latter can also be true, but a good counselor must understand both.)

Furthermore, ongoing litigation, in which confidentiality can be threatened by subpoena or court order, can sometimes force officers to forego counseling that they might really need. This particular breathing method offers an option when counseling is either not an option, or something that the officer doesn't want.

If one can, on a daily basis, "inoculate" oneself against stressful, even potentially traumatic experiences, life will continue to be enjoyable, or will become enjoyable once again, even as you continue to work in a highly stressful environment. The goal is not trying to restore some kind of mythic "innocence," that one had "pre-trauma." The goal is to relegate the experience to its proper place—something ugly that happened sometime in the past.

Team Breathing

This is a simple technique to unify a team before, for example, a door entry. At "go," all officers take a deep breath, whoosh it out in unison, and *then* **GO**. Ken Good,[6] a world-class trainer on tactical entry (among many other skills), states that this helps coordinate the team into one focused entity.

CHAPTER 9

The Intoxication and Joy
of Righteous Anger

Most people consider anger to be a harmful emotion, one that upsets the angry person as well as the recipient. This isn't true for everyone. There is a subset of people, including a fair number of law enforcement officers, who don't mind fighting whatsoever, particularly when they believe their cause is just. These individuals go off-center in an interesting way, becoming calm, even happy, when someone offends them. As a boxer once stated in regards to an opponent, "When he gets hurt, he wants the round to be over. When I get hurt, I get happy." Such people, when functioning in a professional capacity, have an especially difficult task. They must recognize that when they feel *good*, they're in danger of becoming part of the problem. Instead of imposing calm, they escalate the situation, not minding it in the least.

Circular breathing (Chapter 8), for those who are anxious, stressed, or frightened provides a real sense of peace and relief. However, if confrontation feels good to you, such calming breathing, dynamic through it might be seems like the last thing you would like to do. You think, "Center myself? Hell, no. I'm right where I want to be." If this description fits, your task is to recognize the special joy that comes with righteous anger, and bring yourself to a calm state of mind, even though in the heat of the angry moment, it feels like a loss rather than a gain.

Figure 9.1 One Author's Experience

There are times when you are responding to a specific type of call, and you hear which officer(s) are answering up to cover you and you think, "Oh, Lord, this is not going to go well!" They're exactly where they want to be: angry yet safe, because there are other cops around. They're large and in charge, and they become indignant and self-righteous and escalate the situation the moment they hit the scene. Even worse, others are deliberately provocative, provoking the subject, even though they are mentally ill.

I recall being sent to a bar scene to quell a major disturbance. One particular officer was dealing with some un-friendlies in an adjacent alley. As he was defusing one unarmed, highly intoxicated male, another officer blew right past him and using his flashlight, struck the subject in the face just as the first officer was advising him he was under arrest. The startled cop, now wondering what he missed, was told, "I thought he assaulted you." The original officer, a defensive tactics instructor, hadn't been assaulted and if he had been, knew exactly how to remedy the situation.

The righteously angry officer may be known for this type of reaction. He/she is also the one most likely to *not* recognize this, and *not* believe they need to do any breathing or calming. **If this is you, recognize it and fix it.** This isn't about becoming some sort of Zen sage, never angered, never off-balance. Of course, you will be angry. In many situations you *should* be angry. It may even keep you alive. The problem is when anger justifies anything from treating, aggravating or troublesome people with contempt to actions that are either immoral or illegal on the extreme edge.

Figure 9.2 One Author's Experience

I was on the SWAT team in two different police departments, over a span of ten years. Of course, we all got excited when we had a SWAT call out. The adrenalin rush is most addictive. Yet, it is these times specifically that one needs to recognize this addiction and remember the mission and ethics of our jobs. I believe it is 100 percent fine to be righteously pissed off; it is the *action* you take that becomes scrutinized by the world, not your anger.

Circular breathing will assist you when you need it most: in the hairy situations. If any of you are thinking that this talk about breathing is on the New Age or "touchy-feely" side, for the purposes of this book, I consulted with one of our officers, a SWAT sniper who has served several tours of duty in Iraq. He stated, "I know all about what you're talking about, both righteous anger and how good it feels. I learned this type of breathing years ago, although we didn't call it by the same name. I can attest to centering myself lying behind the scope of my rifle awaiting a murder suspect to emerge from a residence."

Protecting Your Family From What You Otherwise Would Bring Home

Another type of righteous anger is that evoked when someone does something so clearly evil that you feel that annihilation of the perpetrator is the only justifiable response. Both of the authors, in varying capacities, have done investigation or evaluation in cases of child rape and murder. Circular breathing most definitely is needed prior to the interview to keep oneself balanced, focused, and thinking rationally rather than emotionally. If you indulge in your emotions, you will very likely blow the case. You want to be able to push the perpetrator's buttons rather than having your own pushed.

Returning to the subject of the last chapter, this is a particularly important example of how such breathing can protect your family. Both of us have felt utterly contaminated by being in the presence of some of these vile perpetrators of abuse. Having done our job well, gotten a confession, evidence to make a case, or ensured that the abusive parent never had access to the child again, we each have left the room feeling a failure because we didn't take the individual's throat between our hands and squeeze the life out of him/her for what they did to an innocent child. Both of us made sure that we never brought it home. Each of us learned to sit in our car, running the breath around our body, maybe going to a quiet place in the house or yard and work through the images in our brain, so that when we walked into the presence of our wives and children, the only thing each of us ever brought home was ourselves. No child molester will ever walk into the house with us.

SECTION III

Dealing With Unusual, Intense, and
Eccentric Communication Styles

CHAPTER 10

Overview

What is a mental illness anyway? Is it any odd or eccentric behavior, or should we not confine the term for more serious disturbances of behavior and thought. It sometimes seems that we lump together mental phenomenon that is as disparate as the distinction between a common cold and lung cancer. Yes, both may be troublesome, and make breathing difficult, but they're very different disorders.

Law Enforcement Officers should not feel that it is required that they diagnose what an individual may be suffering from, even in the most general way. This book focuses on behavior, not on illness.. However, if someone behaves in a way that makes it difficult to communicate with them, or even more problematically, enacts disruptive behaviors, then you should be prepared with several skills:

- The ability to recognize the behavior as showing a pattern.
- The knowledge of best practice communication strategies to respond to a person who is displaying such a pattern of behavior, whatever the cause may be.

Not everyone who needs to be calmed or de-escalated is aggressive. However, those who display unusual or eccentric patterns of behavior are more difficult to communicate with, and when the ability of people to communicate breaks down, the risk of aggression increases.

CHAPTER 11

Rigid Personality

Law enforcement should be aware that you will be seeing more and more socially withdrawn, very intelligent "misfits," who live their lives mostly online. They're getting increasingly involved in computer crimes, particularly hacking.

Although such individuals, who are often diagnosed with Asperger's Syndrome, may possess normal or even superior intelligence, they have tremendous difficulty negotiating social interactions. They find other people to be incomprehensible, confusing, or threatening, and to make matters worse for them, they find it very difficult to know from other's facial expressions, body posture, and vocal tone, what they're feeling or thinking. Other people, particularly some with schizophrenia, often show a similar combination of "cluelessness" and rigidity in communication with others. Such rigid individuals become fixated on their own preoccupations and imagine that everyone else shares them.

Such rigid individuals can also be very literal (concrete) and they can get stuck on certain thoughts and behaviors (obsessive). As one child with Asperger's Syndrome said when asked what he thought the bully who beat him up was thinking, "Oh, he was thinking of Lewis and Clark." When asked with astonishment why he would be thinking of that, the child replied, "What else could he be thinking about? It's the most wonderful story in the world. Lewis and Clark took the greatest journey...." It was a good ten minutes later before the therapist got him off the subject.

Others are simply not interested in or aware of others' feelings. This can lead them to be very blunt, or brutally honest.

Figure 11.1 Examples of Socially Clueless Statements by an Individual Displaying Rigid Personality Traits
1. "What is the bump on your face? It's quite ugly. You know, it could be a melanoma, which could cause your face to simply rot away, or it could infect your brain and then you'd die. I've seen photos of tumors that have actually eaten right through a person's cheek and you can see their teeth and tongue out the side of their face."
2. "You've gained a lot of weight in the last year. I don't mind, but many men don't think that is attractive."

THE THIN BLUE LIFELINE

They have no malevolent intent here. Other people's feelings—unimaginable and incomprehensible—are simply not a relevant bit of data to the person.

Such a person often doesn't appear to be mentally ill. Rather, they're stiff and socially awkward people, who are always a little out-of-sync. Their voice may be too loud, and they may sound odd. Their eye contact may be "off," or non-existent, and sometimes, they're physically uncoordinated. They don't pay attention to the effect that their actions or appearance might have on others. They're frequently insensitive to body spacing. Because they find people unpredictable and unreadable, they are frequently very anxious, and use self-soothing movements, like flapping their hands; rhythmically tapping an object or body part, to help distract them from what us stressful.

Quoting the rules with such an individual is often the best option. Consider this: if you had difficulty figuring out what someone— a police officer, for example—wants you to do, and the officer's body language, tone of voice, and facial expression are incomprehensible, the rules, clearly stated, would be very reassuring. Attempts at validating such individual's feelings, on the other hand, will merely result in them becoming increasingly confused or upset. State each rule in a matter-of-fact way, as if simply providing information. Follow this up with a logical sequence of steps to solve their problem. You must be as concrete and literal as they are. State the obvious. Below is an expanded list for dealing with individuals displaying rigid personality traits:

- In a matter of fact tone, explain the rules. She says, "Why should I lower my voice? I'm angry!" Your reply should be, "Because it is the rule here to speak about grievances with a quiet voice." "That's a stupid rule," she replies. "Nonetheless," you return, "it is the rule."
- Give them a logical alternative way to follow-up on their grievance.
- Even more than with other individuals, try to avoid physical contact. Many people with rigid personality traits detest touch and can react violently. Only touch them if you're taking physical control of them (defensive tactics).
- If they continue to be non-compliant, you may have to physically require them to comply with your lawful order, but take the extra time in the manner we suggest whenever possible.
- If they're doing a physical repetitive movement, such as flapping their hands, understand that it is for the purpose of calming themselves down. Nonetheless, if the movement (hand flapping near the waist or chest) could resemble a move towards a weapon, order them to stop, by telling them that it's against the rules to wave your hands around while speaking with a law enforcement officer. When they ask why, simply repeat that it is against the rules. When they ask if it's alright while speaking on the phone, say that it is alright in that circumstance, but not face-to-face. Understand that their incessant questions are an attempt to try to figure out just what they can and can't do. It isn't game-playing. They feel the need to cover all possibilities. However, after too many questions, you must take over and give a general policy that, hopefully, will cover all variations.

Figure 11.2 De-escalation of Someone With Rigid Personality Traits

Pavel. "I can't go to the hospital now. I saw seven orb spiders in my house, and that is bad destiny."

Officer. "Pavel, you are required to go to the hospital, no matter what number of spiders you have seen."

Pavel. "But this could mean a disaster for someone. Seven spiders is terrible."

Officer. "The rule is that people making suicidal threats must go to the hospital when told by a law enforcement officer to do so, and this applies even when you believe that there are unlucky signs."

Pavel. "Destiny, not bad luck."

Officer. "It is still the rule, be it destiny or not. The rule has no deviation."

Pavel. "How about if a meteor hits the hospital?"

Officer. "Pavel, the rule is ironclad. If you are told to go, you must.

Pavel. "Well, I think that's very irresponsible, that you would take someone to the hospital when a meteor might it!"

Officer. "Pavel, get your coat now. It's time to go. That IS the rule."

Figure 11.3 Review: Dealing with Rigid Personality

You will recognize the person with a rigid personality because they get stuck on subjects that seem rather odd in the circumstances. They seem unaware of their effect on others. Their emotions—if they're even displaying any—aren't those you would expect when someone calls with the complaint they have.

- State the rules in a matter-of-fact way, as if simply providing information.
- Follow this up with a logical sequence of steps to solve their problem.
- Discussion about their feelings will be counter-production. Tactical paraphrasing (Chapter 48) or other ordinary tactics to deal with an angry person tend to make things worse.
- No body contact unless it is part of defensive tactics or physical control.
- Don't get deflected from your task. Like a parody of a lawyer, they may bring up possible exceptions to your order. Remember: They are not playing games. "Step through" the objections and simply state that they're required to follow the rule.
- This type of person is relatively uncommon, unless you are working at a software or other technical site. Use this type of strategy only when it is clear that this is the type of person you are trying to interact with: rigid, stiff, concrete, and socially out of sync. Think of Data on Star Trek and perhaps include in your imagination, what Data would look like while angry, either coldly logical, or if that didn't work, frustrated and out of control. In the latter case, as always, control based on the mode of rage (Section X) they're displaying.

CHAPTER 12

Tell It Like It Is:
Communication With Concrete Thinkers

Concrete thinkers have a lot of difficulty, or even a complete inability, understanding metaphors, slang, or imagery. Instead, they take everything you say literally. For example:

- "Way to go!" an expression meant as praise. The concrete individual thinks, "I'm not going anywhere." Or "Where?"
- "Get out of my face," an expression that means that the person shouldn't be oppositional or aggressive. The concrete individual thinks, "I'm not in his face. I'm over here." Or "How can someone be inside someone's flesh?"

When communicating with concrete thinkers, officers should use short, clear sentences, using simple, yet specific words that are easy to understand. Remember, they will understand what you say in a very literal manner; they can comply with a specific command, but not even understand the general principal. Speak in a firm manner, and refrain from showing too much emotion. If you become angry or frustrated, the concrete individual will react to your emotions, not your instructions.

Figure 12.1 Example of a Dialog Between Law Enforcement Officer and a Concrete Thinker

LEO. "Okay. So you don't have to worry anymore."

Concrete Person. "I wasn't worried. I was upset."

LEO. "On, okay, you were upset. Anyway, the ambulance is coming, and will be here shortly. I want you to sit tight."

Concrete Person. "How do I sit tight? Should I wrap myself in a blanket?"

LEO. *(Sigh)* "No, you don't have to wrap yourself up. I meant you should sit quietly and…."

Concrete Person. "You mean I shouldn't talk?"

LEO. *(Aghhhhh)* "No, you can talk! It's a figure of speech!"

We think you get the idea. Let us take this last example and show what might be a better way to accomplish the task. Imagine this just from the LEO's side:

- "The ambulance is coming."
- "Sit in the chair right here."
- "Yes, sit where you are right now and keep talking to me. No, you don't have to wait by the door."
- "Yes, I can hear them too. No, sit in the chair until they come in the house."

Figure 12.2 Review: Concrete Thinkers

You will recognize *concrete thinkers* because they take what you say literally. Therefore be sure to:

- Use clear, short sentences, with a firm, calm voice.
- Give directions using simple words that are easy to understand.
- Show a minimum of emotion. Don't get irritated when they don't immediately understand you. They respond much more to your tone of voice than to what you say.

CHAPTER 13

Information Processing and Retention:
Consolidating Gains

Many mentally ill people develop the ability to "fake normal." People around them may do frightening things, but they don't show their fear. Other people may anger them, but they smile and pretend everything is all right. Conversations and ideas may be too complex, too fast, or irrelevant to what is going on inside them, but they have learned to pick up the rhythm of other people's speech, nod at the right moments, smile or laugh when needed, and agree with the tag lines that invite such agreement.[7]

Therefore, never assume that a mentally ill person understands what you have told them just because they nod their head at the right moment. You need to verify what they've understood:

- **The least effective method is to repeat using other words.** If they have either tuned you out, or didn't understand you the first time, they may fake understanding again. This is different from the repetition you must do with the disorganized individual, when you DO repeat yourself when giving instructions. Here, you're checking to see if what you said got through. Simply repeating yourself and assuming the other person understood what you said is often a mistake.

- **Have them repeat your instructions.** However, some individuals echo what you say, so this doesn't prove that they actually understand or will follow through.

- **Another method is open sentences.** For example, "So, Diane, if I've got it right, you will go home now and relax. And tomorrow you will…." (If she understands, she will fill in the rest of the sentence.)

- **Write down the most important points.** Many mentally ill people don't assimilate a lot of information that they hear, no matter how hard they listen. It is sometimes useful to pull out a small card and write down the most important points of the conversation or agreement. You give this to them, go over the items again, and tell them to check the card if they have any difficulty remembering what they're supposed to do. (We're aware that there are many circumstances where this strategy would be out of the question, but both of us have used it on occasion.)

Figure 13 Review of Consolidation of Gains

- The least effective way is to repeat yourself, hoping that their replies and head-nods really mean that they understood you.
- Have the person repeat back your instructions.
- Use open sentences and questions, allowing the person to fill in the blanks.
- Write down the most important points on a card.

CHAPTER 14

Coping With Stubborn Refusals

There are many non-criminal, non-emergent occasions when, despite treating your contact with clarity and respect, they refuse to comply. They won't voluntarily go to the hospital, give you anyone to call on their behalf, allow you to give them a ride anywhere, or any one of a number of other issues. Of course, if you have been bossing them around, patronizing them, or treating them with disrespect, it isn't surprising if they resist you. All people, mentally ill or not, have pride, and no one likes another person talking down to them or controlling their lives. However, once you're clear that it isn't your approach that is creating the problem, what, if anything, can you do?

Figure 14 Steps to Compliance

- **Focus on the task.** It is very important NOT to take the impasse personally. If you do so, it just adds additional problems to work out between you.
- **Clarify the message using a calm commanding voice.** Be clear on what you require the person to do now. Stay very concrete.
- **Control the interview.** Stay on topic and don't allow the person to divert your attention to unrelated issues.
- **Dispassionately state the consequences.** When this is an issue of compliance to your legal authority, it must be made eminently clear that sanctions will be imposed for non-compliance.
- **Place the power in their hands.** Again, in situations where this is a question of the person complying with a legal command, step back emotionally and sometimes physically (a fraction of a step). Say something like, "You are absolutely correct. You can refuse. Then you can go to jail. Or you can comply and stay in your home. Looks like you have a decision to make."

CHAPTER 15

Stuck: Coping with Repetitive Demands,
Questions, and Obsessions

Sometimes mentally ill individuals make a repetitive demand for information that you have already answered or explained in exhaustive detail. There can be a variety of reasons for this, and each should be dealt with in a different manner:

- They get "stuck" on an obsessive thought or idea. No matter how many times they get the answer, they have to ask it again. This is often a sign of Obsessive-Compulsive Disorder (OCD). Such people experience unbearable anxiety when they don't give in to the obsession or compulsion. Be aware that some people feel so trapped by their compulsions that they may lash out if they feel themselves impeded in carrying them out. Therefore, while keeping fully aware of the potential for assault, calmly require them to do what they must to comply with your directives. In situations where the compulsion is not dangerous, you can tell them that they can fulfill them *after* they comply with you, as in, "You can count the holes in the ceiling after you give me your hand to take your fingerprints." In other cases, you can allow them to fulfill the compulsion in order to engender more compliance, such as, "You may wash your hands and then you will sit here and answer my questions." However, be aware that some compulsive people never do a "good enough" job, and they will feel compelled to do it again and again. In this case, go back to the first choice, and insist on compliance first.

- Others obsess as part of a disorder like schizophrenia, developmental disability, intoxication, or other serious impairments of cognition. If they are (re)asking the question because they either forgot or didn't understand the answer, it is most reasonable to answer them again. If they are not able to retain the information, their repetitive questions or obsessing on a single point may be due to information processing errors (Chapter 13). These individuals are not playing games; they simply have cognitive deficits that cripple their ability to understand and/or retain information.

- Sometimes people repeat a question *intending* to be irritating or challenging. Say in a matter-of-fact tone, "You already know the answer to that," or otherwise point out that they already have the information, and *move on*. By disengaging, you're saying, "I'm not participating in the game." If they persist, it's necessary to let them know that continued game playing will simply make their own life more difficult.

Figure 15.1 Two Examples

- **Bob has Huntington's Chorea.** Therefore he has no sense of proper body spacing, frequently ask repetitive questions, and make repetitive demands. He knows it aggravates the officers who have contact with him, but he can't modify his behavior.

- **George has OCD.** He has an incessant obsession that he will, one day, choke his baby daughter to death. He has no desire to do so, and is horrified by the thought, but he can't escape it. In his search for help, he calls crisis lines and talks to counselors, and they, understandably, contact law enforcement because they can't be sure that he isn't simply mentally rehearsing a crime. After a divorce, and 2 law enforcement investigations, both of which required an expensive psychological evaluation and legal fees, his finances are devastated and he can only see his daughter under supervision.

Figure 15.2 Dealing with Repetitive Demands and Compulsions

- If the person is obsessive-compulsive in behavior, either offer them a chance to fulfill the (non-dangerous) compulsion after they comply with your requirements, or in some cases, allow them to fulfill the compulsion and then they will comply. If they get stuck, and cannot fulfill the compulsion, take over in a calm way and require them to comply with your first. Be prepared for assault if they become frustrated in response.

- With psychotic or other seriously mentally ill people who get stuck on something, remember that it is not game playing. It is due to their cognitive impairments. It is usually easier to simply answer the question again and move on.

- For those who are playing games, simply reply, "You already know the answer to that" and move on with your task.

CHAPTER 16

The Need for Reassurance

Some people are quite anxious by nature or circumstances. For others, intolerable anxiety is either their primary illness, a side effect of either their medication or some illicit drug they are taking, or one of the most troublesome symptoms of their mental disorder. **Anxiety is living as if something that you're afraid of might happen or is happening right now.** For example, the person reads about an earthquake in Japan and imagines what might happen to his/her town if an earthquake hit, and suddenly it is as if the ground has started shaking.

When dealing with someone afflicted by anxiety, you must draw a graceful line. Imagine this is a witness whom you're trying to convince to testify. Don't coddle the person: if you treat him/her like they are weak, they will probably believe you. They may think that something awful is going to happen, and that is why you're talking in such careful tones. At the same time, don't affect a cheerful, "ain't no big thing" tone of voice. This kind of falsity will make the person either uneasy or irritated. Instead, make your voice matter-of-fact. Take their anxiety into account, but speak with an expectation that they're strong enough to manage what they must do.

Figure 16 Review: The Anxious Person
When the anxious person needs reassurance, use a confident voice that makes the person feel stronger for listening.

CHAPTER 17

Dealing with Mood Swings

People with mood swings display behavior that is sometimes referred to as labile. They're angry one minute, sad the next, and happy a couple minutes later. You will commonly see such behaviors among those individuals with borderline personality disorder, bipolar disorder, or those who have damaged their brains with long-term substance abuse. They can be very difficult to communicate with, much less de-escalate, because just as you try to deal with their current emotions, they shift into another. They can be verbally abusive, provocative, complaining, passive-aggressive, blaming, apologetic, ingratiating, and friendly all in the space of an hour, or less. They often attempt to get control of you even when they have no control over themselves.

Coping with Mood Swings

Rather than reacting to the person's behavior with body language or words that manifest your own anger or frustration, remain balanced and emotionally non-reactive. **You influence them by being exactly what they aren't.** The more you're unaffected by their emotional storms, the more likely that they will calm down (Section II)

Figure 17 Review: Mood Swings

Individuals with mood swings shift emotions rapidly, with no particular relationship to the situation they're in.

- Don't mirror the individual's emotional state, reacting to what they do.
- Control them through controlling your own emotions. Remain powerfully calm.
- Speak in a firm, yet calm, and controlled manner.
- Because they display any emotion you can imagine, use general de-escalation tactics, as described throughout the book, as needed.

CHAPTER 18

They Aren't Moving: What to do?

Y ou've surely been in situations where you tell the mentally ill person to do something and they stare vacantly at you, voice a million questions, express misgivings or anxiety, or drift off into a monologue about something completely different. They simply won't do what *you* think is good for them. They may not even understand what that is.

You have to determine if they're truly capable of doing what you think they should. Expectations do have to be realistic, especially with mentally ill individuals.

Observe yourself as you try to get the other person "moving." Do you like the sound of your voice? Don't sound like a "cheerleader" in an attempt to try to get them to comply. ("C'mon. You can do this!") Don't betray your frustration either. Keep your dignity! Persons with mental illness are far more likely to be compliant with police officers they respect, and from whom they've received respect.

Figure 18 Review: What To Do When They Aren't "Moving"
- Be aware of their limitations. Don't expect the person to do something they can't.
- If you perceive the individual is playing games, don't waste too much time asking repeatedly for them to do something. Furthermore, don't do things for them if they can do it themselves.

CHAPTER 19

Should a Police Officer Ever Apologize?

Some people store up grievances, allowing feelings of persecution and perceived personal slights to affect their entire worldview. With mentally ill individuals, these feelings can be more problematic because their memories may be distorted or even delusional. Frequent complaints about old history can become a significant barrier to compliance with directives, not to mention being extremely aggravating to the police officer who must continually turn the individual's attention back to the reason for the officer's contact with them.

- **Apologize.** When the person you're assisting complains, yet again, about something, think about it very carefully (albeit quickly!). Perhaps, maybe possibly, you should apologize. As one veteran street officer put it: "We're looking to get the situation sorted out as soon as possible without anyone getting hurt. I have apologized to people I believe have mental health issues for what the person describes as a previous officer's behavior, even when I have no knowledge of the incident. It has helped the immediate situation, and I believe the person left with a more positive view of police, that we can be strong enough to admit a possible mistake. Be careful, though. I don't apologize in a manner that blames the officer, undermines my or another officer's authority, or accepts the person's complaint as true. It is an easy matter to put qualifiers in an apology, such as, "If this happened as you describe, that's terrible!" or "'If that's what happened, I'm very sorry that occurred."

- **If an apology is not enough.** You might say, "You're still upset about that. You want to talk about it again, don't you?" Notice that you don't ask the person; you state your understanding. This gives them the opportunity to clarify what they're really upset about so that if their complaint is legitimate, you're able to effectively put it to rest.

Figure 19.1 One Author's Experience

An officer apologizing to the wrong person may be viewed as weak, and this could exacerbate a confrontation. On the other hand, I have apologized on a few occasions. I was in a hurry with one mentally ill man, and he was very slow. I just needed to get him to the hospital so I could get on with my work. At one point I became frustrated and told him to, "Move your feet, not your mouth!" Not only did this get his attention but it actually hurt his feelings, and made things worse. I offered a most sincere apology that he accepted, and we sorted things out.

- **Complaints as their own reward.** Other folks don't want an apology, nor do they want to "make things right." The complaint becomes a "rewarding" activity in itself. Others bear a pervasive resentment towards you personally, towards law enforcement in general, or even life itself. For them, complaints are merely an expression of hostility or an attempt to get power over you by getting you to talk about things on their agenda. In both these cases, simply take it off the table: forever. Call them on the game, and state words to the effect that you have already addressed the complaint so that there is nothing more to discuss.

Figure 19.2 Review: Should an officer ever apologize?

Consider the following:
- If you have wronged the person, if it doesn't put you in danger, and if it enables you to assume tactical strength, then yes you should.
- If another officer is said to have wronged the person, give a generic apology. Maybe it's true, maybe it's not.
- If the person is stuck on the issue, say, "You are still upset about that," or something similar, giving them an opportunity to clarify why it is still a problem for them.
- If they're using the grievance or complaint to get control of the exchange, distract you, or simply complain for the sake of complaining, shut it down. Call them on their game and don't allow it to continue.

CHAPTER 20

Useful Tactics for Dealing With Symptoms of Paranoia and Persecution

---

Figure 20.1 This Chapter Focuses on Paranoia

This chapter focuses on tactics specific to paranoia. We're here discussing an attitude with the following characteristics: a sense of being persecuted, blame of others for any problem, and a hair-trigger sensitivity to being vulnerable.

The delusional paranoid individual (Chapter 28 & 29) has this attitude complicated by fixed false beliefs and even hallucinations.

Dealing with a paranoid individual can be surpassingly difficult. The person's motto of life could be summed up in a phrase: "If there is a problem here, that would be your fault." The paranoid world is one of dominance and submission: the paranoid tries to dominate the other people in their lives, and is terrified or enraged at being forced to submit.

The paranoid individual (even without delusions) has a consistent *attitude* of blame, resentment of authority, fear of vulnerability, and an expectation of being betrayed by people they trust. Stimulant users, notably those addicted to methamphetamine and cocaine, frequently display these behaviors. It is also a very common "solution" that criminals arrive at to excuse any failure. Paranoid people are, at core level, terrified that they will be made vulnerable, but they're aggressive toward that of which they're afraid. One helpful image of the paranoid person is an angry porcupine, all quills, with a soft underbelly, hunched over, ready to strike in hair-trigger reaction.

- **Paranoid people interpret relaxation as vulnerability.** Friendship means letting your guard down. Therefore, they become more paranoid when you begin to establish rapport with them. For this reason, paranoid people are particularly volatile within their families. With paranoid folks with whom you have frequent contact, such as some homeless mentally ill individuals who reside in a downtown core area, don't be surprised if they suddenly flare up with suspicion or accusations during times that are uneventful or even, within professional limits, friendly.

- **Being mistaken or wrong is another form of vulnerability.** Rather than admitting wrongdoing or mistakes, paranoid individuals reflexively *project* negative feelings on the other person. If they feel hate, they believe you hate them. If they have difficulty with their family after you tried to resolve a potentially violent domestic issue, they will claim you set them up by planning this with their family.
- **Paranoid people live like detectives.** They continually search for evidence to prove what they already know is true. They have *ideas of reference*, in which they believe that other conversations, glances, or actions are directed at them. They assume that others are conspiring about them, talking about them, laughing at them. Ironically, their reactions, in response to these paranoid ideas often cause others to act in exactly the way the paranoid person expects and fears.
- **Paranoid people make others uncomfortable and/or afraid.** Because of their aggressive or standoffish behavior, they can make other people uncomfortable or afraid. If they sense fear in you, they expect you to attack, and they will then "attack you back first," because fear drives their aggression. Even in situations when you do feel threatened, *appear calm*. (Chapter 8).

Try to Let Them Know What Is Going On
- Because paranoid people are so suspicious, they will often quiz you concerning why you're doing something. Whenever you can, tell them what you're doing.
- At the same time, you shouldn't accept being quizzed incessantly. You aren't required to explain every action. In fact, it might be a tactic to throw you off guard or distract you.
- It often makes tactical sense to say what you're going to do, so there is no ambiguity.
- Even when you place them into protective custody, explain what you're doing and why —once they're secure. You will be dealing with them again, and if they have a sense that you've treated them in good faith, things are more likely to go well next time as well.

Physical and Psychological Personal Space with the Paranoid Individual
Many paranoid people are preoccupied, even obsessed with fears that they will be invaded or controlled in some fashion. The more psychotic are often afraid that they will be molested or otherwise sexually violated. Some of the following are, of course, relevant when dealing with any individual, but they're doubly important with the paranoid individual.
- **Maintain the angle.** Whether standing or sitting, turn your body at a slight angle, so that physical "confrontation" is a choice rather than a requirement. If you directly face a paranoid individual, you *force* that person to turn away if he/she doesn't want to face you. This usually increases their agitation.
- **Mindfulness.** Never let down your own guard. You're in an avalanche zone, and anything could set off another slide.
- **Differentiate.** Paranoid individuals feel safest when you differentiate yourself from them, so that you aren't interwoven with their delusional fears. Therefore, it is better to be somewhat emotionally distant rather than too warm and friendly.
- **Too friendly is as dangerous as a threat.** Try to be aware when things are getting too relaxed. It isn't only about you maintaining awareness. If the paranoid person relaxes, they may suddenly

startle, realizing that for a brief moment, they let their guard down. They may respond by exploding to make sure you don't "take them over."

- **Cover your triggers.** Paranoid people may try to provoke you. If you lose your temper, they will feel justified in whatever they do to you as well as it keying into their terror-based aggression. A slang expression for this is "fear biters." They bark and snarl and when you react, they attack as if you went after them first.

Is there a specific paranoid rage or violence?

There is no specific "paranoid rage." Instead, paranoia is an "engine" that drives rage in all its various forms, so you will use all the tactics described in Section X. You'll de-escalate the individual using tactics specific to the mode of rage they're exhibiting rather than de-escalating "paranoia" itself. Paranoid individuals can exhibit traits of fear, frustration, intimidation, and manipulation. With their focus, however, they're rarely disorganized. Even so, some disorganized people can experience an "omni-directional dread," a pervasive terror that is inescapable.

Figure 20.2 Review: Paranoia and Persecution

The paranoid individual has an attitude that if anything is wrong it is another person's fault. Whether delusional or not, they see others as conspiring against them or persecuting them.

- Depending on what will prove useful, use any of the standard tactics for delusional people when speaking with a person whose delusions are paranoid.
- De-escalate based on the behavior, not the paranoia.
- Let them know what's going on.
- Speak in formal tones. Don't be too friendly.
- They will try to provoke you so they can "hit you back first."
- Be aware of both physical and emotional spacing. Maintain a correct distancing, neither too close nor too far.
- Differentiate by not being too friendly, and if they're delusional, clearly separate yourself from their paranoid ideas without getting into an argument with them.
- Maintain your calm. The paranoid individual is usually assaultive when they feel under attack, when they perceive you as controlling them, or when they perceive that you are afraid.
- If you do take them into custody, or otherwise control them, let them know what is going on and why. Paranoid individual are most likely to become dangerous when they base their actions on their imagination rather than on reality.

SECTION IV

Recognizing the Strategies of Manipulative and Opportunistic Individuals

CHAPTER 21

Divide and Confuse:
Borderline Personality Disorder and Splitting

Figure 21.1 Authors' Note

Suicidal and para-suicidal behaviors are often displayed by individuals with borderline traits. These behaviors will be discussed in detail in Section VI

People with personality disorders (also called character disorders) have habitual ways of interacting that often cause them, and almost always others associated with them, considerable distress. However, most types of character disorder don't cause behaviors that require police response. One that does, discussed previously, is the paranoid personality (Chapter 20). Another is borderline personality. In essence, such a person believes that whatever feeling they're having right now is the only possibly reality. For example, road rage is a borderline reaction: someone cuts the person off, it makes them mad and instead of cooling down, they chase after the person and smash into their car. On the flip side, the same type of person meets someone attractive in a bar, and within 5 seconds, they know that it is the love of their life.

Any of us can be overcome by feelings that seem beyond our control and make emotional decisions that aren't in our own best interests. Sometimes we're impulsive, angry, or even enraged. For us, however, such experiences are an aberration, while for the individual with borderline personality disorder they're an everyday occurrence.

Figure 21.2 Examples of Borderline Personality Disorders

The main characters in the movie, *Monster,* starring Charlize Theron and Christina Ricci, are portrayals of women with two types of extreme borderline personality. Theron plays Alicia Wournos, a woman who came from a horrendously abusive background, drifted into prostitution, and then murdered six "johns." She had the emotional stability of a toddler, shifting from sweetness and trust to hair-trigger rage. Whatever she felt at that moment was her only reality. Some of her murders, at least, were based on the threat and abuse she *felt* she was experiencing from the johns.

The Ricci character was a woman of almost no character at all. She "templated" to the person she was with at the time. Rather than an "active" borderline like Wournos, she was passive. Like Wournos, however, all her actions were based on feelings alone, not on any rational evaluation on what was good for her.

Those on the mild end of the spectrum will be quite emotional, over-reacting to things that others take in their stride. For those whose disorder is more severe, it is as if their nervous system—at least that which modulates emotion—lacks any protective sheathing. Imagine trying to live your daily life with two layers of skin peeled off. That is borderline existence on an emotional level. One's current emotions are inescapable. The borderline person lives with the intensity, but also with the lack of emotional resilience of a toddler. They experience the world and the people in it as good and bad, perfect and foul.

Because of this combination of character traits, individuals with borderline personality disorder frequently find themselves in various crises. Among them are genuine suicide attempts, para-suicidal acts (self-mutilating behaviors or repeat suicide "gestures" that, however dangerous, are staged in a manner that is sure to be found out—Chapters 38 & 39), impulsive assaultive acts, (particularly those involving family or others close to them), and brief psychotic episodes. Among them are people whom law enforcement professionals call "frequent fliers," people who drain enormous amounts of time and resources from law enforcement. In such cases, it is very common for others (police, mental health professionals, prosecutors, advocates, etc.) to begin arguing in remarkably contentious fashion about what should be done with and for them.

When the individuals associated with a borderline individual get tangled up in intense disputes about what is best for them, this type of conflict is called **splitting**. Splitting should be regarded as a method of defense in which a person presents a different facet of their personality to each person with whom they interact. Although not really conscious of what they're doing, the borderline individual is at the center of the conflict. They don't intend to do this: they simply react. This "divide and confuse" strategy sets people against one another and keeps the "heat" off of the person doing the splitting.

Such cases should be discussed, sometimes with outside consultation, to figure out the best way to manage the person's confusing presentation and apparently endless need for help and attention. Once splitting has been proposed as a possible explanation for confusing and opposing viewpoints about the individual, then a case plan can be developed which really does justice to what the person really needs. Without this consultation, an incredible amount of time can be spent working and arguing about the status of one person.

What has to be recognized is that professionals are full "participants" in splitting, and quite frankly, sometimes it is their actions that create the splitting process. Police officers, case managers, and therapists must be ruthlessly honest with themselves and each other when splitting is a possible issue. The task is to provide an overarching view of the individual that admits opposing perspectives about that person within a larger picture that is based, at core, in ensuring public safety.

Figure 21.3 Example of Splitting

Crystal has returned to her abusive husband on five occasions, violating several restraining orders that she took out on him. Her children are in foster care because she didn't protect them from his sexual abuse.

She shifts from rage at him, to complaints about how the police were too brutal with him during his last arrest; to panic stricken calls to her therapist begging for help; and no-shows to the prosecutor's office for meetings regarding her upcoming testimony in his trial.

- One investigating officer regards her as her husband's partner in crime, saying, "If you let someone abuse your kids, you are as culpable as the abuser."
- A second officer feels sorry for her. She reminds the officer of her own daughter, someone who tries so hard to do things right and fails.
- The prosecutor regards her as a manipulative game player, who is using the system to try to get crime victim's compensation.
- Her psychiatrist thinks her erratic behavior is due to bipolar disorder and is medicating her.
- Her counselor sees her behavior as a manifestation of her childhood trauma, and has accused the police of being insensitive to abuse victims.
- Her substance abuse counselor sees her as co-dependent.
- Her children love her passionately, and have blown out of several foster homes. Crystal has told them that they're in foster care because "the judge said so."

Figure 21.4 Review: Dealing with Splitting

Stay focused on whether or not there is an emergent issue. Remember these people create a lot of drama so that situations seem to be emergencies, even when they aren't.

Don't be reactive to the manipulative complaints or side issues the person brings up. If they're a frequent caller or are involved in a case that brings in players from many different systems and agencies, pool resources to arrive at a common viewpoint and develop a plan concerning the person.

CHAPTER 22

Bad Intentions: Recognizing the Strategies of Manipulative and Opportunistic Individuals

Some people don't mean us well. They view us as opportunities to gain something they want or animated toys to play with for their own amusement. Others live for hate and destruction, but delight most in duping people so that they don't even know how "dirty they were done." Some manipulative people lie so that no one can pin them down, using a "divide and disappear" strategy so that the more powerful beings in their life argue about them, instead of focusing directly on what they're really doing.

A Compendium of Manipulative Strategies

Manipulative strategies[8] are as varied as malevolence, desperation, and/or human creativity can devise. Let us consider the following:

- **Alliance.** Once a working alliance has been apparently established, a law enforcement officer can tend to give their contacts the benefit of the doubt. This is a particular hazard when using confidential informants. What we might not realize is that the manipulative person makes establishing rapport difficult, so that the officer will be grateful when they believe that they finally achieve it. Once set up in this way, the officer rationalizes it when they become aware of their contact doing something outside the rules. In other cases, one is so relieved that the individual finally "gave it up" that one stops looking for anything more serious.

Figure 22 The Tactic of "Making It Difficult"

It used to be believed that sex offenders were "sectored:" that their kink was fixed, so that they could only "get off" on one thing. For example, if a person was a pedophile towards small girls, they wouldn't be interested in teenagers or boys, or if they were fixated on exhibitionism, they wouldn't be interested in forcible rape. Research has shown that this isn't true. To be sure, many sex offenders have victim profiles, sexualized or violent acts with which they're obsessed. However, many are also opportunistic and far more adaptable and/or indiscriminate than used to be assumed.

Therefore, imagine a long-drawn out interrogation regarding a man who steals underwear from the driers at an apartment complex. He plausibly denies the crimes, then, caught out, *implausibly* denies, and finally, after a long time, "gives it up." What a sense of relief: case closed! So one never thinks to ask about the rapes or the molestations or the window peeping that have occurred one township over. Like a magician, he gets you focused on "one thing" only.

- **Lies of omission.** Often their dishonesty is **"lies of omission."** They tell you reassuring aspects of a situation, but not include their intention to harm you. For example, you're on a "check the welfare" call to an individual, and he perceives your caution at entering his house. He says, for example:
  a. "You can come in. The lock doesn't work anyway."
  b. "My roommate's here. She's cool."
  c. "I guess you're a little uncomfortable going into a person's apartment seeing as the crisis line was worried I'm suicidal. You don't have to worry about that. I'm not suicidal."
  None of these statements establishes, in the slightest, that he doesn't mean to assault you.

- **Reassuring promise.** One sign of coercion is a reassuring promise when none was asked for. For example, an individual approaches a police officer in a parking lot and says, "I know you might be concerned about me coming up on you. That's why I waved. I only need to talk with you for two minutes, I promise."

- **Too much information.** One way to manage the perceptions of others is to talk too much, too elaborately. The manipulative person uses charm to keep their victim's attention focused on the relationship, or on the fascinating details of their stories rather than what they're doing.

- **Personal information.** The manipulative person will ask for personal information. This isn't only intimate information, but also everyday stuff. What is off-limits is determined by your job responsibilities and who the person is. Nonetheless, information can become leverage. The manipulator can use this information to further conversational topics, to "find" points in common and thereby, to enlist you in a positive view of them. Sometimes, the information is used to make it appear to others that you have a special or intimate relationship with the person.

- **Behavior observations.** Manipulative people make many behavioral observations. They're particularly interested in who is intimidated, easily frightened, or overly macho. All of these are "off-center." People who are off-center are easy to manipulate, physically or emotionally, because it is easy to make them react to what you do.

- **Blaming.** The more responsibility is theirs, the more they blame others for any problems. Sometimes such people will go on the attack, but when confronted, will straight-facedly deny they did any such thing OR ask a question like, "How come you're so sensitive?"

- **Bitter Complaints.** If manipulators don't get what they want, they may complain bitterly how they trusted you, and this is what happens.

- **Flirtation.** If you don't address flirtation and come-ons right away, it is viewed as implicit acceptance, which leaves you open to accusations of sexual harassment, as well as threats that such accusations will be leveled unless you comply with what the manipulator wants. Some manipulators will flirt with you in front of other people, leading others to believe that something *is* going on, that you're too weak to make it stop, or that the manipulative person has special privileges.

- **Manipulative language.** This can include (in addition to that already enumerated above):
  a. **Denial of direct responsibility.** "I got caught up in something."
  b. **Denial of personal responsibility.** "Nobody told me."
  c. **Minimizing.** "I made a mistake."
  d. **Collusion/Exclusion.** "You know what I mean." Or "You would, if you were hip."

e. **Obsequious non-compliance.** "I don't know." (Said so the wise cop will explain to them what they already knew—a kind of control.)

f. **I'm saying so, it must be true.** "Honestly." Or "I'll tell you the truth." Or "I wouldn't lie to you."

g. **You're like all the rest.** "I should have known you wouldn't understand."

CHAPTER 23

The Psychopath

Figure 23.1 Authors' Note

There is considerable overlap in this chapter with the safety recommendations made throughout this book, particularly in the last chapter on manipulative behavior. In Section X, we will discuss what to do when facing someone presenting with Hot, Predatory, or Aggressive-Manipulative Rage, all modes that the psychopath can manifest when they become dangerously aggressive. In this chapter we're highlighting the most salient point's specific to psychopathic individuals. This information is so important that it must also stand-alone for easy reference. For further information, the authors strongly recommend Robert Hare's illuminating work, *Without Conscience: The Disturbing World of the Psychopath*[9]

The terms psychopath and sociopath[10] are interchangeable and evoke very strong reactions. Estimates are that 1-3 percent of any population, and perhaps 40 percent of the prison population is psychopathic. A small percentage of people commit most of the crimes in any society, and although there is a sociological component to crime, the psychopath, to a remarkable degree, seems independent of such factors.

Over the years the entertainment media as well as sensationalized news accounts of horrendously violent killers and rapists have introduced an image of the malevolent criminal mastermind or the sadistic predator into the public's consciousness. Without a doubt, violent psychopaths do exist, but they're often rather mundane in appearance and affect, blending in with their surroundings without attracting any undue attention.

Figure 23.2 Examples of Psychopaths in the Movies

Instead of thinking of some movie monster such as Hannibal Lector, a much more useful image would be Johnny Depp's character in *Pirates of the Caribbean*. In his role as Captain Jack Sparrow, Depp plays an aggressive narcissist; he is attractive and likeable, but also utterly selfish and quite willing to violate social norms. A second image would be the Matt Damon character in *The Talented Mr. Ripley*, an inoffensive chameleon-like man, who has no *desire* to kill anyone, but when circumstances "require" it, he does so without hesitation.

Although psychopathic individuals can be charming and ingratiating, they can also be violent, provocative, dishonest, arrogant, and quite willing to break the law. Some are remarkably talented, even brilliantly creative. However, the only thing they really care about is themselves. Everything we have just discussed in regards to manipulative strategies in the last chapter is relevant to a discussion of psychopathic individuals. However, the latter presents problems beyond what you will experience with the "ordinary" criminal personality, however manipulative the latter may be.

Just as a cougar is known to attack whenever a vulnerable animal turns its back and exposes its neck, psychopathic individuals feed off vulnerability. Because of their manipulative charm, they can easily get under the defenses of others. They will gravitate to the most vulnerable people on your team. Not only do they lack a sense of remorse at the harm inflicted upon their victims, but also they often take uncommon delight in it.

Don't assume that we're merely talking about the criminal you may be trying to arrest. This may be the lawyer who is defending the criminal, the prosecutor who should be doing his/her job, or even another police officer on your squad. This can be the victim whom you believe you're protecting, who is, in fact, setting you or someone else up.

Many psychopaths are impulsive, and their sense of grandiosity often leads them to ignore consequences. They view themselves as much smarter than you (this is what often gets them caught). They will, however, study everything you do to find new methods to manipulate others. For example, "Hmm, when Officer Gibb's tilts her head and smiles while I'm talking, I find myself relaxing a little. I can use this the next time I'm trying to get close to a child."

Because such individuals are easily bored, they will deliberately agitate people whenever possible (in the police station waiting room, for example) through rumors, initiation of conflict, or provocative actions. Words are tools to them. As far as they're concerned, the truth and a lie have exactly the same importance, because the only thing that matters is their words' effect on others.

Some psychopaths are violent intimidators, but not all are "apex predators," like leopards or sharks. Most are fundamentally parasitic: con-men, petty criminals, or even businessmen or politicians who figure out legal ways to manipulate or rip people off. They may set up others to create emotional drama or conflict, using other people as "human yoyos" to dangle on a psychological string through lies, rumors, or intimidation.

Sexually selfish, psychopaths can:
- Groom others for exploitation or even worse, molestation and rape.

- Attempt to groom and secure a law enforcement officer just for the thrill of destroying their career, or for the purpose of blackmail or privilege (believe us, it's been done many times!).
- Have sex with whomever they can, simply to gratify themselves, heedless of the chaos they create.

Pedophiles can be thought of as "sectored psychopaths:" within their predatory mode, towards children, they display all the characteristics we're discussing here. When interacting with other members of society, they "fake normal" with such consummate skill that outside of their sector, they're, for all intent and purpose, just like you and I.

They have no loyalty to anyone, although they may form sentimental attachments that last until a stronger interest or desire pushes it away. This loyalty is on the level of, "Who do you think you are, patting my dog without my permission." At the same time, many psychopaths are violent:

- Some exhibit an explosive violence; they may lash out with appalling hatred and rage if they're frustrated in their desires, or proven out in some way so they feel exposed.
- Some exhibit expedient, predatory aggression. These individuals see it as either a business or a nourishment problem, either a problem of getting "paid," or getting "fed." They want something, and violence is the means to get it.
- Some exhibit sadistic violence. The act of violence, itself is gratifying.

Beyond all else, their highest goal is the conning, demeaning, manipulation, and even the destruction of other people. It is a marvelous victory if, for example, a psychopath manages to seduce a cop or correctional officer, thereby ruining his/her career; the destruction, of a vulnerable human being is far more delightful than the sex. Couple this with their previously mentioned charming manipulativeness, and the fact that there are NO therapeutic interventions that can "cure" the psychopathic personality, we hope it is obvious that helping professionals are particularly vulnerable to them, something that can compromise your ability to build a case.

Figure 23.3 Substance Abusers May Present like Psychopaths

Substance abusers often act like psychopaths while using. Addicts in remission who truly are engaged in treatment usually begin to abandon manipulative and strategic behaviors. Psychopaths, on the other hand, don't. They may use *different* strategies when they're sober, but they will never abandon a tactical, manipulative approach.

Tactical and Safety Considerations

- **You will be attacked through your "best" and your "worst" points**. The notion that the psychopathic individual will attack your weak points seems quite logical, and they certainly do. If you're insecure about your personal appearance; for example, the psychopath will either make you feel more insecure, or in a more sophisticated tactic, reassure you that he/she, at least, finds you quite attractive. What is harder to notice is when you're attacked through your best points. For example, if you're religious, they will try to consult with you about a passage in the Bible or Koran that they don't understand. If you love children, they will find a way to ask your advice on an alleged phone call from their ex-wife about putting their child on medications. They might really have a child who needs medication. But they're asking you in order to gain some traction: not to get your help. For such an individual, anything can be leverage. Remember, they don't even have to lie. The truth is an even better tool!

- **Notice when others start making excuses for them.** When conned or manipulated, people often find a way to rationalize what the psychopath is doing, or has done. For example, after assaulting another man at the mental health clinic where he goes for their domestic violence group, a counselor says, "You have to understand. He was brought up that way. When you threatened him with an arrest, it was like a flashback to the way his father treated him."

- **Track any manipulative strategies, document them well, and alert all other members of your team to the manipulative strategies an individual is using.** Consult and consult again. Don't discount the observations of other officers or especially those of correctional officers who interact most directly with those in question. Consult yet again.

- **You may be intimidated.** The most obvious manifestation of intimidation is fear. *There is always a reason for fear.* Use back-up. Watch out when you brush aside your fear, talking yourself out of a genuine warning sign that such a person means you harm. However, what is most difficult to perceive is when we unconsciously *avoid* being frightened by colluding or giving in to the psychopath. Ironically, a cop may sometimes claim that they have a special rapport or working relationship with the psychopath. In fact, all they're doing is giving the predatory individual what he/she wants. This is a particular hazard for officers "working" confidential informants.

- **Be aware of grooming behaviors.** The "grooming cycle" is a pattern and is a behavior designed to alleviate the intended victim's fears and apprehensions, all the while targeting them for attack. The predatory individual will make their target feel a little off-balance, anxious, or scared: just a little. Then they lessen the pressure while making a request that the officer would have granted anyway. The predator begins to "train" the officer to experience a sense of relief when granting a request.

Figure 23.4 An Example of Grooming

I stand too close to you (slightly, not enough to require you to issue a command that I back up). Then, simultaneous to moving back to a more comfortable distance, I ask for a glass of water. My goal is to cause you to associate granting a request with a release of tension. If successful, I will make requests that get closer and closer to a moral or ethical line. Once I get you to do something *over* the line; however, slightly, you are now compromised, an object of blackmail or worse. Hard eye-contact, shifting to friendliness, is another common grooming tactic. Another is a subtle build-up towards what looks like aggression, then strategically backing off.

- **Guard all personal information.** As discussed previously, personal information can be used in a variety of ways. The psychopath can use such information to determine points of leverage against you. They can talk publically about you, apparently displaying intimate knowledge of your affairs. In the worst case, such information can be used to track you down outside of your professional life, or make you fear for the safety of your friends and family.

- **Don't get beyond the horizon line.** *Don't meet psychopaths alone!* Have back-up when you meet with them in the field or in the office for an investigation. We're NOT only talking about physical danger. You're vulnerable to false accusations; you're vulnerable to manipulation where, with no one to monitor the interaction, you may not even perceive it happening; and of course, you're vulnerable to attack. Have a cover officer monitoring the contact for officer safety and to protect your career.

- **Calculated splitting.** As stated earlier, the psychopath uses gossip, rumors, misdirection, and blatant lying to set all the players against each other. Regular communication and consultation with everyone dealing with such an individual is the best way to detect and confront, splitting.

Figure 23.5 Example of Calculated Splitting

A psychopathic individual is undergoing preparation to testify against another person. He is lying. He is worried that the police officer has misgivings about the honesty of his testimony. During a meeting with the prosecutor, he subtly lets "slip" that the cop is worried about the case because he doesn't have confidence in women (like the prosecutor) having the strength or authority to convince a jury, particularly because the defense attorney is so good. If the psychopath does his/her "job" well, the prosecutor will no longer pay any attention to the police officer.

- **Don't try to "out-tough" the psychopath.** We have found two types of sociopaths: those who live as if they have nothing to lose, and those who *believe* that they live this way. Even though the latter may not actually have the courage to follow through with their assumed attitude, both types are exquisitely skilled in reading other people: how strong they are; what limits beyond which their target can't be pushed; and what danger they can present. We, who have a lot to lose—our reputations, our careers, and our well-being—can't successfully "bring off" an appearance of being a "pirate" ourselves. We will be seen for what we truly are, people merely trying to be tough. That is different from being strong! Strength carries an added component: integrity. We're individuals who won't compromise our morals, and who strive to be ourselves *as we are* rather than trying to convince the predator that we're something different. Through strength and integrity, we can prevail in an interaction with a predatory individual, and do so all the time!

SECTION V

Communication With Those With
Severe Mental Illness or Other Conditions
That Cause Severe Disability

CHAPTER 24

———

Overview

This section offers detailed descriptions of the most significant behaviors that mentally ill individuals may display, regardless of diagnosis. Along with each description will be suggestions for the best way to communicate with such individuals. Please note a lot of the strategies in various sections overlap. Some are generally applicable, while others are specific to only one type of behavior/symptom. Just because you might be reading about paranoia for example, doesn't mean that a paranoid individual isn't also disorganized, delusional, or manic. What you're trying to develop is a range of communication tactics that cover as many situations as possible.

When people hear the term "mental illness" they think of severely impaired individuals, who may display disordered or unusual behaviors. This is a common misunderstanding. Many behaviors that are a manifestation of a mental or emotional disturbance aren't particularly dramatic. Furthermore, most encounters that law enforcement officers will have with the mentally ill won't be emergencies. Nonetheless, the basic principles of communication presented here will serve with those who manifest a mild level of disorder, as well as those who are on the extreme end of the spectrum.

As the establishment of safety and the de-escalation of aggression are the primary purposes of this book, we focus on general patterns of communication and behavior, **regardless of the cause**. In this vein, we can generally distinguish two levels of concern: mental illness and character disorders. By **mental illness**, we mean any mental condition that severely disturbs the person's ability to *function* in ordinary society. **Character disorder** (also called "personality disorder") means any habitual way of relating to others that *causes significant difficulties*, for either the person or even more often to other people with whom they're interacting.

Mental illness, in this vein, doesn't only refer to such disorders as schizophrenia, bipolar disorder or depression. Character disorder doesn't only refer to such conditions as borderline, anti-social, histrionic or paranoid personality disorders. For example, intoxication can be considered a time limited, substance induced mental disorder or character disorder, depending on its level of severity. Beyond any medical condition, people, otherwise normal, can display acute, "out of character" behaviors, due to problems or stressors in their lives. Thus, for the sake of this discussion, substance abuse, distinct neurological disorders, as well as atypical episodes brought on by stress or other factors, all function as either a mental illness or a character disorder, depending on the individual's behavior. The cause may be relevant if making appropriate referrals for treatment; the police officer, however, should most emphatically focus on the behaviors, whatever the cause.

The Undamaged Self[11]

You're walking outside on an icy winter day. You slip suddenly and spin toward the pavement. You thrust out an arm that breaks your fall. It also breaks your right wrist. Your life, for a few weeks or months, is different. Even the simplest tasks are difficult and may require assistance. Still, even though you're inconvenienced, and the injury probably changes your mood quite a bit, you're still "you," the same person as before your injury. In due time, your injuries will heal, the accident forgotten, as you continue through life. Such is not the case with mental illness.

Severe mental illness can cause mental and emotional disturbances far more profound than the temporary inconveniences brought on by physical injury. One's ability to think is distorted, and with delusions, reality is skewed. Perceptions may be bizarre, even hallucinatory. Emotions swing from high to low, or shift into realms at odds with one's immediate circumstances. **Mental illness is an assault on one's worldview, but there is a still a person behind the symptoms.** They aren't simply bundles of raw emotions or distorted cognitions. There exists an essential part of each of them untouched by their mental illness. We can choose to speak to the illness, or speak to the *person* who is ill. That core part of his or her psyche is the person we're trying to reach, not only out of kindness and humanity, but also for tactical reasons.

Why do they stop taking their meds?

The question has to be asked, doesn't it? Countless numbers of people are leading productive, vibrant lives thanks to psychiatric medications. Why do so many mentally ill people enter a hospital or clinic in a terrible state, and thanks to good care and medications, leave in an exponentially better condition than when they entered the hospital, yet soon after they leave the hospital, they stop taking their medications?

- **Bureaucratic obstacles.** The lack of affordable, accessible community health care is a major impediment to treatment for many individuals, whose lack of insurance and medical coverage prevents them from filling their prescriptions, as well as the byzantine nature of the federal and state regulations regarding Medicaid and Social Security/Disability funding. For one example, if the mentally ill person is on Medicaid, they will be dropped if they are incarcerated, for even the most minor of offenses. To get back on Medicaid (and regain access to their medications), they have to reapply, something that, without direct assistance, they may not be able to do.
- **Unwelcome side effects.** Among possible side-effects are muscle spasms, intolerable itching/crawling sensations in the limbs, tongue thrusting, tremors, impairment of sexual functioning, dry mouth, weight gain, weight loss, skin rashes and lesions, even life-threatening disorders that must be monitored through such invasive procedures as regular blood-draws, to name but a few.
- **No effect (or so it seems).** Many psychiatric medications aren't "felt." They don't make the person high, or even "better." Apart from side-effects, which may be significant, the person simply feels like "himself/herself." Feeling good, therefore, one draws the natural conclusion that the drug has done its job, or in other cases, doesn't work, and therefore can be discontinued.
- **No effect (in truth).** Many of the medications simply don't work for a person. They may have had very high hopes that the medications would have helped, even cured them. All that they got, instead, were the side-effects.

- **The illness is better than the cure.** Sometimes, even apart from noxious side-effects, the illness can feel better than the "cure." Many psychotic individuals find that the medications muffle or suppress delusions and/or hallucinations, but they don't make them disappear. Furthermore, the medications don't touch the belief system around the delusions. Life on medications, for such people, is like living under a sodden blanket. What is reality to them may be muffled, tranquilized, and constricted, but not otherwise changed. For such people, the medications may help them live a more stable, uneventful life, but just as we shake off constricting bedding when we're too hot and constricted, psychotic individuals may discontinue medications, simply to have, in their view, air to breathe.
- **The use of illicit drugs or alcohol.** The person's use of illicit drugs and/or alcohol leads them to discontinue their prescribed medications.
- **Incapable of taking meds.** The individual is simply incapable of taking medications by themselves every day.

Figure 24 Knowledge of Medications as a Law Enforcement Tool

There are many reasons why an officer should pay attention to the medications that an individual might be taking.

- The medications in their possession, if prescribed by a doctor, can reveal some information on what mental illness the person may be suffering.
- If they have their pill bottles, you may be able to find out where they're getting treatment.
- You will have important information to provide corrections staff if you will be arresting them.
- You will sometimes find out information that establishes that the subject is using prescription medications to get high or intoxicated.

The authors recommend that your department or even each division be supplied with *Mosby's Drug Guide for Nurses* or a similar manual, in order to help familiarize officers with the various medications available, and to help identify any pills that may be taken from an individual during a search or an arrest. (Skidmore-Roth, Linda, *Mosby's 2011 Nursing Drug Reference, Elsevier*, 2010). Another option, of course, are a number of on-line resources.

CHAPTER 25

Struggling in a Fog:
Dealing With Symptoms of Disorganization

Figure 25.1 Concerning Chaotic Rage

See Chapter 59 for a detailed discussion of de-escalation of disorganized individuals in a state of chaotic rage, including information dealing with agitated developmentally disabled people.

Disorganization is a general term used to describe what it is like when individuals can't adequately organize their cognitions, perceptions, behaviors, and/or emotions so that they can function well in the real world. Developmentally delayed individuals, profoundly psychotic people, those suffering from any kind of dementia or delirium, as well as those who are severely intoxicated all show disorganized behaviors.

Due to their cognitive limitations, developmentally disabled individuals aren't skilled in problem-solving situations. Furthermore, they often lack the maturity to manage complex or frustrating situations, and the criminal justice process is nothing if not frustrating, confusing, intimidating, scary, and etc.

Psychotic people also become disorganized when they really deteriorate. Oddly enough, their delusions may serve them as an organizing principle. For example, if you believe yourself to be surrounded by enemies, or are out to save the world, you have to concentrate, because you're on a mission, as delusional as it may be. When one becomes disorganized, however, even one's delusions break down into chaotic thoughts, often manifested in incoherent speech. Finally, severe intoxication of any kind is a chemically induced disorganization.

Figure 25.2 A Word About Disorganization

You will know you're dealing with a disorganized person because they're nearly incoherent, or it is otherwise impossible to communicate with them. They may seem to shift from one emotion to another, for no logical reason, and it is very hard, if not impossible, to hold their attention. Disorganization is an "over-arching" category. A disorganized person can be latent, concrete, have mood swings, paranoia, anxiety, extreme agitation, confusion, delusions and hallucinations, and information processing problems to name only a few. We have included specific strategies for those syndromes elsewhere: this chapter is concerned with the overall phenomenon.

Overstimulation

Loud noises, the presence of many people (particularly if more than one is talking), too much background noise, or even bright fluorescent lights, won't only be distracting, but also may further agitate the disorganized person. Whenever safety issues don't demand them, turn off your flashers. Consistent with both control and safety concerns, move the individual to a less stimulating environment whenever it is possible. **It is particularly important with disorganized people that only one person speaks to them**.

Keep It Simple

The disorganized person pays far more attention to your non-verbal communication than verbal. Therefore, keep the emotion out of your voice: self-control is particularly important when de-escalating disorganized individuals. Your sentences should be short, and should only have one "packet" of information. For example: "Sit down," is a good phrase. "You've got to sit down, you might get hurt," is not.

Let Me Repeat Myself

When we aren't understood our usual impulse is to elaborate. We use different words, expressive hand and facial gestures, and the emotional tone of our communication intensifies. **With disorganized people, repeat the same statement or question word-for-word.** When their disorganization is profound, you may need to do this four, five, or more times. The aim isn't to browbeat them. You shouldn't increase your volume, shouting at them to get through to them. Your repetition is a touchstone of stability.

Figure 25.3 Concerning Dealing With Disorganized Individuals

Do not change your vocal tone, or get irritated, or you will defeat the purpose of repetition. The disorganized person will react to your frustrated or angry non-verbal communication, and will become more agitated. You will undermine everyone's safety by rolling your eyes, making side-long glances of amusement at your back-up, sighing, raising your voice, pointing, standing close to them to get their attention, snapping your fingers, or suddenly clapping, to name only a few, whether you are repeating the same words or not.

Refer to the section on latency, which is really one subset of disorganization. By repeating yourself several times, with a clear measured tone of voice, you can have the same effect on the disorganized person as you would were you to shine a light on a footpath in the fog. In this example, you have shown the lost person where to put their feet. By repeating yourself and telling the person exactly what you want them to do, you provide a verbal lifeline that they can focus on rather than the chaos that is otherwise overwhelming them.

Magical Thinking

Magical thinking is a term that overlaps with delusions. It is telling stories that you then believe. It is common among small children, senile and demented adults, and developmentally delayed individuals. People displaying magical thinking don't show the same fixed quality of delusional people (Chapter 28), where a fundamental truth is suddenly revealed and then locked into place in the person's mind. Rather, the disorganized person verbalizes his/her fantasies, repeats them, and then believes them. It is like fable making, the kinds of stories very young people tell, be they young in age or young in mind.

Figure 25.4 Important Note Regarding False Confessions

Research on false admissions to crimes reveals that a large number of such confessions are made by developmentally disabled individuals, particularly when they're feeling emotionally pressured or if they're trying to impress or please you. You will get the most reliable information from a developmentally disabled person when they're calm and feel safe.

Once you've established that a claim or statement isn't true, it is non-productive to argue about magical thinking. Sometimes, just let it go. Other times, you can say, even with a little tiredness in your voice, "I've heard that story before. You don't have to tell me again." Or, "Let's not talk about that anymore."

Figure 25.5 Review: Dealing With a Disorganized Individual

You will know you are dealing with a disorganized person when they're:
- Nearly incoherent, or otherwise impossible to communicate with;
- Shifting from one emotion to another with no logical reason;
- It is very hard, if not impossible to hold their attention;
- Acting in a bizarre or chaotic manner.

You should:
- Divide tasks into small bits;
- Give simple, specific instructions;
- Be realistic about what the person can and can't do;
- Repeat your instructions rather than elaborate on them. Don't change your vocal tone;
- Don't argue with magical thinking; redirect them to discussing what, if anything is emergent;
- Only one person should be speaking to the disorganized person at a time.
- Whenever possible, minimize environmental distractions, everything from the TV in the background, to other people talking, to bright lights.

CHAPTER 26

Dropping Stones in a Well: Latency

Latency is a behavior that is often a manifestation of disorganization, but because of both its significance and its confusing nature, we have chosen to discuss it as an entity of its own. This is a behavior in which people respond to communication in a much-delayed manner. You ask a question, and they talk to themselves quietly as they puzzle out what you might be saying. Perhaps instead, they don't even make eye-contact, and engage in odd movements. Some latent folks may simply stare away, a vacuous look on their faces.

Figure 26.1 How to Recognize Latency

You will recognize latency when the person to whom you are speaking not only delays his/her answers for a long time, but also when they do reply, their communication is somewhat odd and disjointed, not really responding to the questions asked. This is different from being silent or defying you. You will get the sense that they're not "there," that they are attending to something going on inside of them, and not you at all.

Imagine your words to be like a stones dropping into a well. If things go as expected, you hear a splash as each stone hits the water. Now, imagine the latent mind like an old well with bricks sticking out, and a tangle of tree roots halfway down. Each stone hits the roots and bounces off a brick, one after the other. This time, you don't hear a splash; you hear nothing. So you start throwing more stones, one after another. You now have any number of stones bouncing around, colliding into each other, adding to your frustration and their confusion, without the first stone ever reaching the bottom of the well. All that is happened with the latent person is that they get more confused and overwhelmed. In other words, adding more words doesn't enhance communication with latent people.

Figure 26.2 Example of a Typical Dialogue (Law Enforcement Officer and an Individual Displaying Latency

Officers responding to a profoundly mentally ill homeless man:

- **Officer.** "Why are you tying yourself to the stop sign?" (*Thirty seconds pass with the latent man standing and staring at the ground, frozen.*)
- **Officer asks again**, "Why are you tying yourself to the stop sign?"
- **Individual.** (*The mentally ill man slowly raises his head, and his eyes vacant, slowly says*) "Uh, stop sign." (*He then resumes tying himself to the sign with thin string.*)

- **Officer.** "I can take you to the hospital. I know there is someone there that is able to help you."
- **Individual.** *(The mentally ill man stops tying himself, his hands still holding the string in mid-knot. His lips move as if he is talking to himself. He raises his eyes, lowers them, and raises them again. Finally, he says),* "Don't take me, steal me." *(He then resumes his activity without eye contact. Attempts to get the man to provide identification or even say his name are fruitless.)*

Note the officer's exemplary patience. This contact is not a failure. The officer has ascertained that the individual is profoundly mentally ill, and unable to communicate even his identity. That the officer is calm probably keeps the individual from becoming fearful or combative in response.

Coping With Latency: Keep Things Simple

Although communicating with a latent person can be frustrating, and often time consuming, the police officer should remain calm. Indeed, any frustration or anger you display will only further confuse them. Keep your sentences and instructions short yet direct, and minimize the use of qualifiers, such as "you might" "maybe" "kind of," etc., that you ordinarily put in your sentences. Officers should also try to minimize the use of hand gestures or changing facial expressions. This doesn't mean you should speak robotically, but simplicity is best.

It is totally useless to try to "get through to them" by yelling. All this does is drive them further into the latent state, as they get more frightened, overwhelmed or confused by the irate cop yelling incomprehensible things at them.

Latent people usually don't need things explained in further detail; they just don't "get it" the first time. Say the same thing again and again. This is like somehow throwing the **same** stone into the well again, reinforcing the original. Rather than adding a new stone, you have added weight to the one already there. Now that stone can get through the roots and bricks and hit bottom.

If you aren't successful, you have actually established, better than any other method that the individual is incapable of responding to verbal communication, thus warranting an assessment by a mental health professional.

Figure 26.3 Review: How to Speak to a Latent Individual
- Keep your sentences short.
- Don't change your vocal tone.
- Repeat the instructions using the same words and the same tone of voice.
- Pause between sentences. Give the person time to process what you have said.
- Try to get the person to repeat back your instructions (No guarantees on this item!).

CHAPTER 27

Withdrawal From Intoxicating Substances

> **Figure 27.1 IMPORTANT NOTE: The Question of Dual Diagnosis**
>
> Given all the attention paid to this subject, the reader may question why we haven't devoted a large section specifically to the behaviors of "dual-diagnosis" individuals (those with both substance abuse and mental health issues) as a separate concern. There is no doubt whatsoever, that dual diagnosis can profoundly affect every aspect of a person's life. Substance abuse makes it much harder to heal from or even manage mental illness, and mental illness makes it much harder to recover from substance abuse.
>
> This book, however, is concerned with the issues of safety and de-escalation from extreme states. Imagine all the descriptions of behavior necessary to distinguish between, for example, a solvent inhaling person with bipolar disorder, a marijuana smoking person with social phobia, and a schizophrenic who injects a mixture of cocaine and heroin. To be sure, each and all of these concerns are relevant when it comes to treatment. The only thing that we're focusing on however, is **behavior**. Whatever substances they may have ingested, whatever illness or syndrome they may be suffering from, we're concerned with the behaviors that they're displaying. This is the only data relevant for crisis intervention. **In a crisis, deal with the behavior, not the cause.**

People in various stages of withdrawal often come into police department lobbies for help. Police also constantly encounter this type of individual on the streets of their community. Drug and alcohol withdrawal are medical emergencies. Your responsibility is to try to keep the person calm—and non-violent—until the ambulance arrives or until you can otherwise get him/her to the hospital or detox center.

People in withdrawal are often in pain or feeling quite ill. They're also frightened or irritable and very much focused on getting more drugs or alcohol, sometimes by any means necessary. The signs of withdrawal can include:

- **Unstable coordination.** Try to get the person to sit or lie down for their safety.
- **Restlessness and agitation.** Try to reduce any stimulating input.
- **Unpredictable and sudden actions.** Keep your movements calm and slow.
- **Slurred or incoherent speech.** Speak to them in a calm, quiet voice and make an extra effort to understand what they're saying. Provide short explanations of what is going on if they're disoriented.
- **Abnormally rigid muscles.** This type of person will present with tense muscles.
- **Being argumentative and demanding.** Try to redirect them or de-escalate depending on the mode of anger or rage they exhibit.

Figure 27.2 Review: Calming of Individuals in Withdrawal

Be calm and firm. Redirect them when they get very demanding. Reassure them that help is on the way. You are simply trying to delay things until the ambulance and/or back-up arrives. To reiterate, this is a medical emergency. A person in withdrawal may die without help.

There is no specific withdrawal rage. They will display terrified, chaotic, hot, cold, or predatory rage (Section X). Use the tactics that best fit the mode of rage they're experiencing.

CHAPTER 28

Psychosis: Delusions and Hallucinations

Whatever the diagnosis (i.e., schizophrenia, schizoaffective disorder, bipolar disorder, trauma based, depression, drug induced), the syndrome of psychosis is typified by delusions and/or hallucinations. A **delusion** is first and foremost a disturbance in cognition. It is a belief that doesn't fit reality. A **hallucination** is an unreal perception through any of the senses.

What is a delusion?

A delusion is usually referred to as a belief that doesn't conform to reality. Actually, it's a lot more than that:

- People from different cultures have different beliefs. Shared cultural beliefs, however, aren't delusional, even if you can't conceive how others could see the world as they do.
- There is often nothing remarkable about the delusional belief except that it isn't true. For example, everyone knows the FBI follows people, but is the FBI following this particular person?
- Lots of people have eccentric beliefs: unconventional religious rites, non-traditional dietary and health habits, or a belief in aliens, crop circles, or telepathy. Possibly, some of these are *your* beliefs; they're eccentric to others, but not to you. Unusual ideas and beliefs, however, aren't delusional.

A delusion is like being a member of a one-person cult. All the confusing thoughts the person may have had, all their worries, prayers, fantasies, or ideas suddenly coalesce into **THE BELIEF**. Such beliefs are unshakable, inarguable, and unaltered by conflicting evidence.

Types of Delusions

The following is a list of the different types of delusions:

- **Grandiose.** People with this type of delusion believe that they have been appointed to a special mission and that they have extraordinary or unusual powers, or are special, remarkable beings.
- **Religious.** Often linked with grandiose delusions, an individual may become preoccupied with religion, focusing all their attention on their beliefs, which may be self-made or associated with mainstream doctrines.
- **Jealous.** A person may believe, against all evidence, that their partner is unfaithful to them. Jealous delusions surpass the almost always-irrational nature of ordinary jealousy. The jealous delusional person concocts infidelity out of the slightest glance, a change in clothing, or a five-

minute delay in returning home, etc. Male perpetrators of domestic violence, particularly those with a paranoid or borderline character structure (Chapters 20 and 21), often manifest this type of delusional psychosis in periods of stress.

- **Delusional stalking (erotomania).** A person may believe that another person is in love with them, is married to them, or has been somehow designated as theirs, whether they know it or not. Special requirements for communicating with those who display erotomaniac stalking behaviors will be discussed below.

- **Persecutory (paranoia).** A paranoid person may believe that people, institutions, or other powers have hostile intentions toward them or have committing evil actions against them. They often believe that others are sending energy toward them, thinking about them, talking about them, or looking at them with malevolent intent. In addition to general strategies for managing any psychotic person, there are specific strategies for communicating with a paranoid person in Chapter 20.

What are hallucinations?

Hallucinations are perceptions through any of the five senses that don't conform to reality. Hallucinations are often, but not always, accompanied by delusions.

Figure 28 A Word About Hallucinations

It is possible to perceive a hallucination, but be neither delusional nor psychotic. A person may hallucinate, but either has no belief about it, or realizes that it is a disturbance of perception, rather than reality. For example, people suffering from several days of jet-lag may complain of hearing voices. However, they're quite aware that the voices are caused by sleep-deprivation; pay them no more heed than people do when they have a song "stuck" in their head.

Types of Hallucinations

The following is a list of the different types of hallucinations:

- **Auditory.** There are two levels of hallucinations perceived through hearing. The first level is *auditory distortion*. One mishears what is said, something that is frequently part of persecutory delusions. For example, a paranoid person is sitting near someone in a restaurant who says, "Do you want the chicken or the ribs?" They hear, "Let's get this chicken in the ribs." The second level is true *auditory hallucinations*. Close your eyes when someone speaks to you. Do you still hear their voice? Of course you do. When people have an auditory hallucination the voices are equally real: they're experienced, not merely imagined. That is why you can't simply say, "The voice isn't real;" that makes as much sense to them as someone saying "your foot isn't real." *Paranoid people, in particular, often display a "listening attitude."* They enter a situation that evokes their paranoia, and expect to be victimized, accused, talked about or assaulted. Then they either mishear people based on what they expect to hear, or in more severe cases, they actually hear hallucinatory voices uttering just what they expected or feared.[12]

- **Visual.** There are two levels where people may experience ***visual distortions***. The distorted visual image appears to move, melt, emerge toward them, or even speak. Think of a Salvador Dali painting in which the objects melt and flow. **The second level is true *visual hallucinations*,** in which objects or beings appear that no one else can see.

- **Olfactory.** This is sometimes a result or symptom of brain injury, as the part of the brain that detects odor(s) is at the front of the head, a frequent target of injury. If a previously non-psychotic person complains of hallucinatory smells, immediately get them checked medically. With so many of our young soldiers returning from the Middle East wars with traumatic brain injuries (TBI), this is of significant concern, particularly because this is often an emergent situation that, if not addressed, can result in permanent brain damage. Other people, without head injuries and purely psychotic, can get focused on their own body smells, and believe, for example, that they're rotting away. Other times, they believe they can smell poison gas seeping through the walls.

- **Tactile.** These are sensations felt within the body. The sensation of bugs crawling on the skin is a frequent side effect of such drugs as methamphetamine or cocaine. Tactile hallucinations can also be a side effect of a person's psychiatric medication. Tactile hallucinations are incredibly irritating. Remember the last time you had "prickly heat," or some other miserable rash. Remember what it did to your disposition. Now multiply that tenfold. Therefore, always be prepared for anger or even rage on the part of a person who is experiencing tactile hallucinations, even apart from the concern you would always have regarding someone abusing large quantities of meth or cocaine. In any case, a medical doctor should always check this symptom.

The Torment of Hallucinations

Hallucinations torment their victims in a variety of ways:

- For unknown reasons, hallucinated voices are almost always cruel. People can be ordered to do awful or degrading things, or they may simply hear awful sounds and ugly demeaning words. Visual hallucinations can be as haunting as ghosts. Olfactory hallucinations are often foul, and tactile hallucinations are almost always very unpleasant sensations.

- A person tries to tell others what they perceive, but their experience is denied over and over again. They can be teased or laughed at. Ironically, the people they tell often torment them in ways similar to the torment of the hallucinations.

- Psychotic individuals find that their worldview is called into question every day. They don't know what is real and what is not. Imagine reaching to pick up your coffee, and not knowing if the liquid will disappear from the cup, or if the handle will suddenly twine around your finger like a little snake. Imagine this is true of every object in your life. In such circumstances, these people find it difficult to trust anything at all.

CHAPTER 29

Communication With Someone Who Is Experiencing Delusions or Hallucinations

Disengage

It can be very draining to talk with a psychotic individual. Like a cultist trying to convert you to their group, they may try to convince you that what they believe is real. They may insist that you accept their beliefs, or even more problematic, insist that you *do* believe, but simply won't admit it. They become focused on debating your resistance, or furious that you deny what is, to them, absolutely true.

There is often no good reason to continue such a discussion. Delusions aren't like some sort of backed-up fluid that you vent and drain away. The more the delusional person talks about it, the more preoccupied he/she becomes, and more agitated as well. While delusional people may feel locked in their inner world and desperate to communicate what they're experiencing, discussion and argument seem to cement the delusions even further.

Figure 29.1 Rule #1: Disengage

There are many occasions when nothing at all can be accomplished by talking about delusions or hallucinations. There is no emergency, and no need for investigation or information gathering. In such cases, disengage.

Islands of Sanity

Imagine being dropped overboard into the ocean. It is cold and rough among the waves, and there are all sorts of sea-life that demand your attention: everything from sharks to jellyfish. There seems to be no way to escape, and it is so overwhelming that you can't take your mind off your situation.

Even in the ocean, however, there are small patches of land: islands. If you can only get to them, you can put your feet down on solid ground. For psychotic people, too, there are "islands of sanity," areas of their lives where they aren't delusional. They may be convinced, for example, that someone is poisoning their food, and only canned goods are safe to eat; or that someone is beaming messages directly into their brain. But when you bring up the subject of football, and the two of you begin talking about how the Steelers demolished yet another opponent, the psychotic person takes his mind off his delusions without even realizing it. For a brief moment, they have a moment of respite: an island of sanity.

Remember, you and other officers may deal with the same, profoundly psychotic person on a frequent basis. If you have a means of deflecting them out of their delusional rut and into discussing something where they can feel solid, they will begin to associate law enforcement officers as beings who stabilize rather than stress them. This, alone, is a significant factor in risk reduction. Therefore, try to ensure that other officers are aware of what the particular island of sanity is for a potentially dangerous psychotic person.

Figure 29.2 Rule #2: Move Toward an Island of Sanity

Pay attention to subjects where the person is not delusional. Unless there is an emergent issue that must be addressed, divert your contact to those "islands of sanity," whenever possible, rather than allowing the conversation to focus on delusional subjects. Make links with other subjects that are also not tainted by delusions. Think of yourself as expanding the size of the "land-mass:" making an area where it's predictable and safe. If the individual gets stuck within his/ her delusions, you may find that changing the subject requires real finesse. Nonetheless, do so whenever you can, because talking about delusions makes it worse.

NOTE: These "islands of sanity" are not necessarily "nice" subjects. One of the authors worked with a very dangerous man for nine months and the only subjects that he wasn't floridly psychotic were bar fights and motorcycles. It was safer talking about the sound of a cue ball impacting on someone's skull than what he had for dinner or what his childhood was like.

Threat Assessment: When should you talk about delusions or hallucinations?

Some of most dangerous mentally ill people are those whom you see over and over again. They frequently decompensate, or go off their medications; therefore, it is necessary to do a brief threat assessment every time you see them.

Imagine a delusional person who is sure that she is the Archangel Michael. If you recall this biblical story, Michael, the righteous sword of the Lord, casts Satan out of Heaven. Further imagine that this woman believes she perceives Satan's work in the behavior of people around her. Based on her past history, you must be aware when she gets preoccupied with her delusions, because some time ago, seeing evidence of Satan's corruption among her neighbors, she tried to acquire a sword at a pawnshop. Had she not praised the dealer for his help in cutting Satan out of the hearts of the children, the police wouldn't have been called, and the family down the street could have been maimed or killed.

Therefore, whenever this woman begins to talk about God, angels, Satan, or anything similar, it is a good idea to ask questions about that which she is preoccupied. Some questions you could ask her follow:
- Mrs. Hampton, are you telling me that you think you have seen Satan? Where?
- Why do you think that this is Satan's work?

- Do you think you should do anything about this?
- What do you think you should do?

If Mrs. Hampton's answers are bland and not aggressive, then change the subject to an "island of sanity" at the right moment. If her answers seem to manifest dangerous ideation, then you must act to get her help, protecting society in the process. For example, if she to says, "Don't call me Mrs. Hampton, that she-whore of Babylon! I'm Michael, the Lord's most beloved angel. Satan will have no place on this earth when I take my righteous sword in my strong right arm!" Then you will take action NOW. Be sure you have cover officers – remember, she believes herself to be the mightiest angel in Heaven—and complying with policy and procedure, get her evaluated by a professional.

Dangerous answers are an alarm call to get help: alerting her doctor, her care team, or take her into protective custody. She may have to have her medications adjusted, or needs to stay in the hospital for a brief or extended period of time. But whatever the appropriate response, you must act when she is dangerous again.

Figure 29.3 Rule #3: Talk About the Delusions to Assess Risk

Talk about the delusions as a means of threat assessment. Ask direct questions, particularly in regard to the person's intention to hurt him/ herself or others. When contacting such an individual bring up the issue of concern yourself if they don't do so on their own, just to see if they have become seriously delusional again. For example, "The last time we talked, you told me about the Angel Michael and Satan. Are you worried about the Devil today?" Remember, the distinction between this rule and the previous two is that in this case, you are assessing risk, not just indulging in a conversation about their preoccupations.

Don't Agree: At Least Most of the Time

It might seem to be easiest to take the line of least resistance, simply agreeing with the delusions, or pretending that you, too, perceive the hallucinations rather than get caught in arguments with a mentally ill person about reality. There are a number of problems in doing so, however:
- When you agree with delusions and/or hallucinations, you will entrench them deeper into the person's belief system.
- When you agree with delusions or hallucinations, *you* can be incorporated into the delusional system. Sometimes this can be ostensibly benign, but wearying. All that happens is that the person incessantly wants to talk with the only person who seems to share their point of view. In other words, they'll be waiting for you after your shift in hopes the conversation can continue. In other cases, this can become more toxic. You become a necessary part of their delusions, and they begin to stalk you.
- In other cases, you make a "misstep." For example, they believe that you, an emissary of Satan, have invited them to rule Hell along with him. However, when you don't deliver on what they

believe is your promise, they turn on you in rage, suddenly realizing that you were, in fact, an agent of Heaven sent to stop them from ascending to their throne.

- It can be dangerous in other ways. Just because one is mentally ill doesn't mean the person is gullible or stupid. Some street-wise mentally ill people soon realize that you don't really believe in their delusional world. They see you as scamming them or making fun of them. You can create someone focused on you as an enemy.

Figure 29.4 An Exception to the Rule

Sometimes the mentally ill person will incorporate a police officer into their delusions in a positive way. For example, an individual believes he has a secret team of advisors who tell him what to do. Recently, he announced that the officer was on the team, and he had therefore decided to listen to what she said and follow her advice. Don't try to "prime the pump" by claiming a positive role in their delusions, or simply accept it if the person so "appoints" you. Rather, even if you just have a few seconds, consider this development from all sides. In some cases, it may be worth consulting with their treatment team or a mental health professional. You have to assess if there is any risk that the delusion might "mutate" in a dangerous way. If, in your considered judgment it does make tactical sense, at *most* you accept this information silently. Don't say it yourself. In the example above, you might reply, "Well, all I know is that if the doctors think you should take your medications, then I think that's a very good idea."

Figure 29.5 Rule #4: Don't Agree With the Delusions

In almost all circumstances, don't agree with the delusions. At most, if you have a consensus that it is worth the risk, passively accept their perception in the interest of their complying with something that will keep everyone safer.

Don't Disagree: At Least Most of the Time

Common sense seems to demand that you speak for reality. When people see something that isn't there, shouldn't you tell them so? If they have an irrational belief, why not argue them out of it, or at least, diplomatically point out where they're wrong. This is problematic, however, because you're arguing *reality* with the person.

If you are having a conversation with your daughter, will you believe us if we tell you that you're talking to yourself, that there is no one else in the room? If you're sick of driving that ancient Crown Vic, will you believe us if we tell you that you're really riding in one of those road-hugging, lightning fast Dodge Chargers?

The problem with arguing with delusional or hallucinating people is that you're telling them that their perceptions are lying to them. If they had any trust in you before, it is unlikely that telling them that the world as they see it isn't real will improve that rapport.

Sometimes, however, delusional people may ask, even plead with you, for disagreement because they don't want to believe what their delusions seem to tell them. At other times, a hallucinating person can make a tenuous distinction between real perceptions and hallucinations and will ask if you think something hallucinated is real. In these cases, *when you have been invited*, it is acceptable to state that not only do you not perceive the hallucination or believe the delusion, but also that you don't think they are real.

Figure 29.6 Rule #5: Don't Disagree—At Least Most of the Time

Don't engage in arguments about whether the psychotic person's perceptions are real. However, if they <u>ask</u> you for a "reality check," then you can state that you don't believe that the delusional belief is correct or the hallucination is real. In this case, you are helping the person understand that what he/she perceives is not the "rule" of the world.

An Important Exception to the "Don't Disagree" Rule: Delusional Stalking13

All stalkers should be viewed as potentially quite dangerous, and, in addition, they have an absolutely selfish, entitled sense of their own right to approach, or harass the victim, either in person, or as is becoming more common, through the use of electronic media such as text messages, email, or social networking websites. **This is a crime, and the victim needs to be protected.**

A small subset of stalkers is neither obsessed nor trying to regain control of a relationship they have lost. They're truly delusional. They truly believe that the object of their interest is married to them, destined for them, or that there is some absolute condition that justifies their pursuit. Whether you're in a position to arrest them at that time or not, you must directly say that it isn't true that the victim is destined for, in love with, or otherwise involved with them. Don't get into long discussions, much less arguments. Simply state that it isn't true. Anything less than complete contradiction will be taken as agreement by the stalker. They may take this "agreement" as license to further stalk the victim, or even worse, as approval of their intended act of violence.

Figure 29.7 Rule #6: Exception—Disagree with the Delusion of Erotomania

Calmly and directly tell the delusional person they have no right to the victim they stalk. Define to them that what they're doing is stalking, and if you aren't able to arrest them, do whatever you can to ensure the safety of the victim, including consultation with experts in threat assessment of such cases, the possibility of a forensic mental health evaluation, and the establishment of a safety plan with the victim.

Differentiation: Distinguish Between Your World and Theirs

Delusional beliefs are nearly inescapable. When people experiencing psychotic symptoms attempt to discuss their delusions with others, they're often brushed off, minimized, or even ridiculed. Of course, officers should never act so callously or dismissively, although as we just learned, you can neither agree nor disagree with them either. How can you get the mentally ill person to recognize the distinction between your world and theirs, so you aren't merely wrapped up in their psychotic world? **Differentiate** yourself from them.

Simply stated, to differentiate is to perceive or express a difference. As used in this context, the authors mean that the police officer (you) should acknowledge the person's perceptions and beliefs, while also informing them that although you don't share their perceptions, you aren't arguing that theirs are invalid, unrealistic, or fantastical. You're however, attempting to have the psychotic person also concede that other viewpoints do exist. Here are some examples:

- Alice, I see the table and chairs, the pictures on the wall, and the books on the floor, just like you do. But you see something that I don't. I don't see a vat of boiling oil in the corner of the room. No, I'm not saying you don't see it. I believe you do. I'm just saying that it's something you see that I don't. I don't know why, but that's the way it is. Why do you think you see it?
- Sal, I only hear two voices in this room: yours and mine. I don't hear a woman's voice at all. What do you hear her say?
- Jamey, I know about the democrats and the republicans. I've never heard of the Illuminated Ones. I'm not arguing with you here. I'm just saying that I've never heard of them, so I'm not the person to talk about them.

Remember, the point here isn't to convince them that their delusions aren't real, or even that they're wrong. Basically, differentiation helps you keep the lines of communication open. Think of two people from different cultures, trying to explain what it is like to live in their respective worlds, or even two beings from different planets. If the mentally ill person finds himself/herself shut-down or discounted when they try to talk about their perceptions or beliefs, it is likely that they will try to shut you down in return. If you are, for example, investigating a crime, you've just lost your witness.

In some circumstances, you can act in concert with their belief without endorsing it. For example, "I can't see the laser beams, but I know lasers don't pass through solid objects. Maybe you will feel safer sitting in that ambulance over there."[14]

Figure 29.8 Rule #7: Differentiate

Give the individual the "right" to their own perceptions and beliefs. Inform them that you don't perceive what they do, you aren't arguing with them about what *they* see or believe. In some cases, take their delusions into account without agreeing with them. Example: "I don't see any razor blades on the tree branches, but if I did, I wouldn't walk around in the park after dark where I couldn't see what I might run into. I'd stay home when the sun went down."

Steam Valve: When the Pressure is Too Great

Some people, either psychotic or manic (Chapter 30) are so full of things to say, think, or feel that they seem like they're going to explode from the pressure. Their speech can become pressured as well. Words burst out of them in a cascade.

- Sometimes they make sense, but they totally dominate the "air time" in the room, talking over other people. Even if there is a task to be done, they can't focus and they make it nearly impossible for you to focus as well.
- Other times, they make no sense whatsoever. Their words may sound like poetry as they link words by sound, not by meaning.
- They may jump from idea to idea, in what are called "loose associations," or "tangential thinking."

With some such people, you sometimes have to take over, saying, "You have talked enough for awhile. It's time to be quiet." This sometimes works quite well for both sides. It is honest, it is direct, and it sets a limit. At other times, however, one needs to let out a little pressure like opening a valve in a steam pipe. Then you take over, saying one portion of what you have to say.

- First, put out a hand, palm down, fingers curved at waist level to interrupt them. If they don't perceive it, put up both hands, using a little drama in your facial expression to get their attention and interrupt.
- In letting them speak for a little while about their preoccupations, you've let out a little pressure, so to speak.
- Sum up what they said in a sentence or two. Use a little energy in your voice to prove that you're really "with" them. Then, ask or say something, getting either some compliance or a bit of information. "That is serious. Politics right now are terrible! You HAVE to tell me more about the left-wing conspiracy, but before you do, did your brother come home last night?"
- In exchange for this information, let them return to their cascade of ideas, allowing a little more pressure to be released.
- Then, once again, firmly interrupt.

In essence, you sum up what they said to prove you were listening, and *then* ask your question or make your statement. Steam-valving is for the purpose of letting the person tell enough of what is pressuring them internally so that they don't fight you for the conversational floor.

Figure 29.9 Rule #8: Steam-valving

This is useful with people whose speech is a cascade of words and ideas that are either all over the place (zigzag) or delusional. Listen and then interrupt. Sum up what they said, and tell them you want to hear more, but before they do, you have a question (or instruction) for them. Then let them return to their cascade of words. Listen a bit more, then interrupt again. Continue with multiple sequences of release of pressure, interruptions and questions until you get the information you need.

Figure 29.10 Example of Steam-valving

Larry (Subject). "And then the Berlin Wall came tumbling down and the spirits of dead communist babies flew over the rubble…."

LEO. "Larry. Wait. I want you to tell me more about those communist babies, but before you do, did you leave the gun in your house?"

Larry. "Yes, the gun is in the house, and dead communist babies have flown into the ears of all the children of the West and that is why they no longer respect their elders or money or eider down pillows, or…."

LEO. "Larry, I'm worried about the children too! There IS something different these days. I want to hear more, but first, what room is the gun in?"

Larry. "In the living room, because the gun is a life taker, so it stays in the room that lives, where there are no kids, and…."

Physical Space, Physical Contact, and the Use of the Eyes With Psychotic People

Concerns about eye contact and physical contact are incredibly important in regard to people with psychosis.

- Even more than in ordinary circumstances, be acutely aware when you're inadvertently "pressuring" the psychotic person by standing or sitting too close to them. Consider this *your* responsibility; don't expect the psychotic person to necessarily tell you. The first sign that you're too close—**if you aren't paying attention**—may be an attack as the psychotic person believes they must protect themselves from your "invasion."
- Other psychotic individuals aren't aware whatsoever of personal space, and stand or sit too close to you. Firmly, without aggression or heat, tell them to move back. "Monty, I really want to hear what you're saying. But you're standing too close to me. Step four steps back and tell me more."
- For many psychotic folks, direct, sustained eye contact seems to pierce them to the brain. It's as if you can read their thoughts. Other mentally ill people can misinterpret direct eye contact as aggressive, threatening, or seductive. Therefore, if they're uncomfortable with being directly looked at (you'll know it!), occasionally "touch base" by making brief eye contact, then ease your eyes away, and then back again. **Of course, never take your eyes off of the person in a manner that would make you unaware of any precursors to assault.**

Figure 29.11 Rule #9: Body Spacing, Body Contact, and Eye Contact

Be aware of physical spacing; don't stand too close, and don't accept the person standing too close to you. Most psychotic individuals are made anxious by direct eye contact, experiencing it as either a threat or a challenge. Limit eye contact when it is not emergent so that you have to establish control through command presence, a situation where direct eye contact is a necessity.

CHAPTER 30

Tactics for Dealing With
Symptoms of Mania

Mania is a state of high energy. People in this condition need little sleep, and can be excited, grandiose, agitated, or irritable. They often have flights of fancy, which can be either creative or completely irrational. Their speech is often pressured. Not only is it rapid, but also there is a sense that there is more to say than they can get out.

They're usually extremely confident, even to the degree of believing themselves to be invulnerable. Manic people are often selfish. They feel wonderful, and their own needs and desires are the only things that matter. Their judgment can be extremely poor and they engage in behaviors that can put them or others at risk.

The manic state is associated most commonly with bipolar disorder (manic-depression), in which periods of mania are one-half of a cycle in which the other is periods of depression. **Some drugs can also cause manic episodes (particularly stimulant drugs such as amphetamine or cocaine), and not infrequently, mania can also be a side effect of psychiatric medications.**

Figure 30.1 Beyond Mania is Chaos

People with different brain malfunctions can have periods of agitation that may look very much like mania, but this kind of delirium is usually more extreme than the classic manic state. Such individuals are usually quite confused and disorganized. On the other hand, manic people can get so agitated, called "manic excitement," that they shift into a delirium state. All such individuals, whatever the cause, are de-escalated using the strategies described in Chapter 59 on Chaotic Rage.

Manic people are particularly vulnerable because they're most in danger when they feel wonderful. Imagine the best spring day of your life. The sky is blue, birds are singing, and a gentle breeze keeps things just cool enough to be comfortable. You wake up and literally jump out of bed, happy to be alive. You have so much energy that it feels like there is champagne in your veins. You know you will make some new friends today, so you're going to go to the park, the club, and the bar, whatever you decide, and just enjoy life. Imagine that feeling day-after-day, multiplied 10 or 20 times. Can you see how easy it would be to begin to make unwise choices, how your confidence could lead you to, for example, hijack that freight train because you always wanted to be an engineer?[15]

When you feel this good, it seems like a good idea to feel *even better*. Thus, manic people very often want to party. Drugs and alcohol are very tempting, spending money to buy anything and everything you want leads to credit cards run to the max, and often the energy turns sexual and the manic person gets involved with people who may be inappropriate for them or even dangerous. On the flip side, manic people—stimulant drug users or not—sometimes try to calm themselves with other drugs: barbiturates, heroin, and alcohol. Alcohol can have a "paradoxical effect" on some manic individuals, further exciting rather than sedating them.[16]

Manic people often talk in rapid cascades of words, a waterfall of ideas leaping from one area to another. Sometimes you can follow their thoughts, although they're speaking very rapidly, but at other times, they verbally zigzag, making connections that have little or no meaning. In extreme manic states, people can become psychotic, with all the symptoms of grandiosity, persecutory, paranoid, and religious delusions that any other psychotic individual might have.

Some manic people become very irritable. They can have a hair-trigger temper, and may also be provocative. Rather than merely being reactive, some will aggressively tease and taunt other people. It may seem to be in good fun, at first, but it goes way too far. Others may simply try to pick a fight.

Brittle Grandiosity

Manic people can act as if they don't have a care in the world. They spin ideas, one after another, and expect both agreement and admiration. They seem utterly self-confident. However, truly self-confident individuals are resilient; unfair criticisms seem to bounce off them. They can respond either with a gracious laugh or a dignified response. Think of manic grandiosity, however, as a fragile structure, like a tower made of spun sugar. It glitters, it glows, and it's huge! But tap the wrong strut or beam and the entire tower falls down in shards. For example, if you bluntly criticize individuals who are manic, they can experience your criticism as a personal attack, and from giddy happiness, they suddenly turn on you in rage. If you tease them about their somewhat irrational ideas, try to joke around with them, or laugh at something funny that they said, they easily misinterpret this, too, as an attack, thinking you're making fun of them.

In other words, consider the manic flight of words to be a kind of hysteria. Even when they appear happy, it is as if they're on a giddy flight hanging onto a helium balloon. It certainly is thrilling—until they look down! Miscalculated teasing or criticism is experienced as if you're poking at the balloon with a needle.

Figure 30.2 One Author's Experience: Be Careful—All Is Not What It Seems!

WARNING: They may be acting like comedians, but they aren't trying to be funny!

One of the writers recalls a little guy who had lined up over five thousand "matchbox" cars on every projecting surface of the inside of his house. None were glued, but they were perfectly balanced, even on the molding on the walls! Because he had overdosed, we took him to the hospital. He was given charcoal, and as he sat on a gurney, belching black fluid down his chin into a pan, he was talking non-stop, chirping like a little bird, asking why, if this medicine was so bad, they had given it to a man like him? It was both a reasonable question and under the particular circumstances funny. One of the nurses began to laugh, and he threw the metal basin he was holding right at her head, and still spewing black vomit, grabbed her by the throat, screaming, "This isn't funny. Nothing's funny!"

In other words, it is an act of a professional to not laugh at the inadvertently funny things that many mentally ill people say. This particularly concerns those in manic states. There is no doubt that you may have a story to tell back in the car or the station, or that at times you have to cover up your laughter with a cough, but laughing at another's expense, particularly one both vulnerable and volatile, may provoke them to an act of violence.

Watch Out! Mania Can be Infectious

Being with manic people can be very exciting, particularly if they're at low or moderate levels of elevation. They can be brilliant conversationalists: witty, sexy, provocative, and entertaining. They're fast on their feet, bawdy, and full of fun. It is easy to catch the mood of someone like this, easy to begin to feel grandiose and over-confident yourself. Getting swept up in this energy is just as dangerous as it would be on the highway; once you've jumped in the back seat and are zigzagging down the road at 90 miles an hour it's pretty hard to get back out of the vehicle.

Many manic people assume, when you "hitch a ride," that you're in absolute agreement with them. They assume that what they want is what you want. However, when you object, they can suddenly turn on you in ferocious, betrayed anger. There is an old expression: "He's a drag" referring to someone who slows the party down. That isn't a bad idea with the manic person. Therefore do the following:

- Stay centered.
- Don't get swept away.
- Focus on slowing things down. Speak slower, and take things step-by-step.

It is possible to use humor in a tactical way with manic persons. But you need to be calm and centered, as described in Section II. If you have "caught" the manic contagion, and are trying to match wits with them, the funny statement you make will backfire on you. **Your purpose must be to catch their attention and slow things down, not have fun with them.**

Medication and Bipolar Disorder: It's Not Like Diabetes

Bipolar individuals have a unique problem: medication can usually control their symptoms, but they're most ill when they feel wonderful. Perhaps they will be calm, more organized, sleep more hours, and not get in trouble if they take their medications, but life will lose a wonderful glow. Unlike almost any other condition, profoundly "ill" manic individuals often feel right with themselves: in a state of mystic transport, ecstasy, or just plain fun. People with bipolar illness won't take medication unless their lives on medication are rich and interesting, so much so that they're willing to spurn the dangerous wonders that the manic state seems to offer. For the bipolar person, going *off* their medications is the equivalent of the drug addict using again.

Once off their medications, folks with bipolar disorder can crash down into severe depression, leading to an apocalyptic attitude that there is no hope that things will ever get better: suicidal ideation or rage toward others can easily follow. Even more dangerous, they may quickly amp up into a manic episode that can combine grandiosity, elevated mood, high energy, poor judgment, irritability and psychosis. As a young woman with bipolar disorder, who also had affection for methamphetamine in large doses stated, "The difference between meth and mania? Well, mania is MUCH bigger. Huge!"

When encouraging a bipolar person to take medications, many professionals and family members say, "It's a condition like diabetes. You need to take it every day to maintain yourself. It's not like medicine for a sore throat that you take until you're cured, and then never have to take again." This is true, but there is a very profound difference between diabetes and bipolar disorder. If you don't take your medicine for diabetes, you very quickly become seriously ill—and this illness feels awful too. If people with bipolar illness discontinue medication, very often they will feel much better than when they were on the medications. Unfortunately, all too often, that puts them and many others at risk.

Figure 30.3 Review: Dealing with an Individual in a Manic State

You will recognize the manic person because they will display super high energy. They will often be talking very fast and their ideas will "zigzag" from one to another. They often act like comedians, with a rapid-fire delivery. Their behavior may also be either sexualized or hair-trigger aggressive. In either case, they will very likely be provocative. Here are some things you should do:

- Remain calm and centered.
- Be conscious of their "brittle" state of mind, in spite of how confidently they behave. Grandiose doesn't mean strong!
- Don't bluntly criticize their actions.
- If you use any humor, it is for the purpose of slowing them down, not joking around.
- Don't laugh at them, either deliberately, or involuntarily.
- Don't join in what sounds like fun. It isn't.
- They may try to provoke you (think of the Road Runner and Coyote).
- They can be very volatile, exploding into rage with the slightest provocation. Be relaxed but ready for the worst.
- If the manic person is also psychotic, the latter syndrome will probably take precedence. In these situations, you essentially have a hallucinating or delusional person who also happens to be moving and talking very fast.

CHAPTER 31

Communication With Elderly
Demented People

Effectively dealing with elderly people in a law enforcement context, particularly if they're also mentally disabled, is one of the most challenging situations an officer might face. Officers will almost always outweigh and outmuscle them, but even if they have retained substantial strength, they may be physically fragile.

Figure 31.1 Example of an Officer's Encounter With a Demented Elderly Women
Officers were dispatched regarding a disorderly elderly woman, 83 years old, refusing to leave a store. She was suffering from dementia. The responding officers eventually got her out of the store. They called the woman's family, but they refused to come. They had been trying for years to get her to the doctor, yet she would refuse to the point of rage. She had spit on her grandchildren, accused her son of having sex with the neighbor, and had tried to throw boiling water on her daughter-in-law, the last time she came to bring her some food.

The family said that they could do nothing, and social services told them she had a right to refuse services. So they said, "Arrest her." The officers advised the elderly woman that she was under arrest for trespass. At which point, the little old lady kicked the officer square in the groin, something that the onlookers somehow missed. They did, however, witness the officer use his conducted energy device on the little old lady, resulting in a media uproar.

So what do you do? If in the above example the officers had applied a come-along hold, they easily could have broken her wrist or arm. If they had manhandled her to the ground, imagine the outcry that a broken pelvis or thigh might have engendered, injuries that have killed elderly individuals!

Are there any verbal interventions that might possibly keep the situation under control at a lower level of force with an elderly, demented individual? Remember, older adults aren't a monolithic category. They're people, just like us, simply older. Every character type, every mode of aggression, every mental syndrome, and every de-escalation strategy applies to elderly people as well as those of other age groups. Despite their age, elderly people do assault others, particularly those involved in their care. Their rage can emerge from dementia, medical conditions, pain, adverse drug mental illness, pure meanness or hate, or any number of stressors.

Many elderly people are prescribed a number of medications, from a number of doctors. Not all the medical practitioners may be aware of one another, and the elderly person, rather than being demented or mentally ill, may be suffering from a complication from drug interactions, or, due to age and confusion, taking the prescribed medications improperly. Don't rule out the possibility of a medical emergency due to such medication problems. They're quite common.

Figure 31.2 Concerning Physical Force and the Elderly

If physical force is required to safely bring an elderly person under control, then so be it. However, because of the particular vulnerabilities of elderly people, your defensive tactics instructors should consult with medical specialists, particularly paramedics and emergency medical technicians, regarding the type of physical guidance and restraint that offers the least risk of injury. This should be integrated into your training scenarios.

Figure 31.3 Human and Tactical Concerns With Elderly, Aggressive Individuals

Be aware that the elderly may be resistant to help. This may be due to disorganization and confusion brought on by dementia, by a combination of severe depression and fear, or by pride ("At least I still have the strength to refuse someone."). The following will be helpful in handling the elderly:

- Speak respectfully, befitting the age and seniority of the person. Too many people speak in a patronizing demeaning tone to elderly people, and even if cognitively impaired, they know they're being talked to as if they're children.
- Don't forget that they may be hard-of-hearing. What you think is resistance may be due to them not being able to understand or hear what you are saying.
- Use their honorific and last name unless specifically invited to use their first name. If you wish to achieve a more informal relationship, ask "Would you prefer to be called Mrs. X or by your first name?" Let them *offer* the first name.
- When it is not an immediately emergent situation, take a little bit more time. Attempt to "nibble around the edges," talking about life, about family. Sometimes the volatile rage that elderly people display comes from a deep depression; they're isolated, confused, and no one seems to care if they live or die.
- Be prepared to get enormously frustrated at their leaden stubbornness, that "they simply won't do what is good for them." What appears as inertia may be a profound expression of fear. Remember that the most proximate change that many old people are concerned with is death, and therefore, any situation provoking anxiety evokes the fear of death. **You may think they're defiant; they may simply be scared out of their wits.**
- Don't talk around or about the person to others as if they aren't present.
- Don't barrage them with choices, decisions, or too much information.

- Paranoia, (Chapter 20) whatever the cause, is one of the frequent triggers of rage in elderly people, particularly with older adults with dementia or adverse drug reactions. As the person becomes suspicious, you can often change the subject, so that the object of their suspicion recedes from their awareness.

- The rage and violence that emerges with elderly people is frequently chaotic. Please refer to Chapter 25 on details regarding communication with disorganized people and Chapter 59 on de-escalation of people in chaotic states.

- Be aware that the person's behavior may very possibly be brought on by improper use of their prescribed medications, or interactions between different prescribed and over-the-counter medications.

- **Do not under-estimate the risk of assault with elderly people. Tendon strength is the last thing to go, and some frail-looking people can have grips like a mangle. And of course, it doesn't take that much strength to pull the trigger on that firearm that was concealed under the cushion.**

SECTION VI

Suicidal Individuals

CHAPTER 32

Why Is Suicide a Concern
of Law Enforcement?

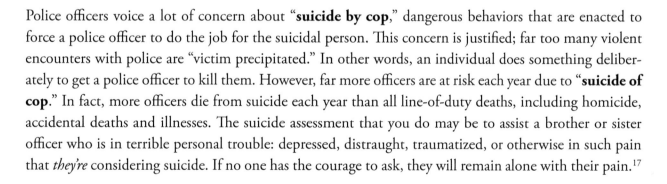

Suicide is an apocalyptic action. It is literally self-annihilation. For the suicidal person; however, suicide is an attempt to solve a problem. They find themselves in an intolerable situation and nothing makes their pain any less.

Law enforcement officers aren't counselors. Therefore, one could legitimately state that suicide should be the responsibility of a mental health professional. However, mental health issue that it is, and problem-solving activity that it might be, suicide is also the killing of a human being. That it is done by one's own hand doesn't make it less murderous. This is a particularly important consideration because, given that there is hatred and often a weapon, you must consider the safety of others who might have any connection—even mere proximity—with the suicidal person. In short, the difference between murder and suicide is often no more than what direction the weapon is pointing.

Police officers voice a lot of concern about "**suicide by cop**," dangerous behaviors that are enacted to force a police officer to do the job for the suicidal person. This concern is justified; far too many violent encounters with police are "victim precipitated." In other words, an individual does something deliberately to get a police officer to kill them. However, far more officers are at risk each year due to "**suicide of cop**." In fact, more officers die from suicide each year than all line-of-duty deaths, including homicide, accidental deaths and illnesses. The suicide assessment that you do may be to assist a brother or sister officer who is in terrible personal trouble: depressed, distraught, traumatized, or otherwise in such pain that *they're* considering suicide. If no one has the courage to ask, they will remain alone with their pain.[17]

Warning Signs

What should make you consider the possibility or even likelihood that someone might be suicidal beyond them bluntly stating that fact? Below are listed some warning signs:

- Significant negative changes in the individual's life: divorce or a romantic break-up, events such as fights at school or the workplace, an incident that is humiliating, a large disappointment such as being dropped from a team or club in the case of youth, or fired in the case of an adult, etc. Personal losses aren't only of social position or status: due to a deterioration of one's physical or emotional health, it may have become difficult, if not impossible, to do the things one used to do.

- Warning signs that suggest such negative psychological changes even when you don't have concrete information: a radical change in clothing or appearance, particularly styles that sets one apart from the society of which they were previously a member, a lack of care about one's appearance, hostility towards peers, workmates, family, or social services staff, social withdrawal, social isolation, giving away prize possessions, writing or drawings with morbid or despairing themes, a depressed demeanor, allusions to a lack of a future or to the "pointlessness of it all," or reassuring statements when you know nothing has changed for the better, such as "you don't have to worry about me anymore. I'll be taking care of things. It's not an issue, anymore," etc.

- Sometimes, without knowing why, you have a sense of foreboding, or at other times, one thinks something "ridiculous," like, "I don't think that kid will live to see 20," or "I wonder if this is the last time I will see this person." Such thoughts are often, let us emphasize, **very** often an intuitive sense that something is very wrong. Asking someone if they're suicidal when your "evidence" is so vague requires some tact, but approach you must.

- Statistically, suicide is the eighth leading cause of death for adults in the United States and third for adolescents. It is important to note that 3-5 percent of those who are suicidal don't seek any help and successfully kill themselves; in addition 30 percent leave it to chance whether someone intervenes; and 65 percent don't wish to really end their lives. Eight out of ten suicidal individuals give some form of warning as to their intent. Hopelessness, helplessness, and not seeing a solution to their problem(s) are the hallmarks of a suicidal individual.[18]

CHAPTER 33

The Basics of Intervention With Someone You Believe Might Be Suicidal

Are you the proper person to ask this individual any questions at all? This isn't the place for grandiosity, where you believe that because you're "good with people," that this person will open up to you. Do you *know* that this person respects you? If not, you're probably not the person to speak with them. To be sure, there are people who are isolated and alienated, and it is *only* through the asking of the questions of concern that respect between you will be born. But you must at least have a sense, knowing this person, that he/she doesn't hold you in either personal contempt or indifference.

If you're unfamiliar with the person, having "met" them on a welfare check, or in a crisis negotiation, if you become aware that you can't establish any rapport or mutual respect, then you need to pass this task on to another officer.

If however, you're the person who has to speak with the suicidal person, what must you do? (Note: Some of these strategies may seem contradictory. As you read them, however, you will be able to imagine or recall the type of person to whom you should approach in that specific way.)

- **Concentrate and get them to concentrate on you.** You won't get to choose where you engage the individual: a bridge, hotel room, roof top, from outside their car, in a park, etc. The environment may be loud or otherwise distracting. Onlookers may be yelling at the person to jump from the bridge or shoot himself/herself. Use circular breathing to simultaneously give the person close, attention while remaining aware of your surroundings: where your team is and what potential threats are nearby. Whenever the person becomes distracted, get them to focus on you.
- **Demeanor.** Too much direct eye-contact, close physical proximity, an overly-gentle, "concerned" voice will shut them down. Speak easily but not over confidently. If you present yourself as too "together," they may experience this as a slap in the face, their lack of ease contrasting negatively with you. If all you do is stare in their eyes, they will experience it as a constant, intrusive examination.
- **Meander.** With any reticent or wary individual, your conversation should "wander around," talking about this and that. As long as they're talking, they aren't killing themselves. This gives you time and also helps to build trust.
- **Ask direct questions.** When you have a real concern that an individual is considering or planning suicide, you must be more direct. Don't tiptoe around the subject, as vague statements leave the person an "out." The following would be an example of this mistake with the individual's inner thoughts place in parentheses:

    a. Police Officer. "Are you thinking of hurting yourself?"

    b. Subject. "No, I'm not." *(Soon I'll be feeling no pain.)*

The correct question to ask when a true concern about suicide arises is, **"Are you thinking of killing yourself?"** Being asked questions directly is a relief because it indicates that you're someone who is strong enough to listen to what is really going on inside them. If the person is not suicidal, they will let you know. They should be able to give you a clear explanation why you don't need to be concerned. If they're outraged, explain why you were concerned. One final point: It ***won't*** put the idea in their head if it wasn't there to begin with.

- **Speak in a calm matter-of-fact tone of voice.** If you sound nervous, you'll appear unreliable. If you're joking or off-hand, the person will feel that you aren't taking them seriously. If you're overly concerned, overly warm, or "sensitive," you'll sound like a hovering counselor, that soft-voice, earth-tone wearing, gentle soul who can't be trusted to stand up and fight, but seeks refuge only in being "nice." A calm, matter-of-fact tone shows that you aren't panicked by their situation and that you can handle anything they say.

- **Act as if you have all the time in the world.** If you act like there is little time, the person you're talking with will believe you, and they'll rush to a decision or conclusion. When you take time, you give time. The suicidal person begins to believe that there is enough time to figure out a better solution than suicide.

- **Don't give advice too soon.** Until you know the situation, don't hand out advice. Even then, keep it to a minimum. If you immediately say, "Think of your family," the individual might mentally reply, "Yeah, they'll be sorry. Their tears dropping on my grave are the best payback I can think of!"

- **Never dare them to do it.** That kind of stupidity only works in the movies. The classic stupid sentence is, "Cutting? If you were serious, you would cut your wrists lengthwise, not cross-wise." The idea here is to "scare the person straight." The aggressive intervener thinks that they're obviously attention seeking and not serious, and they try to shock them with the reality of what they're doing. In all cases we can recall, such "interventions" are born out of frustration, irritation, burn-out, or plain dislike of the often repeatedly suicidal person. It is a statement for us, not them. One of the authors met a man who took such advice regarding lengthwise cuts. His crippled arm looks like corduroy, due to seven elbow-to-wrist , bone-deep razor slashes.

- **Don't get in a debate, particularly a religious debate.** Some people use suicidal behavior as a way to feel some power in a world over which they have little control. Debates about the meaning of life, the nature of heaven, or the immorality of suicide will break rapport, particularly if you're "winning."

- **The most powerful intervention with suicidal individuals is that you're talking**. The suicidal person, almost invariably, feels completely isolated, cut off from life and from people. A respectful conversation conveys on an almost primal level that they're still worth something because you find them worthwhile. Communication itself heals.

Figure 33 Warning: Concerning Suicide

One of the behaviors that officers encounter is suicide from a high place: from a window ledge, a bridge, or a building. Officers can get so focused on saving the person, particularly as the hours pass and a powerful intimacy grows, that the intervener suddenly tries to grab the person and pull them back from danger. This can get you killed. As one 25 year veteran negotiator wrote to us, "I don't really see that as an option for the officer doing the negotiating. That officer's focus must be absolutely on communication. If he/she is simultaneously trying to line up to grab the person, their communication will be off, and so will their focus for the grab. The suicidal person may very possibly end up "pushed" off the ledge as you try to help them, or even worse, they may grab the intervener and take them along. To be sure, other officers and firefighters may become the "rescuers," getting nets out, and making a move to grab the person while they're focused on the negotiator, but the person talking to them shouldn't be doing the grabbing. Beyond the immediate safety issues, such incidents have opened up police agencies to huge liability suits."

CHAPTER 34

Essential Questions

> **Figure 34 Important Note**
> Your jurisdiction may have hard and fast rules on what police should do when contacting a suicidal individual. For example, you may be required to take them to an emergency room as soon as you ascertain that they're suicidal. In other jurisdictions, particularly when there is a CIT team as well as coordination with the mental health system, some of the responses below will result in the person being linked up with a "next day appointment" or a mental health outreach team.

The following are the standard questions for assessing suicide risk. As you can see, there is a progression in which greater specificity indicates greater danger. You're assessing if the individual is safe, and if not, your next step would be to get them to a mental health professional, or place them in custody, depending on the level of risk. Your tone should be calm and straightforward.

Don't use the following questions as a "checklist." Instead use them in the natural flow of the conversation while understanding that the individual may wander off on all sorts of tangents before being ready to answer the next question.

The Four Questions
1. "Are you planning to kill yourself?"
- "NO." If they answer no, follow up with questions and statements why you believe they might. If they can't satisfactorily counter your suspicions ("Your boyfriend called and stated that you told him that you were going out in a blaze of glory tonight. And then you said, 'Don't look for the body.'"), regard this the same as if they admitted to suicidal ideation.
- "I DON'T WANT TO KILL MYSELF, BUT I PRAY I JUST WON'T WAKE UP IN THE MORNING." This could be termed passive or soft suicidal ideation. Don't minimize this. The person's pain is very real. At the same time, these individuals can usually be linked with a mental health intervention, such as an outreach worker or an appointment the next day.
- "I'M NOT TELLING YOU." Hospitalize if you have collateral evidence that they might be suicidal, so that they can be linked up with proper personnel for a full assessment. It shouldn't be your job to beg them for an honest answer. If you have enough collateral information to suggest that they might be suicidal, you can insist that they be placed in protective custody for an evaluation, despite their refusal to answer any of your questions
- "YES I AM." **This is a clear red flag.**

2. "How would you do it?"

- "I DON'T KNOW." This, too, usually means you have time. You should be able to negotiate an agreement to seek or accept treatment after further discussion. You have to find out if there are any impediments to seeking treatment, such as "I'm not going to see a counselor. All they do is look at you and repeat what you say," or the ever more common, "I don't have money to pay for counseling."
- "I'M NOT TELLING YOU!" Same as above.
- "I COULD DO IT ALL SORTS OF WAYS." (They then give you a list in a rather defiant or bored tone.) This is game playing. It doesn't mean they won't make a suicide attempt, but it usually comes more from an "I'll show you!" attitude than a genuine desire to die. At this point, you must make it clear to them that such suicidal threats are taken seriously. (Depending on the overall situation, the response can range from hospitalization to possible prosecution for false reporting.)
- A CLEAR METHOD. "Yeah, I'm going to cut my wrists. I'll be sitting in a bath of warm water, and I'm hoping I'll just drift off." **Sure second red flag.**
- METHOD AND BACK-UP PLAN. "I've thought of jumping off the Aurora Bridge, but if I don't have the guts, I'll use pills." Same as above, **second red flag.**

3. "Do you have the means to do it?" such as "Do you have a gun." Or "I don't see a car. How are you going to get to the Golden Gate Bridge?"

- "NO, I DON'T." Once again, that gives us some time. Despite the serious nature of the first 2 red flags, you may be able to negotiate with them, following up with treatment, or the dispatch of a mental health outreach team. In other cases ("I don't have any pills, but the pharmacy is half a block away and I've got money in my pocket."), you must hospitalize.
- "YES." If they're talking about guns or knives, immediately find out if they have the weapon, or where it is located. Alert your back-up officer(s) and emergency response personnel of the potential threat.
- "I'M NOT TELLING YOU." Same as above.

4. "When will you do it?" This question helps you gauge immediacy, how established the plan is and if there is anyone else who is "timed" to suffer. (e.g., "ON MY MOM'S BIRTHDAY")

The more "positive" answers you get to these four questions, the greater the risk of a lethal outcome.

Follow-up Questions
In most cases, particularly when interviewing a subject of an investigation or welfare check, you will have fully accomplished all that you need to do. You know that the person is or isn't suicidal, and how close to the act they are. In many cases, however, you may have to keep talking:

- They're struggling and trust someone and want to talk more.
- They're on a phone and you're trying to keep them on the line.

- It is a barricade situation, and the person is talking on the other side of a door.
- They are a fellow officer and you, as a friend, are trying to help them and convince them to seek services.

The following questions are designed to get more information and to keep them talking. As people continue to talk, they often pull back from the intent to kill themselves on their own, or they'll be more amenable to de-escalation because they feel that at last, someone is willing to listen to them. Simple communication brings people away from suicide, even without a solution to the problems that drive a person towards it.

- "Have you tried to kill yourself before?"
- Have you ever tried to kill yourself another way? Desperate people become very concrete and literal, only thinking of their chosen method. They may have made several attempts before, by other means.
- Have you ever *felt* like killing yourself before?
- What stopped you? Who stopped you? Be sure not to make them feel like they "failed" when they weren't successful in a previous attempt. When they recall someone or something that stopped them, this may help them regain a sense of responsibility for the people who care for them, or some other factor that kept them alive in the past.
- "Has anybody in your family or someone you cared about ever tried to kill themselves?" Such people have "shown the way," making it seem almost reasonable to the survivors.
- "Have you been drinking? Using any drugs?" *(Don't push this one if you have a sense that the person will be more worried about getting arrested for use or possession than finding a solution to the situation.)*
- "What's happened that things are so bad that suicide makes sense?" OR "What happened TO-DAY that you decided to kill yourself?"
- "What else did you tried to do to get yourself out of this situation?" (Be careful: an angry person could respond by thinking or saying, "Now I have to explain myself again. I don't ***know*** why having a great family, a beautiful girlfriend and a fine career isn't enough!"
- Other areas to talk about include if the individual has suffered any recent losses, is ill, or has little or no social/family support.

CHAPTER 35

The Art of Communication
With the Suicidal Person

The following will be helpful in communicating with the suicidal person:

- **Dialogue is the lifeline.** Suicidal people feel profoundly alone. They believe that nothing can end their pain, but death. They're often depressed or very bitter and angry. These emotions isolate them. When one is isolated, one doesn't even feel half-alive, because to be human is to be in relationship with others. <u>When you're able to begin a dialogue with the suicidal person, your real power is that you're speaking together.</u> By definition, the person is no longer alone. Someone is hearing them out. Someone grasps how terrible life is for them. As time passes, the very fact of talking with you makes them feel alive again, and this gives hope, even when the person's situation has otherwise not changed.

- **Don't make guarantees of how wonderful life will be or how easy it is to recover from one's pain.** When the suicidal person makes demands of you, don't give a guarantee of results. Explain the difficulties instead. For example, "No, I'm not guaranteeing counseling will help. And you will have to work to find a **good** counselor. Even then, it won't be easy. It might be the hardest thing you've ever done. But it's something you haven't tried."

- **Be very careful about making promises about what will or won't occur if they end their suicide standoff.** For example, you say, "I promise you will be able to see your child at the hospital once you come down." Later you find out that his wife has a court injunction against him seeing the child, as part of their bitter divorce battle. Once trust is destroyed, the person will be more at risk and less trustful of getting some help next time.

- **Don't be a cheerleader.** If you're too active, too "positive," it is as if you're "in it together." Their success will be your success. Paradoxically, if you act as if things are *too* important, the suicidal person begins to feel that they're doing things for you, not for themselves.

- **Don't try to bolster their "self esteem."** You may know that they've got a talent, that they're attractive, or have a wonderful family. If you point this out to them—"You have so many reasons to live!"—you will most likely break rapport entirely. It is very likely that they know these things themselves. They look in the mirror and they see the beautiful face, but inside, they feel corrupt and foul. They look at their mom and dad, whom they painfully and deeply love, and think, "They would be so happy without me." They have a talent, and they know it, but even as they play the piano or paint or score 30 points in a game, they merely feel an aching misery.

Figure 35.1 Deepening Rapport With the Suicidal Person

Once you have achieved a deeper level of rapport, it is quite sound to talk about what the person loves: their vocation, hopes, and dreams, their family, or their talents. The goal here is to participate in reminding the person of the value of their life. However, they have to realize this, themselves as they talk about these things. It isn't effective to tell them what is special about them. If that were all it took, they wouldn't be suicidal in the first place.

- **Frame things with negatives.** "You've had a bad time. There is no doubt about that. Yet, somehow, you held it together all these months. What's different about today?"
- **Identify the intended "victims."** Try to ascertain whom the suicide is intended to hurt. You will be able, thus, to get a better sense if the person is also homicidal, or on the cusp between self-harm, and an intention to take others along. We can tell if there are others intended to suffer when we ask:
  a. "Who will find your body?"
  b. "Who will identify your body?"

Some people are utterly shocked at these questions, so preoccupied with their own pain that they didn't even think that their children, for example, who would be the one to find them upon returning home from work. Others describe that same scene with happiness, hoping thereby that their family member will never have a good night's sleep again.

- **When you should talk about their family.** A natural follow-up of the last question is to begin speaking about their family and what will be the implications of their suicide upon the family. You must be careful here. The suicidal person may become enraged with you, perceiving this as a manipulative trick to make them feel guilty. However, once you get a sense that the suicidal person does care for his/her family, particularly children, such talk may be very powerful. For example, one intervener asked a man on a bridge what he would say to his daughter were she the one standing on the railing. As he began to think about this, the intervener was able to suggest that she would probably want to say that to him as well.
- **Suicide is selfish.** If you get a sense that they do love their children, partner, or friends, but are so preoccupied by their own pain that they don't realize the implications of their suicide on others, one can ask, "What happens to your pain if you do kill yourself." Quite frequently, the suicidal person says that their pain will be over. The reply to that, in a regretful tone, is, "That's not really true. You just wrap your pain up in a package and hand it to your loved ones to carry." This can sometimes shock the person to considering the implications of what they're doing. **Caution:** This type of intervention only comes after some long talking. Many suicidal people are so preoccupied with their own painful situation that they become too preoccupied with their own pain to care about their family. Rather than a healthy shock, they will resent you for reminding them of what they're trying to extinguish.

- **Suicidal threats without following through are not a betrayal of *you*.** You will deal with people who dramatize their problems, only later to minimize or discount those who gather to help them. Particularly with people who make repeated attempts or threats, this can enrage or frustrate us. It is ironic that contempt, irritation, or frustration is exactly what they expect from people, and that is what their behavior elicits. One of the occupational hazards of working with people who suffer is that not all those in pain are endearing. Some are frankly quite unlikeable. Others don't even have the ability or resources to accept help when it is offered. It is the hallmark of a professional that you don't become burned out simply because some people either play games, or are playing on an entirely different field than you thought.
- **How to respond to internal questions that sidetrack us:**
  a. "I don't know if I would want to live in such a miserable situation." It's not about you! The fact that they're talking with you means they still have some hope for another answer.
  b. "Why is it important that they live?" OR "I know I should care, but I don't." In cases like these, make death itself your enemy. Your attitude should be you will do your best to speak for life. You're a voice from the land of the living to one trying to cross over into the land of the dead. *Not on your watch!* If they wanted to die, they shouldn't have come into contact with you!

Figure 35.2 The Experience of One Officer

NOTE: The officer involved in this incident has very graciously given us permission to use this story.

A passerby saw the abandoned car stopped on the side of the road with the engine still running. Then they saw the man standing outside the railing on the freeway overpass. This particular bridge is like so many in nearly every community dispassionately called "suicide bridge," arcing approximately 100 feet above an 8-lane highway. The officer had only just arrived on-scene when he suddenly realized he knew this would-be jumper. They had attended high school together, one of the hazards of policing in the same town in which you grew up. Not only did they share high schools, but they shared the same first name. The suicidal man recognized the officer as well. After talking for a long time, the suicidal man said, "Don't blame yourself, Paul. This is about me and not you. Please don't take this personally. Tell my wife and kids I love them and I'm sorry."

The officer stated, "I knew that precise moment I wasn't going to be successful. It was like our minds met, and I could feel the intense pain he was living. It was as if he wanted me to feel it. It was profoundly ugly. I knew this would be over soon and I wouldn't be able to convince him to crawl back over the railing. We kept talking, but I knew I wouldn't be able to save him."

"Eventually, a crisis negotiator on a countywide SWAT team arrived. He assessed where I was with this guy, and could see I needed a break. He took over, but about 90 seconds later, the guy let go of his grip and fell to his death. I had no idea that this was someone I might know. I wasn't prepared for my not being successful in convincing him to not to jump. Nor was I prepared to feel the emotional attachment to him as we talked. I wasn't prepared to watch him jump from the overpass. Nor was I truly prepared for what happened next. The overpass and the freeway had been shut down and it was dead quiet. When he hit, it sounded like a shotgun blast. Officers one hundred feet up heard it. Officers in their cars on the freeway heard it. It sounded like an explosion. It stayed with me for a long time. I can still hear the sound. My mind comes back to it and in spite of what I know, I keep asking myself if I could have done anything more."

Officers are sometimes (more than we would like to be) with someone at the precise moment when life passes. Whether you personally know the individual or only know them because they're frequent contacts in your world of policing, it can have a devastating impact on you. Intervening with a suicidal person can create a powerful intimacy, in which it feels like your two lives are intertwined. A successful suicide while you watch or that they actually force you into participating, can cause you to question yourself: "What did I say? What could I have said? What could I have done differently?" These events can profoundly impact an officer's personality, family life, and career. Even though your logical mind may tell you that there was nothing you could do, the deeper part of you, so powerfully focused on drawing this person away from death with your voice alone, may not believe it. Seek assistance for yourself. Whether it is a critical incident stress debriefing, peer support, your personal doctor, psychologist, or whoever, seek it out. Other officers around you may not say anything because they may not know what to say. Don't be too "macho" to accept help or be in denial. Remember, suicide is an act of violence and often there is more than one victim. Do what you must so that you aren't one of them.

CHAPTER 36

Suicide as Self-murder: A Taxonomy

Figure 36.1 Concerning This Information

This is a tool that can be used to help gauge the seriousness of the person's suicidal intent, and what type of suicide it might be. Given that suicide is a form of murder—of oneself—let us categorize it by roughly the same sub-divisions that we do homicide. This type of information can help you know what you should be talking about and how to approach the person. Furthermore, it can be invaluable information to pass onto those who will be working with the person next, from crisis negotiators, emergency room personnel, mental health professionals, and corrections staff.

- **Aggravated first degree self-murder.** This would include killing oneself in a heinous or torturous way, drinking acid or lye, for example, because the person believes he deserves to suffer. Another example would be a suicide calculated so that a loved one will find the body. A third would be a suicide-murder killing oneself after killing family members or other people.

- **First degree self-murder.** This would include any planned suicide. The majority of the people to whom you speak will fall into this category that is why the standard assessment questions are concerned with planning.

- **Second degree self-murder.** This includes impulsive actions that are usually due to extreme emotion or intoxication. Precipitants would be something like a sudden business reversal or a break-up of a relationship. One's world has suddenly turned upside down, and the person's impulsive solution is to "get out." It is rare that you will be on-scene *during* an event like this. It would require that the person goes into an explosive personal crisis in your presence. For example, you go to arrest a woman in front of her family and she is so humiliated that she ends up on the apartment roof threatening to jump.

- Self-harm with intent to commit mayhem. The person doesn't mean necessarily to die, but they do something horrible to themselves, often with the intent to show others, "See how much I'm suffering!" Or "See how much you make me suffer." We're aware that the distinction between the previous item and this one is a hard call. You may not even be able to make it at all. However, if you're aware that the person didn't consciously intend to die, a professional would work with them in a different way. The professionals to whom you might refer such an individual would also find this useful information, if you happen to acquire it.

Figure 36.2 One Author's Experience

One of the authors recalls a case where a young man returned home to find his father on the couch having sex with the young man's new girlfriend. (He was unaware of their shared affection for crack cocaine. When she entered the home, they recognized each other as kindred spirits immediately.) The young man pulled out a fish boning knife and yelling at the two of them, stabbed himself right in the abdomen. Miraculously, the flexible blade threaded its way between his internal organs and all he needed was a few stitches. He said to me, "I didn't want to die. I didn't even think of that. It's just that my dad has always done stuff like this to me. Every time I trust him, this is the result. I guess I didn't know whether to stab him for doing it, or stab me for being so stupid as to trust him again."

- **Assaultive self-harm.** This includes suicidal gestures, cutting oneself and other self-mutilating actions. (Chapters 38 & 39)
- **Self-sacrifice.** Rare though it may be, this would include actions that have the intention of helping others—like throwing oneself on a grenade to save ones comrades.

Figure 36.3 An Example of Self-sacrifice

A young girl, age 12, disclosed sexual abuse by her father, and her mother slapped her in the face for "talking dirty." She suffered it for years, but when her father began turning his attention to her younger sister, in that magical thinking of a child, she thought that if she did something as awful as suicide, maybe someone would save her sister. Her mother had made it clear to her that disclosing didn't help. Thankfully, her attempt to kill herself failed, and a very good hospital social worker asked the right questions, thereby getting both girls out of the house.

- **Self-execution.** This includes suicide that is primarily directed by a sense of guilt. Such an individual believes that they deserve to die for some unforgivable transgression. We're confining this category to those who have actually done something terrible, not someone who, due to a sense of pathological guilt brought on by mental illness, decides that they don't deserve to live.
- **Survivor's guilt.** This particular form of "self-execution" is usually the outcome of a traumatic event. It is particularly common among frontline war veterans. The intense bonds between soldiers are among the most profound relationships that humans can experience. Facing death, only the trust and dependence upon one's comrades may keep one alive. A powerful sense of being "of one flesh" develops, where the man on the right is one's right arm and the man on the other side is one's left. When comrades are killed, one can simultaneously feel like a part of oneself has been killed, but at the same time, one feels terribly guilty to still be alive, as if one abandoned them. One feels like one doesn't have the right to the joys of life. And that the other person or

people were better than them, or perhaps worst of all, life-and-death is a random throw of the dice, which suggests there was no meaning to one's comrades' sacrifices.

- **Mercy self-killing.** This category includes so-called "assisted suicide" or other suicides in which the person is seriously ill and wishes to "die with dignity."
- **"I'm taking my body out of here."** This is an attempt at final control over one's fate, something that can range as an act of heroism against intolerable violation or oppression to the act of a psychopath in prison whose only way of thwarting the people who hold him against his will is to kill himself/herself.

CHAPTER 37

Suicide by Cop

Victim-precipitated homicide, also known as suicide-by-cop (SBC), is a phenomenon where an individual bent on self-destruction will act in a threatening manner to force a lethal response from law enforcement. This is a case where the police officer is also a victim, either through harm directly exerted by the actual perpetrator (the suicidal individual) or through the possibly traumatic experience of being forced to wound or kill another human being.

The statistics on the rate of suicide-by-cop are hard to come by, because the criteria used in various studies can be quite different. Most studies focus on situations where an individual plans a confrontation with the police, intending to force the police officer to shoot them. In such studies, the rate of SBC among police shootings usually falls within a range of 10%-18%. In a recent, very prominent study by Mahondie, Meloy, and Collins, 36 percent of all police shootings of males in a sampling of 707 cases in North America were classified as suicide-by-cop.[19] This number, compared to other studies, is startlingly high. Unlike many other studies, they also included another type, the "spontaneous" SBC (81% of all events in their study), where the subject, perhaps distraught or angry, did not plan to die, but somewhere within their interaction with police, officers apparently decided to confront them in a way that required the police to respond with lethal force, i.e., whirling around and lunging at the police, yelling, "Alright, f*ck it. Just shoot me then!"

Mahondie et al's study established:
- Suicide-by-cop cases were more likely to result in the death or injury of the subjects than regular officer-involved shooting cases.
- Findings confirm the trend detected in earlier research that there is a growing incidence of SBC among officer-involved shootings.
- SBC individuals had a high likelihood of possessing a weapon (80 percent), which was a firearm 60 percent of the time. Half of those with a firearm discharged it at the police during the encounter.
- Nineteen percent simulated weapon possession to accomplish their suicidal intent.
- The study also highlighted that many engaged in SBC can severely injure or even kill innocents, in order to elicit a lethal response from police. Ninety-seven percent of those who did victimize innocents were then killed by police.
- Most SBC cases were spontaneous, but had clear verbal and behavioral indicators that occurred prior to, and during the event.

Captain Rick Walls[20] of the Los Angeles Police Department notes a number of causes that may drive an individual to attempt suicide by cop. Among them are:

- Religious Beliefs – killing oneself in some religions, for example, may bar one from Heaven. The individual intends to "con" God into thinking their death was not a suicide.
- Many survivors of such an incident state that they attempted to kill themselves by their own hand, but couldn't summon up the "courage" to do it. The police officer, therefore, becomes a suicidal implement to accomplish what they couldn't do on their own. Related to this is a concern that they will fail in their own attempt, but they can trust the police to "finish the job."
- If the individual succeeds in engineering an incident that makes the police look at fault ("He was reaching for his cell phone!"), one's family may financially benefit in the subsequent lawsuit.
- Many life insurance policies will not pay on suicide
- The individual wishes to be portrayed as a victim of police actions or a martyr. In other situations, perceiving the police to be agents of injustice, they wish to create an incident that will draw attention to what they perceive as police malfeasance.
- Some individuals are outraged by previous encounters by police and wish to punish officers by a) harming them b) making them responsible for the suicidal person's death
- Going out in a blaze of glory.

Figure 37.1 How SBC is relevant to officer safety: It's not just the weapon that can hurt you

Officer safety does not only concern what might happen to a first responder under attack. Two other aspects of officer safety are psychological well-being and legal liability. That an assailant may have intended to engineer their own death is very relevant to these latter two components of officer safety. Until you have faced a situation, you have no idea how you will react.

If, through an investigation, including a "psychological autopsy," it is determined that deceased or injured individual intended to force the law enforcement officer to kill them, the driver being any one of the causes listed above, this can, in many situations, help with any post-traumatic reactions the officer might have. Furthermore, this can protect the officer(s) in any of the more abstract harm they may suffer: lawsuit, fitness-for-duty issues, internal investigations, etc.

There are two types of suicide by cop: the pre-planned event and the spontaneous event. In the former, the individual acts in a way that requires police response. They have no intention to escape, and in some situations, have event written notes in advance, addressed "To the officer who killed me . . . ." They generally confront the first responding officers immediately, to prevent back-up from getting involved. Armed with a weapon, or feigning the same, they advance towards the officer, making it impossible for them to withdraw or escape. As noted in Mahondie, et al.'s study, many will threaten innocents to force a police response.

A sizable number (22 percent) of individuals involved in suicide by cop have previously been diagnosed with mental illness. Captain Walls, however, notes an important caveat, regarding alleged suicide by cop and the mentally ill. He states that over 95 percent of calls for service for persons with mental illness come from family members and caregivers and 97 percent of police shooting involving the mentally ill occur in their home or perceiving living space (the latter can be anything from a patch of ground under an overpass to a shopping cart). Suicide by cop requires intent, and in encounters with severely mentally ill individuals that result in shootings, some at least were the result of the ill person acting in a terrified rage, seeing themselves as protecting their domicile or well-being. This, of course, underscores the need for both caution and good crisis intervention techniques when called out to the home (real or perceived) of someone you know to be mentally ill.

The second type of suicide by cop is often a barricaded individual. They may or may not have planned the incident as a suicide. They are usually individuals who are unable to escape prior to police arrival and also are individuals who, at least in the moment, prefer death to incarceration. This may include those who have committed a heinous crime such as child abuse, and the thought of both the humiliation they will experience and how they believe they will be treated in prison drive them towards death. Others, like the characters portrayed in any number of Hollywood movies, want to "go out a hero" rather than a suicide. These individuals may have already killed family members or are threatening to do the same. They may demand that police kill them, or brandish or fire a weapon to elicit this. They may tell hostages that they want to die, or "we are all going to die." They tell the negotiator that there is no way they are going back to prison, and when the negotiator attempts to get them looking to a future *beyond* a potential incarceration, they emphatically state that this is "not an option." They express a virulent hopelessness, either embittered or despairing, in which they see no other options for themselves. Captain Walls also notes that they will frequently "offer to surrender only to the person 'in charge.'" Some will engage in self-mutilation. Unlike the often-calculated actions of the parasuicidal individual, who usually acts while alone, these mutilating acts occur with police present, as if to underscore how little the person has to lose and how dangerous and aggressive they are. Many will verbally identify with others who have killed themselves or been killed by police.

Beyond these more subtle indicators are those which demand immediate police response: reaching for or pointing a weapon, or acting in another matter that makes it clear to police that they are about to be assaulted, advancing towards police when told to stop, refusing to negotiate assaulting or harming hostages with police present,

Perhaps the most important information for first response officers is that those who engage in suicide by cop attempts are reported to have frequently made suicide attempts or suicidal statements proximate to the current incident. This is, of course, moot if one is involved in a gun-fight. However, if there is a static or barricade situation, or if the officer(s) have any time to gather collateral information, interviewing family/friends whether the subject has made such an attempt or statements is invaluable in helping determine if the subject actually intends to survive the confrontation.

It is sadly necessary to cite one more aspect of Captain Walls' research. He notes that returning veterans from war zones are showing a suicide rate twice that of the general population. Walls' current research indicates that 8 out of 10 police shootings involving veterans have aspects of suicide by cop.

Figure 37.2 An Experience of Suicide by Cop at Close Range

Officer Tremain was dispatched to the local hospital, after a security guard called, stating that a mother, who had just dropped off her 42 year-old son, told the nursing staff she thought he might be carrying a gun. He had been brought in for a reported head injury, and he had been drinking. He had made a suicide attempt nine days before, having slashed his neck with a box cutter. The suspect was wrapped in a large blanket (it was cold that night). Upon contacting the man as he exited the bathroom, Officer Tremain put him up against the wall, and conducted a pat-down for weapons. Tremain found a small loaded revolver in his right pocket. He hand-cuffed the suspect, and continued the pat-down, finding another loaded revolver on the left side. He found no more weapons.

During an interview with hospital social workers, the suspect was mostly unresponsive, but stated several times, "I just want it to be over." A mental health hold was eventually placed on the sub-ject, who was kept for about two hours in the secure room of the hospital and watched by Officer Tremain. At one point, Officer Tremain left the room to retrieve his paperwork. A nurse was in the room trying to convince the suspect to put on a hospital gown. He said he didn't want to change his clothes, and became agitated. The nurse exited the room, and summoned Tremain, who reen-tered the room just in time to see the suspect pulling a revolver from his waistband (subsequently it was learned that he had a handgun secured with a bungee cord around his waist. He had hidden this third gun in a bathroom prior to Tremain's arrival and retrieved it later). Tremain grabbed the barrel. The suspect silently attacked, and the two of them slammed into the wall and down to the ground, the suspect on top. Tremain pulled his service pistol, and jammed it into the attacker's ribs, and pulled the trigger once, killing him.

For yours and others' safety please note the following:
- Contacts with suicidal individuals should never be treated as routine.
- Remember that suicide is a form of murder.
- Murderous people are often hopeless, desperate, enraged, and/or hateful.
- Often, the only difference between murder and suicide is the direction the weapon is pointing and that can shift in an instant.

CHAPTER 38

Self-mutilation and
Para-suicidal Behavior

One of the most confusing actions that a person can do—at least to those outside the situation—is self-mutilation. When it is more severe, looking like a suicidal act, it is referred to as "para-suicidal behavior." This primarily includes cutting ones wrists or other actions that, taken to an extreme, could have resulted in death. Among self-mutilating actions we have encountered are:

- Rubbing an eraser on the wrist until all the skin is peeled away and one has a weeping lesion in the flesh.
- Stabbing oneself repeatedly by dropping a knife between the fingers, any error resulting in a wound in the web between the fingers.
- Running a needle in–and–out of the flesh of one's belly.
- Burning the face and genitalia with lit cigarettes.
- Hacking over one's wrists on the corner of a table, and then, after being stitched up, tearing out the stitches with one's teeth and attempting to spray blood on nearby corrections officers.
- Literally slicing open the abdominal wall all the way to the fascia that holds the organs.

The hallmark of all of these actions is that the person doesn't intend to die. Even in the last horrifying example, the woman in question, a former nurse, called for help after she's made the cut. There are a number of reasons why someone would do such acts:

- **Self-hatred.** The individual punishes himself/herself through self-torture and disfiguration.
- **Attention seeking.** These cases usually are typified by more superficial wounds. Such individuals "require" others to pay attention to them, particularly family members or loved ones who become afraid that they will be responsible for their death if they don't act. The case, cited above, of the young man who threaded a needle in-and-out of the folds of his belly was an unpopular, socially inept boy who, by means of this action, got some attention from schoolmates.
- **"Primitive medicine."** Like ordinary Europeans and Americans a mere 150 years ago, they're metaphorically "draining out" the poison by "bleeding" themselves.
- **A struggle to feel something.** Some people, in the throes of deep depression or trauma, literally feel numb. The torturous acts help them feel alive.
- **Stress Reduction.** Physical wounding, like many other stresses on the body, result in the release of endorphins, neuro-hormones that are close analogues to opiates such as morphine and heroin. People can become habituated to endorphin release, and activities that stimulate it can become addictive; one cuts to feel a sense of well-being.

Figure 38.1 One Author's Experience: Stress Reduction by Self-wounding

A young woman told one of the authors that, after years of verbal and emotional abuse by her father, "I felt like I was walking on egg shells all the time. Then, when my mom and I finally left, it was like I couldn't stand any emotions at all. Even when I was happy, I would still feel like I was going to explode." She described one day cutting herself on the forearm with an Exacto knife, and to her shock, felt a sense of warmth and peace. Not psychological warmth alone, but a warm floating sensation as well. Several weeks later she tried it again, and it became an addiction.

- **Rehearsal.** Some people want to commit suicide, but they also want to live. Over and over again, their feelings at war within, they make hesitant attempts to harm themselves, and fail.

Figure 38.2 The Line of Self-mutilation has "Moved"

We must be aware that the line of self-mutilation has "moved." We see individuals with multiple piercings, including one's tongue or sexual organs, who have voluntarily branded themselves, and others who some even have implants of metal placed under the skin, to end up with "devil's horns." Most of these people talk about endorphin release. Many claim that they're making their own bodies into works of art. As strange or repulsive as we may find some of these body modifications, this isn't an emergency, unless the person puts themselves at medical risk.

In an ambiguous situation, you need to ascertain if this is a suicide attempt, and also try to determine how seriously they're wounded.

In short, action is necessary if you have either a psychiatric emergency (a genuine suicide attempt) or a medical emergency, either intentional or accidental. Imagine an person who had NO intention of suicide, but decided on a do-it-him/herself splitting of their tongue in emulation of a snake (one author has seen such an unlovely sight. It takes a lot of days and a fair amount of dental floss.). However, when you arrive for a field-check, you find that the bleeding isn't stopping and they're toxic with some sort of infection.

CHAPTER 39

Crying Wolf: Identifying and Helping
Para-suicidal Individuals

Y ou surely have some people in your community who seem to be in or seem to create constant crisis. One of the most troublesome behaviors of such people is repeated suicide attempts or threats or self-mutilating behaviors that we referred to in the last chapter as "para-suicidal" behaviors.

Many of the problems engendered by such behavior are unsolvable. In Western society, we view this as a manifestation of mental illness or emotional desperation, and generally speaking, believe ourselves required to try to help the person. This requires our law enforcement and emergency medical personnel to strive to intervene, repeatedly, in the actions of people who either reject our help, or repeat the actions as if all our interventions are irrelevant. Let us consider the damage their actions cause:

- **Compassion burnout.** We get sick of such people. We see them only as manipulative, self-involved pathetic losers. Beyond whatever justification one might find for that point of view, it unfortunately expands. Many officers begin to view all mentally ill people, all suicidal people through the distorted lens that burnout creates. One loses compassion. This becomes a safety issue. When we begin to view others with contempt, they may respond with their own negative emotions. Thereafter, interactions between law enforcement officers and the mentally ill become increasingly volatile. Don't forget that the, suicidal, perhaps mentally ill, person might have a negative interaction with one contemptuous officer, and decide to take it out on another, at a later date.

- **Damage to society.** Suicidal threats, alone, can take up an enormous amount of man-hours, not only for law enforcement, but also for the emergency medical system. With our economy severely stressed, and our medical system currently in unknown financial waters, the hundreds of thousands of dollars that may be needed, every year, to manage the behavior of a single para-suicidal individual make such acts, however unintentional, an act of violence against our society. The bottom line is that hard-working citizens pay for any public service.

- **Officers out-of-reach.** Although to the best of our knowledge, such research has never been done, but it is a fair assumption that, in the hundreds of thousands of hours that officers have spent dealing with para-suicidal individuals, crime victims have been hurt elsewhere because officers haven't been available. This doesn't even have to be something so dramatic as "the officer wasn't there to stop the crime." Rather, there was no presence of officers in that neighborhood for a period of time, giving the criminals an opportunity to act.

When such individuals come to the attention of law enforcement, a committee needs to be set up to figure out the best way to deal with the situation. Ideally, this committee should include representatives from law enforcement, emergency medical response, hospital ER, the mental health system, and the prosecutor's office.

- If the person has made repeated suicidal threats without action, and no other effective intervention has been achieved, they should be prosecuted. Among the charges that can be levied are: false reporting, abuse of the 9-1-1 system, interfering with medical care. While in detention, it is the responsibility of the mental health system to maintain contact with the person, and begin to work with them so that they get a sense of reward when NOT using suicidal threats to get attention. If the reader's response is that it isn't practicable in your community, your police agency should initiate a coordinated effort between law enforcement, mental health professionals, and prosecutors/district attorneys to make such action possible in the future.

- If they have actually enacted suicidal gestures, even wrist scratching or taking a few pills, no one will prosecute them.[21] The risks of a more serious suicidal attempt will be viewed as too high. However, a comprehensive plan can be set up so that the individual gets more emotional rewards and attention by NOT engaging in para-suicidal gestures, and far less reward when they do act out. We have included a description of such a situation in Appendix B that highlights well how such a comprehensive community response can be set up.

SECTION VII

Recognition of Patterns
of Aggression

CHAPTER 40

The Nature of Aggression

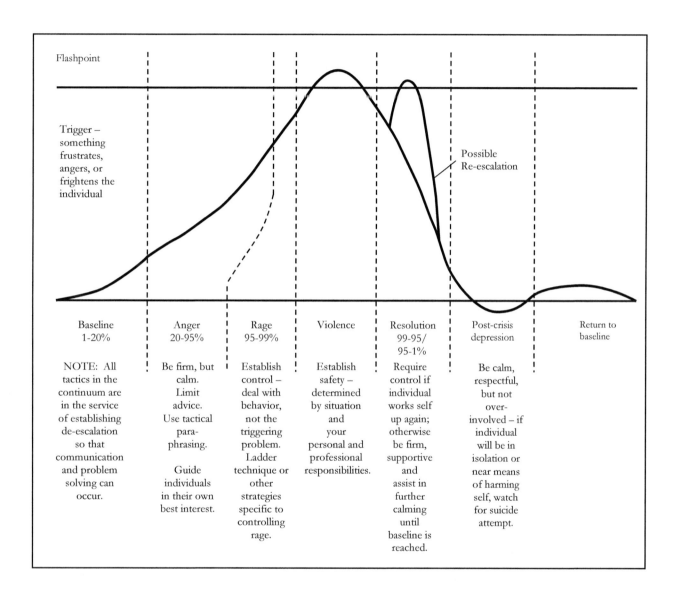

Flashpoint						
Trigger – something frustrates, angers, or frightens the individual				Possible Re-escalation		
Baseline 1-20%	Anger 20-95%	Rage 95-99%	Violence	Resolution 99-95/ 95-1%	Post-crisis depression	Return to baseline
NOTE: All tactics in the continuum are in the service of establishing de-escalation so that communication and problem solving can occur.	Be firm, but calm. Limit advice. Use tactical para-phrasing. Guide individuals in their own best interest.	Establish control – deal with behavior, not the triggering problem. Ladder technique or other strategies specific to controlling rage.	Establish safety – determined by situation and your personal and professional responsibilities.	Require control if individual works self up again; otherwise be firm, supportive and assist in further calming until baseline is reached.	Be calm, respectful, but not over-involved – if individual will be in isolation or near means of harming self, watch for suicide attempt.	

An outburst of aggression occurs in a cycle that starts with relative calm and ends with relative calm. Although the aggressive cycle often appears to start with a clear *triggering event*, the crisis may have been burning for some time beneath the surface. The reader may be familiar with the term "trigger" in terms of relapse in regards to substance abuse. In fact, they're similar. Many addicts have triggers that elicit the urge to use drugs: similarly, aggressive individuals, particularly the habitually violent, have triggers that cue them to become violent.

Calm/Baseline

When we're calm, we're at **baseline.** We use the parts of the brain most responsible for our better human characteristics: thinking, creativity, and forming social relationships. You can certainly have a fair amount of energy in a dialogue, and still be fully rational: a heated discussion, for example. For this reason, on a scale of 1 to 100, we approximate Baseline as 1-20.

Anger

A triggering event elicits a change in both thinking and feeling. This event can be something that threatens an individual's sense of safety, infuriates him/her because they haven't gotten what they want, or are simply a cue that they're now justified using a skill (aggression) with which he/ she is confident will allow them to achieve dominance or total victory. Once aggression is triggered, the person becomes irritable, then angry.

If violence is given the number "100" and baseline starts at "1" then ANGER is 20 through 95, with irritation at the low end of the scale. If the person at baseline is eminently human, the angry individual is a "mammal." The primary social focus for mammals is their place in a pack. It's the same for us human animals when we're frustrated, threatened, or believe we are being ill-treated. That is why angry people use such expressions as "taking a stand," or "I won't be pushed around," or "who do you think you're to talk to me that way!"

Nonetheless, the angry person is trying to communicate with us. Because we perceive them to be obnoxious, domineering, or just plain irrational, we often discount what they're doing as communication. They, on the other hand, experience an increasing sense of frustration or desperation, and not infrequently, a sense of helplessness. From their perspective:

- When you don't agree with them, you're resisting what is clearly true or right. Certain individuals cannot accept anyone disagreeing with them, experiencing it as a kind of attack.
- When you don't seem to grasp what they're saying, you're showing that you're disinterested, too stupid to understand, or your lack comprehension implicitly accuses them of stupidity.
- When you don't agree or comply with them you're frustrating them in achieving something they want.
- They have a sense of being wronged, experiencing a direct threat to their "position." Dominance hierarchy, for humans, includes not only one's position vis-à-vis others, but also one's self-image.

As people become more agitated, the areas of their brain that mediate basic emotions take over. At this point, equity, negotiation, or compromise becomes less and less attractive. In their frustration, individuals shift, increasingly, to attempting to dominate you: to *make* you see things their way, or to comply with them. Their domineering behaviors are, as much as anything else, an attempt to "get through" to you.

Think of arguments you have had when, frustrated, you said such things as: "No, that's not what I'm saying! Do I have to explain it again?" Or "Let me put it another way!" Or "You just don't get it! What do I have to say to make you understand?" Although counter-productive, you probably became more intense because you wanted the other person to grasp what you were saying.

Anger is accompanied by physical arousal, which functions as a feedback loop to drive the brain toward further arousal. When the heart rate rises 10 percent to 15 percent above baseline due to emotional excitement, angry people no longer care about the truth. We only care about being "right" and proving others "wrong." Communication is seen as a "win-lose" situation. We interrupt more frequently and cut other people off; we only listen to others to pick out the flaws in their argument.

Tactical communication with an angry person, particularly one who is mentally ill, focuses on "lining up" with them. You prove that you comprehend what they're trying to say. In other words, you're taking them seriously. This in itself is powerfully disarming, not only calming them down, but also helping you to work together to actually solve the problem.

Rage

Rage is a set of behaviors, including both physical actions and verbalizations that serve to disinhibit people so that nothing holds them back from violence. They are no longer trying to communicate: they're working themselves up to an attack. Their rage is almost instinctive; they desire to destroy, not merely become dominant. Some people slowly build themselves into a state of rage as a prelude to violence. Others lash out violently with seemingly no prior warning, verbal or otherwise. Even non-communicative aggressors will usually signal their rage through their body language and other non-verbal forms of communication. Officers should be aware of these warning signs of impending assault, as manifested on the intuitive level (Chapter 3) and based on observable behaviors, as described in the remaining sections of this book.

Human beings have various inhibitors that check the desire to commit mayhem on another person. The prime inhibitors are:
- **A fear of consequences**. The fear of counterattack, legal consequences, social disapproval, and a host of other possible negative outcomes.
- **Morality**. Toxic ideologies and cultures often define one or another type of individual as less than human, and therefore "fair game" for violence. Nonetheless, almost all human beings possess a core set of more principles, and when face with the vulnerability of another human being, face a "demand" to treat them without violence.[22]
- **Self-image**. A man may see himself as the kind of person who doesn't hit women, make a public display of aggression, or lose control of himself.
- **The relationship**. A feeling of responsibility toward the other person: friendship, love, family may hold them back from violence.

> **Figure 40.1 Relationships Can Sometimes Save Lives, even in the Most Unlikely of Circumstances: An Officer's Account to One of the Authors**
>
> I was working for many years in a drug task force. We raided this one house, and there were some pretty heavy drug smugglers there, guys from Mexico, mostly. We had a couple dozen guys hooked up in the yard, and as I walked past one guy, he looked up at me and said, "Officer, my kid's sleeping upstairs. There's an attic room. He's five years old. He's not a part of this. I shouldn't have brought him along. His mother lives in X (a couple of hundred miles away). I just had him for a visit. She's not a part of this. Please, sir, take him home to his mother. If you don't do that, he gets caught up in the foster system, he'll be hurt. I'm not legal. Please."
>
> The officer told him he'd do what he could, but he wasn't making any promises. He found the child upstairs, and after the immediate business of the raid was done, he cleared it with his superiors, called the mother, verified the story (she was horrified), and he drove the child home to her, on his own time.
>
> A number of years after this incident, this officer was working undercover, in another area of the country, making a drug buy. He felt a gun on the back of his head, and was dragged into a van. Eventually, he found himself kneeling in an open field, a circle of men around him, one man about to shoot him in the back of the head. Suddenly he heard ratcheting sound of another gun, and a man stood over him, pointing his weapon at his assassin. It was the father of the little boy, who said, "I know this guy. He saved my son. Back off. We're leaving." And they left him kneeling, alive, in the field.

- **Learned helplessness**. Some people, abuse survivors, for example, have tried to defend themselves in the past and have failed repeatedly. They may believe that they can't fight back. Their rage, however, is there. We have unlovely phrases like "a cornered rat," or "the worm turns," which describe a person who has suppressed their rage, sometimes for years, because fighting back always meant failure, pain, even destruction to them. Given enough frustration or threat, such people, may explode in a fit of uncontrolled anger and violence.

In short, rage is a transitional phase between anger and violence. For this reason, we assign it the numerical value of 95-99. What is the difference, then between rage and violence? Anger is a rocket ship all fueled up with some fumes coming out, and the countdown initiated. Rage is right before lift-off. The rocket has not yet moved, but there are flames and steam billowing out, making a terrible roar, so loud the ground shakes. It is a roiling moment of explosive, tenuous equilibrium. Fuel could still be cut to the rocket engines so that it sits silent on the launching pad, but there are only a few moments to act, because the rocket is about to lift off. Lift-off is the equivalent of the initiation of **violence**.

What you should experience in the face of rage is fear. This isn't a bad thing. Fear tells us that we're in danger and that we must do something—NOW! We will most likely be able to handle it, but we had better pay attention. Fear switches us on so that our emergency response systems are activated. [23]

Fear doesn't mean we won't be able to handle it. All fear really demands, is attention. A sense of power-lessness, on the other hand, is a *conclusion* that some people believe when they experience fear. Imagine two people about to get punched. One feels a sense of helplessness, a crumbling inward. The other feels a sense of outrage and at that instant knows that they will somehow win. That person has an internal sense that even if the body is wounded, the spirit will never be overcome. Fear can and should be a call to arms, not a sign of defeat.

Figure 40.2 The Difference Between Anger and Rage

Imagine someone hands you a huge plastic container. Through its translucent sides, you can see a dark, hairy shape, a Goliath Bird-Eater, the world's biggest spider. It rustles around the container shifting in your hands like it's filled with mercury. Is it creepy? Sure it is. Is there any reason to be afraid? Not really. As long as the lid is on the container firmly, you are absolutely safe. This is the equivalent of anger. Internally you say, "I'd better keep the lid on this thing."

Now, imagine your "friend" takes the container back, and to your surprise and horror, takes off the lid. The spider emerges onto the floor right next to your leg. It raises its front legs in threat-display and opens and closes its ¾ inch fangs. There is something poisonous, hairy, and mean in the room, and it is not enclosed in any container! The spider is out of the box. This, metaphorically, is rage.

However, the fear that now arises within you doesn't mean that you are helpless. You can step on the spider or jump up on a table. If you are ticked off enough, you can grab your "friend" by the neck and make him sit on it! A belief that you are helplessness near the spider is an interpretation, not a fact. Fear is simply the warning cry—the drums at the brink of battle—that demands that you *must* act right now.

To deal with the enraged person, you must establish *control, especially if,* their behavior presents an immediate threat to you, to themselves, or to others. Control tactics—be they verbal or physical—are geared to establish the conditions that make the aggressive person no longer dangerous. In essence, using our metaphor above, we say, "Put the spider back in the box. Now!"

Violence

Violence doesn't begin when someone is hit or injured. Violence starts when you have good reason to believe that you or someone else is about to be hurt. It is violence when an individual has violated the "safety zone" (the space between you at which you could credibly avoid an attack) and refuses to retreat. If the person doesn't have a weapon, we're talking about someone who is at about three arm's length distance and approaching in a menacing way. If armed, the distance can be much greater.[24] Your guiding principle is **SAFETY,** which is defined by what you must protect. This includes yourself and other people for whom you're responsible.

This is when all your training comes into play. Your tools, both your verbal skills and the ones on your belt, are at your disposal. Your department's use of force policy as well as all the requisite defensive tactics and combative skills are hopefully drilled within you at a pseudo-instinctual level. There are times when you should be talking. There are definitely times when the officer rightly decides that the best thing to do is to remove themselves from immediate threat, and return with back-up and the tactical advantage. There are other times that the officer uses less-lethal or lethal force. There are active "shooter situations" which require you to move in the direction of danger at risk of your life. You do whatever is most effective to protect yourself and the people around you.

CHAPTER 41

Why Would Someone Become Aggressive?

Aggression is not an alien or unnatural emotion. Without a capacity for aggression, humanity would never have survived. Yet, much aggression seems far apart from the basic activities of hunting or self-defense. Why would someone be swept by rage when it causes so much harm? Why would people be prepared to throw away a future, even their lives, driven by emotions that they themselves might be horrified to have expressed even a few moments later? Why would people choose to take on police, even in situations that they have little possibility of winning?

As you know from your own experience, there are many reasons to become angry or even enraged. We can better control aggressive people when we can communicate with them and we can do that better when we understand what set them off in the first place. Anger and rage can develop because a person

- **Feels confused or disorganized**. They can't understand what is going on around them or "inside" them due to cognitive distortions or a chaotic situation (too much information for them to figure out). Among those who experience this confusion are those who are seriously mentally ill, autistic, developmentally disabled, intoxicated, or others who are overwhelmed by emotion, or an incomprehensible situation in which they find themselves. Imagine a huge spider web dropping onto you. You thrash and struggle chaotically trying to get free.
- **Feels helpless, enclosed, trapped, or overwhelmed**. This is similar in effect to disorganization, but it is accompanied by a particular anguish, because the individual usually perceives someone as the agent of their situation. This sense of desperation could be elicited by being stopped, either physically or through intimidation from leaving a situation, or becoming enmeshed in an argument that gets worse and worse and continues to escalate. In the latter case, people feel unable to speak sensibly and make others understand their point of view. Arguments between intimates, called "emotional flooding," evoke this type of anger or even rage, where whatever one person says is "checkmated" by the responses of the other.
- **Perceives an invasion of personal space.** Every human being has a sense of personal space (Chapter 3). If someone moves inside this space, the other individual will experience it as an attack. In volatile situations, no matter what your intentions, you will be perceived as an attacker if you step in another's personal space.
- **Demands what they perceive as justice.** It is rare that an angry person doesn't believe himself/herself to be justified. Demands for justice are usually a complex sense of victimization or grievance and can include:

a. *The individual feels that they're losing their autonomy and power.* In this case, the person feels dominated and oppressed, and regards themselves as fighting for their freedom. This sense of loss of power is a personal reaction. It doesn't have to be "true" in an objective sense.

b. *The person feels that their rights are either denied, or being taken away.* Many people, mentally ill or not, experience a sense of violation when they're being limited or forced to conform to rules. Such individuals believe that something that is vitally their own is being stolen away even when, in truth, it is for their own good.

c. *A "self appointed" revolutionary feels the world is unfair and rebels.* The best sense of power that many people can achieve is in opposition to others. In this sense, they welcome an opportunity to designate others as enemies: legitimate targets for their own hate. Paranoid people view themselves and others as being oppressed by systems or powers beyond them. They "designate" you as a representative or exemplar of those larger forces.

- **Becomes intoxicated.** A "self-induced" delirium, intoxication causes poor judgment. For other people, drugs and alcohol aren't a "problem:" they're a solution. They drink or take drugs to "liberate" their brutal desires, something observed frequently among perpetrators of domestic violence.

- **Perceives a material threat.** People will fight to defend what they have or that to which they believe they're entitled. Many people regard violence as a legitimate response to the loss of one's home, job, or freedom.

- **Experiences organic stressors such as loss of sleep, insufficient or un-nutritious food, and/ or fatigue.** Brain chemistry changes when the human organism is stressed. In turn, this causes changes in perception, mood, and cognition, and among these changes can be an increase in irritability or hypersensitivity.

- **Experiences emotional stressors and losses.** Anything that elicits profound emotion can cause a person to become volatile. This can include a recent loss through the death of someone close: job loss, divorce, infidelity, or feelings of profound insecurity. The legal system certainly elicits strong emotions and each and every interaction with a law enforcement officer brings those emotions to the forefront. All too often, the law enforcement officer becomes an available target for an individual who has lost something important, as if to say, "As long as I'm suffering, why don't you suffer along with me." Anything that would drive a person towards suicide can drive them towards violence as well.

- **Feels a sense of entitlement.** For many people, entitlement is intertwined with desire. Their motto is, "If I want something, I deserve it, and if I'm not getting it, I have a right to be more forceful in my demands so that it is given to me."

- **Responds to their ideology.** Religious and cultural factors, be they the larger culture of a society, religion, and nationality, or the smaller culture of a community or family can provide an ideology that legitimizes aggression, even violence. Many cultures offer its members an "operating system" that expects a violent response in certain situations. Furthermore, cultures often define certain people or classes as inferior, even less than human. All too many cultures sanction violence against women as a matter of course.

- **Is flamed up due to family interactions.** One of the biggest motivators of aggression is what occurs in families. There is the friction of arguments regarding everything from house rules to who "owns" the house, irritation due to living too close together, past grievances brought up with no resolution, and a host of other issues. An argument starts, but it degenerates quickly into a demand that each concede that the other is right. Each feels flooded emotionally and becomes more and more irrational and furious because of their inability to "get through" to the other. This becomes all the worse when one or more family member is mentally ill, because what they're arguing about may be irrational or delusional. Families often function as emotional traps: there is no escape from the people who, although loved, cause one the most pain.
- **Is flamed up due to things occurring within their romantic relationship.** People in relationships often demand that the other person submit to their wishes. There are numerous grounds to fight: money, sex, childcare, infidelity, snoring, whatever you can imagine.
- **Has "given up."** For some, aggression, like its mirror-twin, suicide, is a "problem-solving" activity or a "what the hell" response when one can't find any other solution. Related to this is a person's belief that he/she has no effect on the world. Violence ensures that you will make an impact. Depressed people, particularly males, often manifest this type of aggression.
- **Hallucinates (command hallucinations).** The person is tormented by alien voices that assert an all-powerful identity The person may feel compelled to comply with the voices, which urge violence, or in trying to make the hallucinations stop by any means, becomes violent. On other occasions, the voices, visions, smells, or sensations are simply distracting and irritating. Imagine a mosquito whining in each ear, crawling deeper into the ear canal, unreachable, unstoppable.
- **Feels shamed or humiliated.** One of the most powerful driving forces of aggression is a sense that one has been shamed. Shame isn't a mild sense of social embarrassment. It is a sense of being exposed and victimized by others, with no way to make it stop. It is a driving force for revenge-based aggression and is also a prime motivator for attacks when a person identifies you with someone who shamed or violated them in the past. They may have been brooding about it for years, exploding into rage like an underground coal fire exposed suddenly to the air. This is a particular problem for law enforcement officers, where people who may bear a grudge against a previous officer, try to take it out on you.
- **Has been set-up by others.** This can occur for a variety of reasons:
  a. People are provoked by family members or friends. For example, a wife says, "I thought you were more of a man. I can't believe you let that cop talk to you like that. He made you into a little bitch."
  b. Other people do this to *themselves* by "fronting," making a scene in front of others (friends or family, for example) to increase their status in their "pack." Out in front, they're afraid to back down. Others carry the "audience" inside their imagination, demanding they conform to a" macho" self-image.
- **Thinks "life is war."** Some criminals see themselves in a war, seeing the cop as a combatant on the other side of the lines.

- **Uses violence as recreation.** For some person, hurting others is perhaps the most pleasurable activity in their lives. There is a joy in making others submit, and for some, a delight in causing pain.
- **Uses surgical violence.** This is a conscious tactic of intimidation. "I won't hurt you if you do 'x' but if you don't do what I say, I will hurt you very badly."
- **Is acting out of protective rage.** This is the rage expressed by one trying to protect another perceived as being victimized. The closer one feels to the perceived victim, the more one's identity is "merged" with them, and the more fiercely aggressive the "protector" will be.

CHAPTER 42

What Does Escalation Look Like?

What do people do when they become aggressive? As people escalate, their bodies become activated to fight, to posture, to intimidate, or to flee. They can show a variety of different behaviors.

Mood Changes

- **Atypically withdrawn.** Some people avoid eye contact, stop speaking, or only respond with short phrases, or even monosyllables. **Note:** Some people are quite withdrawn by nature. What makes this significant is when an individual who has hitherto been friendly or engaged lapses into sullen hostility or refuses to respond to a greeting. This would be something most relevant to a school resource officer or walking-patrol officer who sees certain individuals every day.

Figure 42.1 Example of Making Contact With an Atypically Withdrawn Person

Approach them and ask in the following manner, "Hey Tim, every day when I come down the hallway, you say, "Officer Sorrentino, what's up? But today, you turned your back when I came near. Something's going on."

Note that you didn't say, "What's going on." All this does is give the person an opportunity to ignore or discount you. By treating the behavior as both factual and meaningful, you are more likely to get a truthful response, such as a) "I just had a really bad phone call from home and don't want to talk about it." b) "You know what's going on! You know what you did!" (Such a response is the quickest way of ascertaining if the person is a threat to anyone.) c) "It's that dude down the block, not you officer. He's got no right to talk to my girl. He thinks this is over? No way."

- **Nervous, anxious, even frightened.** Such people usually lash out in defense. They're not looking for a fight; they're trying to protect themselves.
- **Overwhelmed or disorganized.** Such a person begins to speak in repetitive loops or pace and babble or talk to themselves. This is a manifestation of intoxication or a chaotic mental state.
- **Hostile.** Hostility is the open expression of dislike, hatred or threat.
- **Seductive.** Seduction is when an individual tries to get you to collude with them, for example, "C'mon, it's just a pipe. You aren't going to arrest me for smoking one pipe." Often this is just manipulation, but some people shift to overt violence when their "masked aggression" fails. NOTE: There are some situations where the officer plays the same tactic back, thereby getting

information from the subject. All we are saying here is that seduction is a form of covert hostility, so be ready for the individual to try another, more aggressive tactic when their seduction fails.

- **Exhibits mood swings.** (Chapter 17) This means rapid shifts in mood, for example, boisterous and loud to morose, then shifting to depressed and quiet, to once again, loud, this time belligerent. Such individuals present a particular risk because they're both unpredictable, and unable to control their own emotions.

- **Hypersensitive to correction or disagreement**. (Chapter 20) Hypersensitive people are very reactive to other people around them. Such individuals feel perpetually under attack. When there is no enemy, they will find one, or even create one. Paradoxically, they don't feel right with themselves unless they discover who is attacking them: in their world, someone always is.

- **React to authority issues.** These individuals become very frustrated or outraged, refusing to comply with rules. Their motto of life can be summed up in the phrase, "No one can tell me what to do."

- **Electric tension.** This is that intuitive sense you get when you're approaching a dangerous situation, the feeling you get before a thunderstorm hits. (See, in particular, Chapter 3). **If you feel it, ALWAYS trust it**,

Changes in Thinking

- **Cognitive distortions.** Negative self-talk that makes the situation seem worse. Such cognitive distortions heighten the individual's belief that they're being abused or threatened.

- **Interpersonal cognitive distortions.** The person hears the worst possible interpretation in what another is saying. For example: "Mia, you're trespassing. If you don't leave, you will be going back to jail." And her response is, "You're arresting me!!!!!!!"

- **Becoming less and less willing to negotiate**. The individual focuses increasingly on dominating the other, on winning the argument, or taking out their frustrations on the object of their anger rather than trying to find a way to a peaceful resolution.

- **Concentration and memory deteriorate.** It becomes more difficult for them to communicate, to solve problems, or to recall past problem-solving skills.

- **The angrier they are, the lower their ability to listen.** One focuses on being "right," not on finding out the truth. Without the ability to hear the other's perspective, they become either irrational or self-centered. In the latter case, only their own ideas and desires have any importance to them.

- **Judgment becomes worse and worse.** As their information processing skills deteriorate, their judgment consequently becomes worse and worse. They can't evaluate what is really in their own self-interest.

Figure 42.2 Example of Impaired Judgment Due to Escalated Anger

An officer was arresting a male suspect for an assault on his wife. On the way to the police car, still furious, he told the arresting officer, "If you take me to jail, she's going to throw away my dope. I paid good money for that." The officer re-contacted the victim's wife, and retrieved some methamphetamine, resulting in a second charge.

Words or Lack of Words

- Behaving with morose, sullen **silence,** accompanied by hunched shoulders, knitted brows, and glaring at the floor or at other people.
- Becoming **sarcastic.** Sarcasm is hostility shaded in humor or passive-aggressive phrases. They jeer at you, or sneer scornfully, demeaning your strong attributes and highlighting your weak points.
- Becoming deliberately **provocative**, by doing and saying things to upset or irritate you. Provocation is a challenge, trying to elicit a response on your part that will justify them becoming increasingly hostile, if not violent. They twist what you say deliberately, trying to confuse you or make you feel ridiculous.
- Becoming increasingly **illogical**. This isn't like deliberate tactic of playing word games. Swept by anger, they misunderstand or misinterpret what you're doing or saying or veer off on a tangent whenever you try to offer calming words or a way to restore peace. They become unable to explain what they're doing or trying to say.
- Becoming **loud and demanding**, with a belligerent tone.
- Using **abusive or obscene language**.
    a. When the individual uses terms that are vile and degrading, they're trying to make you "less than human." They might not do violence to a human being, but if you're a _____ (fill in the blank), then it is no more wrong to be violent than it would to exterminate vermin or a wild beast.
    b. In other cases, the obscenities and slurs are a focused weapon. The aggressor uses the words to shock or stun, so that you focus on what they say and not on what they're simultaneously doing. While you're preoccupied with their vile language, you don't notice that they have shifted their feet and slipped a hand into their pocket.
    c. Note, however, that some people use obscenity as adjectives and punctuation. They swear to illustrate their own emotions and ideas and truly aren't using their words as a form of attack. In the first two cases, you must deal with the verbal attacks as part of their mode of assault. In the latter event, correcting someone's rude way of speaking can escalate something that wasn't a problem in the first place.
- Making repeated **demands or complaints.** Of such people, we often say, "They have an attitude." This person is trying to legitimize a pervasive sense of grievance so they have an excuse to argue or fight.
- **Refusing to comply** with rules or directives. In their mind, it is all or nothing. If they comply, they lose. Only resistance is victory.
- **Denying totally** either the facts or the implications of what they're doing. They're so angry that reality is irrelevant to them. They're right and you're wrong.
- Using **clipped, pressured speech**, thereby presenting as "over-controlled," even as they have the pent up energy of a volcano. Such people often use very formal or stilted language. They sometimes seem to be biting off their words as they leave their mouth.
- **Implicit threats**. Boasts of past acts of violence or warns that they might not be able to stop themselves from doing what they did before.

Physical Organization—Disorganization

Facial Expressions. Facial expressions can vary a lot, depending on the mode of aggression. Facial expressions will be discussed in more detail in Section IX. The following list isn't hard-and-fast, but there is real likelihood when the following facial expressions are displayed the person means what follows:

- **Clenched teeth.** An attempt to contain or control intense emotions.
- **Bared teeth.** A threat display. You may have noticed certain people smiling who are really baring their teeth.
- **Frowning.** Is often associated with anger.
- **Knitted brows.** The eyebrows are pulled together, and the person looks out from under the eyebrows, associated with smoldering anger.
- **Staring eyes.** (Particularly if there is tension in the cheeks and all around the eyes. Can be an attempt at intimidation or manipulation; targeting the other as prey).
- **Biting or compressing the lips.** Is associated with barely controllable intense emotions.
- **Quivering lips.** Is associated with fear or unhappiness.
- **Tightening the lips.** Is associated with an attempt to control or contain intense emotion.
- **Pulsating veins in the neck.** Is associated with building anger and rage.
- **Dilated pupils.** Is associated with drug intoxication.
- **Avoiding all eye contact.** When coupled with other expressions of aggression, this can be associated with planning an attack, hiding intentions of an attack, or, paradoxically, an attempt to disengage so that they won't be forced to fight.

Voiding. When angered, some people have an urge to void themselves, clearing their bodies for the fight. Nausea and vomiting can occur with reduced blood flow to the gut. Other people feel a need to urinate or an onset of diarrhea. These behaviors occur when an individual is in a state of intense fear or otherwise full of adrenalin.

Breathing.
- Those shifting into offensive anger often breathe deep in the chest and down into the belly. This can be slow or fast, depending on how fast their anger is building.
- Those going into defensive aggression usually breathe in a shallow, rapid, and irregular pattern—almost like panting or gasping. Some hyperventilate, breathing so fast that they go into an acute anxiety state. They may become violent out of a terror-induced panic.
- Psychopathic individuals and others who are "professionals" at violence often maintain a smooth easy breathing pattern throughout.

Actions

- **Tense.** Most aggressive individuals become **tense and/or agitated**. Sometimes people try to discharge the tension by pacing, usually typified by rapid jerky movements, or even exercise that clearly isn't for fun.

- **Posturing.** Those who are getting angry, as opposed to enraged, begin to posture, inflating the chest, leaning into the other, thrusting their chin forward. This is an intimidation pose rather than a fighting pose.
- **Fighting pose.** Some will take a **fighting pose:** a combative stance, as opposed to posturing, is often a crouch, with the chin tucked in. In other cases, the aggressor brandishes a fist or a weapon.
- **Relaxed.** One subset of aggressors, the predatory (Chapter 62), tends to **relax** when they're preparing for an attack. They're at home with violence, like a tiger or a snake. These individuals sometimes smile while making eye contact with you.

Figure 42.3 One Author's Experience

Those best at being dangerous often don't act dangerous! One of the authors was acquainted with a man with a reputation in some circles as the best street fighter in a section of Tokyo. He was middle-aged, short, pudgy, and out of shape. He couldn't box or wrestle. However, every morning, for one hour, he would stand in front of a mirror, and practice smiling, relaxing, or gazing with a puppy-dog-like apology—perfecting utter harmlessness. Right beside the mirror was a small leather bag at head height. That was how he practiced his nearly perfect sucker punch (which was always followed by a head stomping).

- **Implicit physical threats.** Hard eye contact, intrusion into your personal space, cracking knuckles, clenching fists, etc.
- **Ritualized behavior.** Men, in particular, though not exclusively, will begin to **ritualize** their behavior, going into a stereotypical "war dance," puffing up their chests and spreading their arms to make their torso look bigger, invading their "victim's" personal space, pacing, smacking their fist in their hand, breathing faster, etc. They may move in quick jerky starts and stops, making movements toward their victim and then back, as if working themselves up to attack.
- **Positioning.** Those looking for a fight or confrontation square off directly in front of their target, while those looking for a victim tend to move to their "corner," so that they can attack where they're vulnerable.
- **Glaring.** Some individuals glare into your eyes with a direct hard stare
- **Trespassing.** Some aggressive individuals will trespass on personal space, even "accidentally-on-purpose" bumping into or jostling their prospective victim.
- **Power testing.** Picking up, mishandling, or even breaking the other's possessions. An example would be leaning on a police officer's car.
- **Visual rape.** Some men use their eyes to trespass on women, running their gaze over their bodies in what is a "visual rape." The implicit communication is, "What I'm doing with my eyes, I could do with my body any time I wanted."
- **Displacement activity.** Hitting, kicking, or throwing objects. This is done to discharge tension, as a threat display and as a "warm up"

- **Scapegoating.** This is a form of displacement activity expressed on living beings rather than objects. For example, a man, furious with a police officer, screams at his wife, "Would you shut that damn kid up!"
- **Making a dramatic scene.** The individual "acts crazy," either to get closer to you than you'd let someone who was purposefully targeting you, or to get you so preoccupied with calming them down so you lose sight of larger tactical concerns.

The Edge of Attack

- Angry or otherwise emotionally upset people have a **flushed** face, the pale-skinned turn red, and the dark-skinned turn even darker. In essence, blood at the surface of the skin is threat display, as if to say, "See how angry I am!" If people **blanch**, light-skinned people turn bone-white, and dark-skinned people get a grayish tone, this indicates RAGE. The threat is not potential: it is NOW.
- Increased **pacing**, while muttering to oneself, is arousing, bringing oneself closer and closer to the edge or attack
- Some people engage in **more and more displacement activity**, hitting, kicking, and throwing things.
- Others will **internalize** all signs of incipient assault, and thus, it seems to come out of nowhere. Right before the attack, these people stop breathing a moment. They can be utterly quiet and still: the "calm before the storm." It's as if you aren't there. In the latter case, the subject will sometimes have a "thousand-yard stare," where they seem to look beyond or through you.
- Some people, particularly, but not exclusively, the psychotic aggressor, get an **eerie smile** on their face, one that holds no mirth.
- As the attack is incipient, the aggressor can **"lose it"**—shaking, yelling, and acting berserk.

Explosion and Resolution

The crisis will be some form of assault, either verbal or physical. Of course, at this point, you will do whatever you must do to establish safety. After the explosive episode, the aggressor moves to the *resolution* phase in which they gradually, sometimes *very* gradually, return to baseline. Their body relaxes, cognitions improve, and their actions are less stereotypical. After resolution, there is often a *post-crisis depression*, which is due partly to physical depletion (the stored nutrients in the body are used up), and is partly psychological. The individual may be remorseful, apologetic, resentful, or merely withdrawn (Chapter 64).

SECTION VIII

De-escalation of
Angry Individuals

Introduction

All the techniques in this section are for angry individuals (mentally ill or not). Some work for low to moderate anger (*irritation*), and others across the entire range of anger. Remember they're a response to the angry person's attempts to communicate. We control them by establishing that we "got" the communication, so that there is no longer any need for the anger.

Note that methods used to de-escalate angry people do not work with enraged people. In fact, they will very likely further escalate the situation. Imagine saying to the berserk methamphetamine intoxicated psychotic, "I see you want to rip my brains out of my skull and smear them on the walls. You've been having a rough day today."

Conversely, using strategies that are suitable for enraged people (control tactics) with angry people will flame them upwards *into* rage. Imagine coming home and your spouse tells you that he/she is not happy at all that you forgot the groceries in the trunk of the car, and you say, "Step back. Give me five feet right now!" (It's going to be a long night, isn't it?)

CHAPTER 43

Core Principles of Intervention
With Angry People

When dealing with potentially aggressive individuals, safety must supersede all other concerns. If you don't establish safety for yourself and others, you can be of no assistance to anyone. This doesn't mean that you shouldn't be talking with the aggressive individual, reassuring them, or negotiating. However, everything you do must have a tactical basis: even reassurance or validation is in the service of safety. Solving problems must wait until safety is established. In the material that follow, there are page after page of techniques for de-escalation. Some are widely applicable, whereas others may only be useful in very specific situations. This is a catalog of techniques, not a sequential series of procedures. Think of them like the scales and octaves of music that must be mastered so that you can improvise freely.

- **Knowledge.** For field contacts: Officers should obtain as much information as possible from dispatch.
- **De-escalate, then solve the problem.** Your focus should be on what the subject is doing, not the cause of the upset. You can't solve a problem with an angry person. De-escalate first, eliminating the anger, and then engage in problem solving.
- **Watchful waiting.** Sometimes the best control tactic is letting them control themselves. You remain centered and ready as the angry person calms himself/herself without any assistance from anyone else. This doesn't mean that you ignore them. You're ready to suppress any action on their part that would indicate that they're ramping up instead of down.
- **Trust your hunches.** If you have a vague sense that something is wrong, you're probably right. You're becoming aware of the first behaviors that they display when getting angry (See Chapter 3).
- **Only one person should talk to the angry individual.** Trying to talk to two or more people at once will cause the angry person to become more and more confused, as well as making him feel attacked and surrounded.
- **Be what you want them to be.** Embody exactly how you want them to behave: calmly, with slow breathing, and upright posture. People tend to mirror the behavior of the most powerful individual with whom they're interacting. If you, the officer, are out of control, the angry person will be even more so. Conversely, if you're calm and powerful, other people tend to calm as well.

CHAPTER 44

Physical Organization in the
Face of Aggression

How you stand, how you breathe, how you use eye contact, your gestures, and your posture are all essential factors in calming aggressive people. You can say all the "right" things, but if you look like you're afraid, irritated, or angry, your verbal interventions will have no effect whatsoever and the situation will only get worse.

Breathe Smoothly. When you breathe rapidly with your chest, you tend to hyperventilate, which "informs" the brain that you're in trouble because **you need more oxygen now!** Deep, powerful chest breathing, on the other hand, excites the more primal areas of the brain: not flight, but fight. In Chapter 8, we describe a comprehensive method called "circular breathing." We strongly recommend that you master this method. However, for those who aren't able to effectively use circular breathing, or when one has to teach people in a short time, a more simple method[25] is to inhale on a four count, pause your breath on a four count, and exhale on a four count, As described in the last chapter, people tend to calm around people who are powerfully calm themselves. Proper breathing is the quickest avenue towards that end.

Be at an angle to the upset person. Standing, this is sometimes called a "blade stance," because you stand with one foot in front of the other, the back foot at a 45 degree angle with some space between them (don't put the two feet in one line!). Of course, your gun should be furthest away from the subject. Paradoxically, this is both calming (as people can tolerate your proximity better than if you were standing "squarely," confronting them), and also a much better stance to appear and feel strong (because you're both more balanced, and better prepared to protect yourself from a blow or a kick).

If you're seated. In any situation where the officer is seated, here, too, one uses a "blade stance." Sit on the edge of the chair, with the lead foot (opposite your weapon side) flat on the floor, and the other on the ball of the foot. You don't look ready to fight, but you are. You simply look relaxed and alert, and you can get to your feet without your hands, thereby being able to employ them in any way necessary.

Use the stillness of your hands as a calming agent. Clasp your <u>wrist</u> with the other hand. You can stand this way relaxed for a long time. By clasping your wrist, you slightly broaden yourself, and you will feel solid rather than nervous. Furthermore, you're ready to bring your hands upwards to fend off or block a strike *without looking like you're ready to do so*. In other words, there is no apparent fight in your stance: just strength. It is being tactical without looking tactical.

Use Your Hands as a Calming Fence. You can use your hands as a fence in a "natural" way by "talking" with them. [27] The hands are held up in front of the chest, with the backs of the hands forward. You move them in tune with what you're saying, sometimes turning one or both hands forward, or little-finger-edge towards the individual. However, **keep your movements slow and small.** You're rotating your elbows, not swinging your arms from the shoulders. People will become more agitated, if the officer is waving his/her arms in what appears to be threatening or chaotic gestures.

If the situation is getting more heated, and the person is increasingly encroaching in your space, place both of your hands, palms out, in front of you to set a boundary between you and the angry person. The arms should angle from the body at about 30 degrees, and the hands should be relaxed and curved slightly. *Both the hands and arms should be relaxed, like a flexible willow branch rather than like iron bars.* Of course, you can use these upraised hands to push back away or fend off if you have to. The hands shouldn't be in a "fighting stance" nor stiff in a rejecting gesture.

Figure 44.1 Don't Use Only One Hand Unless the Danger is High

When trying to de-escalate someone when the situation is not too heated, holding up *one* hand is more likely to provoke the individual. Rather than a fence, a single hand becomes the leading point of a triangle, your shoulders being the other two points. Many people experience this as aggression on your part. That one hand is "in their face."

If, however, the situation has gotten so volatile that you need to place a hand on or near your weapon, the single hand is simultaneously a calming gesture, a warding-off gesture and a fighting stance. Of course, do not over-extend the hand, or the aggressor could snag it and pull you off balance.

Be aware and sensitive to body spacing.

- Don't get in people's face. Don't get so wrapped up in communicating with them that you're unaware of their agitation. They may be shifting back and forth, looking down or away, begin to tremble, have their eyes go flat, or sway backwards. **Give them space unless there is a good tactical reason to take it away from them** (Chapter 3).
- Are they too close to you? If they keep trespassing in your body space, tell them that you're happy to talk about the problem, but they should step back—they're standing too close.
- Try to distinguish between the mentally ill individual, who is unconsciously too close (and needs to be *taught* space issues), and the person who is consciously trespassing, and needs to be *ordered*. It's the difference between saying, "You are standing too close. Move back, Arnie" and "Step back! Now!" Of course, never forget that mentally ill people can be aggressive or predatory just like anyone else!
- As escalation and danger increase, establish the ideal space to create an authoritative presence so as to keep yourself out of harm's way and most effectively control the other person. Not too close

or too far away. This is generally two arm lengths apart with adults. With small children, try to assume a low posture, so that your head heights are equal.

Figure 44.2 One Author's Experience: Intercultural Rules of Spacing

Various cultures have different "rules" regarding physical proximity and distance. To make matters more complicated, people within any culture are more diverse than you could possibly imagine. For example, I lived in Japan for well over a decade. It is a truism that people from East Asia don't like direct eye contact as much as people from America. This was certainly accurate with most people. However, I have had some Japanese people stare so deeply in my eyes that I felt like they were counting the wrinkles in my brain. So don't assume that someone is close to you "because they're from 'x' culture. Someone *from* 'x' culture may be getting close to you with the intention of harming you, just like someone from your own.

To be sure, you should be aware of cultural conventions so that you don't unnecessarily offend people. At the same time, such individuals are now living in this culture (wherever my reader resides) and therefore, in setting your own limits regarding space, you are teaching them how better to survive in their new home. Therefore, if someone is too close for your comfort, whatever culture they're from, tell them, tactfully, to move back so that you can continue your conversation with more ease, and conceivably, safety.

Try to move slowly and smoothly. Agitated people startle easily. If you're breathing slowly and moving smoothly, however, they will tend to calm in rhythm with *you.*

The art of eye contact. In almost all cases, it is best to have direct eye contact with the angry individual you're trying to calm. You must be both non-threatening and non-threatened. In other words, to use your eyes to calm someone else, you must show that calm and strength in your own eyes. There are several exceptions to the eye-contact rule:

- Some psychotic or disorganized people find eye contact to be very invasive. When they're calm or only slightly agitated, angle your body in such a way so that they don't feel confronted or forced to make eye contact with you. If they escalate into real aggression, you must make eye contact to establish control, whether they're mentally ill or not.
- There is a disinterested "no-eye-contact" that can be used with *aggressive-manipulative* people (Chapter 61).
- There are some people who are so frightening that you feel your will is breaking and your mind taken over when you make eye contact with them. Others are so chaotic, manipulative, or confusing that you find yourself unable to maintain a solid sense of what to do or say when you make eye contact. If you're facing either of these types of individuals, **look between their eyes**. When you look into someone's eyes, you're establishing a human connection. If that connection

puts you off-balance, then it's dangerous to you. When you look at their forehead, you're just looking at layers of dead skin. You will find yourself far calmer, and the subject, *if aggressive*, will still think you're looking in their eyes. You will just appear very strong.

CHAPTER 45

Tone and Quality of Your Voice
for De-escalation

Talk as a professional. An angry person will focus on your tone rather than the content of your words. Don't betray any negative or angry emotions. For example, a bored tone with either impatience or condescension is guaranteed to evoke more anger, not less.

In most situations, try to pitch your voice a little lower than is usual for you. Under stress or intimidation, our voices tend to go up in pitch. When you pitch your voice lower, you will feel a little vibration in your chest. You get immediate feedback that you have taken control back of your own body. In addition, a quiet, but strong, low-pitched voice—only a little lower than normal, not necessarily a baritone—communicates that control to the aggressor. This is the voice you use to deliver strong unambiguous verbal commands.

Slow down. It is often useful to speak a *little* slower than they do. However, don't speak in slow motion or in such a way that they think you're trying to hypnotize them. You're trying simultaneously to get them to resonate with your slower energy and also to keep yourself from being swept up in theirs. (As will be described below, there are other times that you want to "catch" the other person up in your energy. In these cases, you may speak with speed and/or enthusiasm.)

Don't be "saccharine." Unless you're dealing with a small child in distress or someone severely developmentally disabled, don't use a soft, nurturing voice. When you talk to people as if they're children, incapable, helpless, and/or fragile, they will either feel that way, or feel that you're trying to make them that way. People who feel incompetent believe that they can't make things better. This includes calming themselves down. That overly sweet vocal tone can provoke the aggressor to regress to a more child-like state, which can easily deteriorate into hysteria or a tantrum, which in an adult body means an assault. Others, insulted at what they perceive as condescension, become angrier.

When necessary use a dramatic voice. When should you use such a voice? It'll usually be effective with someone who is developmentally disabled, childlike for some other reason, or an actual child. It will feel like the right thing to do. Make your voice a little louder, and use charisma to grab attention.

Figure 45.1 Example of the Use of a Dramatic Voice

A mentally ill woman is upset because she thinks people in a courthouse lobby are laughing at her. You say, "Claire, I SEE you are upset! I'D be upset too if I thought those people were laughing at me! Now COME ON over here!" Indicate with your body where you want her to go, moving as if you are absolutely certain she will comply. "C'mon. I want you to tell me EXACTLY what happened! EVERY word! Let's go over here where no one can bother us!"

Show her that not only are you giving her your complete attention, but the drama means that she is important, the center of the action. By moving her somewhere else to talk, you remove her from the scene that is upsetting her.

When to use the "battle cry." With few exceptions, the major time you would be yelling at an individual is combat. This is the battle cry, an emergency shout of "NO!" or "FREEZE!" or "STEP BACK!" You only use this when an aggressor is attacking you or otherwise presenting immediate danger to someone. You roar like a lion to startle and momentarily freeze their motion, so you can evade attack and escape, put them in custody, or deploy a weapon on them while they aren't moving.

- Open your eyes WIDE!
- Slam your stomach BACK to try and connect your navel and your spinal column.
- Tighten your throat. (This will be a little painful to some people, leaving a raw throat for the next day, but it's worth it if it saves you or someone else from harm).
- **ROAR** a command.

Figure 45.2 The Choice of Words for a Battle Cry

When an attacker, already close to you, is moving toward you with hostile intent, don't command that they "Stop" or "Freeze." They may comply and still be too close. Instead, command that they **"Step Back"** or **"Move Back"** or **"Back Off."**

The commands **"Stop"** or **"Freeze"** should be used to arrest an action that will, in itself, result in harm; for example, if an attacker is about to assault another person, throw something, or simply run out into traffic. You are trying to shock them into momentary immobility, so that you can effectively get hold of them or deploy a weapon to stop their threat.

CHAPTER 46

Dealing With People Across
the Spectrum of Anger

Sometimes an early intervention moves an individual to a state of calm. You avert the crisis before it happens. You should be able to imagine scenarios when you interact with angry people, mentally ill or not, where one or another of the interventions in this chapter fits the situation.

An attitude of calm. An essential factor to lining up with the aggressive individual is *your* attitude. They're in an emergency state and believe there is no time left. If you also believe there is no time, you're both in crisis and you won't be able to act as a stable person to help them get back to a peaceful state.

Greet them and work your way towards the subject. In a situation where an individual appears to be brooding or preoccupied about a grievance or perhaps a delusion or obsession, it is often not a good idea to immediately start talking about what you believe is upsetting them. Instead, start with a greeting. It's common courtesy. Start talking about something, like the weather, or sports. This is also an informal assessment tool: if they resist your attempt to redirect them, this informs you right away that the situation is becoming serious.

Use a "door opener." State in an impartial way what you observe or believe is disturbing them. For example, 1) "You looked like you were getting upset with that girl;" 2) "Something just happened between you and your P.O. I saw you guys talking in the street." Notice that in both cases you don't ask if there is something wrong or a problem. When you ask a question, you give the person an opportunity to simply close the door by denying what you observe. An open-ended statement implies that it is self-evident, as if to say, "We're already past the argument whether my perception is real or not. At this point, we're discussing what this perception means to you and to me." Follow this question with *silence*, accompanied by an open inquiring expression on your face, as if the next move—them replying—is a given.

Don't touch the irritated person hoping to calm them down. There are very few occasions where touching angry people will make the situation better. Such situations do exist—with distraught children, perhaps—but not with adults, and *particularly* not with aggressive individuals. The only times you will touch a potentially aggressive person should be to handcuff them, control them, or protect yourself.

Don't make sudden moves, unless the fight has started. A sudden move may be interpreted as an attack. When you move with measured calm, you slow the process, and hence the individual down.

Tell me; you don't have to show me. As elementary a suggestion as this might sound, the following illustrates the power of this intervention. A very upset individual begins swearing at a police officer on the phone. She replies, "Al, it is absolutely clear that you're upset. Furious! And I'm able to help you with this. But I can't and won't do that when you swear at me. Tell me why you're upset. You don't need to show me."

Demonstrate empathy. Empathy isn't the same as sympathy, that feeling of sorrow for the person's plight. Empathy simply means that you grasp, approximately, what other people are feeling based on their physical organization, what they say and how they say it. Use phrases such as, "I understand you're…." or "What you're saying really makes sense." Or "I imagine I'd feel the same way…." We thereby demonstrate that we grasp what the person is experiencing without necessarily agreeing with it.

Figure 46.1 CAUTION

There are some police de-escalation systems that make this a centerpiece of their training methods. However, if you overuse this you will sound like a parody of a "therapist in blue." Like everything else we have discussed, it is a tactical communication that is to be used sparingly at just the right time, such as, perfectly timed, during an interrogation.

Let them tell their story. Sometimes people simply have to say their piece. There is no need to problem-solve and no need to interrupt. In such cases, listening with attention and respect is all that they need.

Be professional. Some officers act in far too friendly and informal a manner. Professional distance gives the subject of your attention a clear understanding of the true nature of your relationship with them. Police officers shouldn't allow people to call them buddy, pal, dude, babe, or any other form of casual address that implies a friendship or intimate relationship. Conversely, the officers should address citizens with the respect they deserve. Use their name, not just "Hey you."

Ask what kind of help they need. If a mentally ill person is only mildly upset, of course you can ask questions. Ask what they want or need. If you have a solution to the problem, explain it clearly to them, give them an idea how long it will take and what they should do in the interim. Always try to explain the process. Many folks walk around frustrated. With the proper information they de-escalate on their own. This is particularly valid with service-level complaints.

Team up with them. Incorporate them into your "team" by using the word "we." When they accept this unconsciously, they begin to feel that they're working with you, not against you. A couple of examples are: "Let's you and me sit over here." And, "Yes, we do have a problem. Let's see what we can do to figure this out."

Humor. This is the ability to see a situation from another perspective, can sometimes work like magic. However, you must be very careful—it only is helpful when the person is at low levels of escalation—irritation—rather than strong anger. If they're too upset or agitated, their response to a joke or humorous comment is likely to be, "You're making fun of me," or "This is serious. You think this is a joke?"

Figure 46.2 One Author's Experience

Many years ago, one of the authors was a member of a mixed-race group when one of the men, an ex-con with a history of assaults, started singing a little song, "I got a bullet here for every white man here, because everyone should die." I smiled at him and said, "That won't work on me. I can only be killed by a silver bullet, followed by a stake through the heart." I looked at him blandly, and he gave me a momentary hard stare. Then we both broke into laughter, and the atmosphere in the room lightened considerably.

Distract. Particularly with young or cognitively impaired people, it is often best to simply distract them. This is sometimes useful even with people who are experiencing a delirium state, where you distract them long enough so that they can be restrained safely. Their anger is driven by feelings and sensations, rather than by what they're thinking. If you can change the focus of their attention, their anger often dissipates.

Honesty is golden. Don't promise what you can't do or otherwise try to fool the person. If you suggest a solution to the problem, be clear what the limitations are. Don't leave them feeling betrayed later; it can come back to bite you or another officer the next time there is a confrontation with the individual. Furthermore, be absolutely clear. "You can do this or that, but not the other." Many people take negotiation as concession, believing they will get everything they demand. If they don't clearly understand their options, they will later experience a sense of betrayal when they're refused something they want.

CHAPTER 47

Diamonds in the Rough:
Essential Strategies for De-escalation of Anger

Codes for Living

People live by codes, and paradoxically, those leading outlaw lifestyles cling to codes even more than others. Some of those codes are based on the culture into which they're born, and others are based on the culture or lifestyle they adopt. Some of these codes are passed down within a family, while other people may create a code in resistance to those they were bequeathed. Some people's codes are impeccable principles of personal integrity and others are eccentric rules congruent only with their mental illness or character disorder.

The heart of their code is often a phrase of one or two words that sums up their deepest values. When people talk about themselves, their codes of living are often woven throughout their speech. This is especially true when people are angry. The reason for their outrage is often their belief that their code is being threatened or compromised:

- They perceive that others are demanding they violate their code.
- They take offense when others don't conform to their code.
- They think another's actions require them to respond or they will violate their code.

Angry people will very often proclaim their code for living in their explanation or tirade.

Figure 47.1 Examples of Individuals Proclaiming Codes and Values

Person 1. "I'm a man. He can't talk about me that way."

Person 2. "Think of how I feel. If someone did that to you, wouldn't you be upset?"

Person 3. "Are you saying I'm not going to get paid? I did the job and you owe me. Whether you like it or not isn't the issue, you owe me!"

Person 4. "I was standing there all alone. Everyone was looking at me. Talking about me!"

You should be able to describe their code in one or two words. What is most important to each of these people in the above examples? Individual #1 is focused on pride; #2 on empathy, that others should understand his situation; #3 is focused on obligation and an implicit contact being broken; and #4 is focused on humiliation.

This code is an access route to the person. When you incorporate it in your response, they feel understood. Another way to think of this is that you're filtering out the static and noise to get to the real music. Take note of the following:

- **Personal integrity.** Frame your suggestions with the same theme. "I wouldn't want people talking about you as a man who can't control himself."
- **Respect.** "Man, I can see how angry you are. I'd be angry too if someone said that to me. If you break into his room to hurt him, though, you end up losing. You lose your room and you're going to jail. Yeah, I know you think he *disrespected* you, but if you assault him, you would be letting him 'own' you. He says three words, and you end up losing your home, and your education at this school. No, I'm not saying to let it go. Let's you and me figure something out, so you win in a real way, so you keep your room, your education, and your respect."
- **Situational.** The dominant metaphor here is that it is "hot and tired." "Look, Frank, I know it's a hot day, I'm tired, and I guess you are. I don't care who's right here, really; I just want to finish this investigation so you can get back to your house where it's cool. These hot days are a killer. Here you and I are stressed out just cause we're both hot and tired."
- **Tunnel vision.** A person can get so focused on an issue that it is all they can think about. "Disgusting. Absolutely right. Those meds are disgusting. They must taste terrible, and don't let anyone tell you different. If they didn't work so well, the doctor would never tell you to take such disgusting tasting things. But they do work, don't they?"

Break the Pattern

An aggressive person, set on conflict, often attempts to enmesh you in an inescapable system. Consider the following:

- **Aggressive man.** "What are you looking at?" "Nothing," replies the intimidated other person. "What!!!!! You called me nothing!!!!?'
- **Aggressive man.** "What are you looking at?" "I just looked in your direction," replies the intimidated other person. "What!!!!! There's something on my face you don't like!!!!? Or are you just calling me ugly?"

In "breaking the pattern," you do or say something that makes continuing the dispute absolutely impossible. In many cases, you will use a dramatic voice or display somewhat uncharacteristic or outlandish behaviors. It is hard to describe *how-to* do this. Here's a few examples:

Figure 47.2 One Author's Experience

A very aggressive, manic individual, after jumping around my office while verbalizing very dangerous fantasies, whirled around and said to me, a grin of delight on his face, "You are scared, aren't you?" I blurted out, "Yes, I am," (That statement, from very early in my career, was clearly a mistake, one I would not make today.). He then started to stalk menacingly toward me. Realizing I was in danger, I jumped up, and yelled in a dramatic voice "You know what I'm scared about? I'm scared what's happening to kids today! They're being murdered in wars throughout the world. But we don't even have to go that far! They're cutting school lunches and little children who go to bed hungry aren't even being fed in schools!!!!! I'm scared what's happening to kids today!" With a look of shock on his face, he dropped into a chair, and said, "I like kids. What are we going to do about that?"

Figure 47.3 Example of Breaking the Pattern

A police officer was arresting a hostile man, who was twisting away, trying to avoid having handcuffs put on him. The methamphetamine-intoxicated man yelled an obscene accusation about the officer's assumed sexual predilections. The officer jumped back and said, "Goddamn it! You make one mistake 20 years ago and they never let you forget! The man held up a hand and said, "Whoa, whoa brother. That's okay. These things happen to everyone. It's okay," and turned around, offering his hands to be cuffed.

Figure 47.4 Example of the Use of Humor to Break the Pattern

A police officer was arresting a drunk when he called her that word that, more than any other makes many women incensed. With a look of puzzlement on her face, she said, "Jimmy, do you spell that with a K or a C."

"K," he replied.

She answered, "Jimmy, if you are going to use big boy language, you should at least know how to spell it. Now when you get released tomorrow, you ask your wife how to spell it."

He responded "No way! She'd kill me. She don't like that kind of talk. . . Oh yeah . . . I'm sorry officer."

Figure 47.5 One Author's Experience of Breaking the Pattern

A man came into a clinic, drunk and belligerent. I came out and yelled, "Man, WHAT have you been DRINKING? Me—I like Ten Canes Rum. Whoa, <holding up two hands and yelling boisterously> Not your turn yet! I'm talking about my rum! Ten stalks of sugar cane for one bottle of rum. It is SWEET as sin and gold as a tiger's eye. Man, I love my rum. I go home, take two ice cubes and put them in a glass. When the rum hits that ice, I hear a crack as clear as the bell in a church and I know everything is going to be alright!"

What have YOU been drinking?"

He blearily looked at me and said, "Whiskey."

"What KIND of whiskey. I need to know WHAT you have been drinking!"

"Four Roses," he slurred out.

"AHH man, not Four Roses! Sit down here and tell me why you've been drinking that stuff."

We ended up sitting on two chairs, laughing and talking about our favorite drinks. When the police arrived, I requested they trespass him from the location. He was having so much fun with me at this point, that he accepted this, still laughing.

Breaking the Pattern seems like magic, a highly developed intuitive skill that some of us imagine we would never be able to do. You can't have an array of special catch-phrases ready to disarm any aggressor. It is pure improvisation, like jazz or rap. However, the key isn't how creative you are, as if only brilliant people can possibly bring this off. It is actually the outcome of the same powerful calm that we have written about throughout this manual. When you're *trying* to be creative, you may say something witty, but it will be at the wrong time, with the wrong timing, and to the wrong person. When you're in control of yourself, with the mainline skills of de-escalation at hand, such improvisation will simply emerge, an idea or sentence that "demands" to be said. You will be wrong: off-center, or off-target if you're *excited* about what a cool or funny thing you're about to say. Although the story you tell later about what you said may be dramatic or hilarious, you aren't a comedian trying to be entertaining.

Silence

Sometimes the most powerful thing you can do is to be silent. Be sure that you aren't being passive-aggressive, or fuming in silent anger. Instead, you're powerfully, quietly waiting. Such silence can evoke curiosity, anxiety, or a desire for a response. Keep your face calm, your posture centered, and be aware, and truly interested. Calmly nod your head as you listen. Do this slowly and only several times, intermittently. In many cultures, including America, if you nod your head too rapidly and often, it means that you want the other person to hurry up and finish, or simply shut up.

Silence, however, isn't that easy. There are three ways to listen silently, and two of them will make people very angry.[26]

- **Contemptuous silence**. You're tired of the dispute, or may be tired of the person. You fidget, you sigh, and most significantly, you twist one corner of your mouth, and roll your eyes upwards to one side. In all cultures that we're aware, this facial expression and behavior expresses the attitude that you hold the other in complete contempt. It is guaranteed to provoke rage.
- **Stonewall silence.** When you stonewall, you ignore the person or make it clear that you wish they would shut up. You can also appear to do this inadvertently when you're inputting data, listening on the phone simultaneously or to another conversation, or taking notes. Stonewalling evokes incredible anxiety in the other who wants to get through to you, finding that there's a "wall" in the way. They will do anything to get "through," and this includes yelling, hitting, or begging.
- **Interested silence.** *The Right Way.* When you have been listening well, the angry person often ends up asking, "Aren't you going to say something?" or "Don't you have any ideas." If they don't ask, and continue to talk and talk, interrupt them. Do this by advancing a hand slightly at your waist level or a little higher, fingers curved, palms down (you don't want the individual to interpret your hand movement as a "shut up" gesture). Your shoulder also leans in just a little. In effect, almost subliminally, you're indicating that it's your "turn." In either event, you say, "I *do* have something to say." **The first thing you should do is to sum up your understanding of what he just said. You have to prove that you were listening.** This becomes the perfect lead-in to "tactical paraphrasing" (Chapter 48). If they're talking really intensely, put up both palms, open your eyes wide, and say something like, "Okay man, okay! It's my turn."

Some officers find staying silent difficult, particularly when the other person is talking nonsense or making a fool out of themselves. Remember this is a tactic: if nothing else, be interested, as a "street scholar," studying how people can come up with the things that they're saying.

CHAPTER 48

Tactical Paraphrasing:
The Gold Standard With Angry People

Paraphrasing is perhaps the most important technique for calming really **angry** people. You sum up in a phrase or sentence what the angry people has just said in a paragraph. If you paraphrase accurately, you have established that you have "gotten" it that far, so they don't have to repeat it, or try to say it in other words. It is like peeling off a single layer of an onion so that you can be shown the next one. If you don't show that you "get" it, the angry individual will feel compelled to repeat and/ or elaborate that layer of the problem with more and more intensity. As they get more intense, they usually get more irrational, and their ability to communicate breaks down even further. The wonderful thing about paraphrasing is that you don't have to be "smart" and interpret anything. You simply have to listen carefully.

Figure 48.1 Paraphrasing Versus "Mirroring" or "Active Listening"

Many people refer to this method as "active listening" or "mirroring." We have chosen another phrase to describe it to highlight some important differences between the proper use of this method in a law enforcement context and that of many others.

- Mirroring often entails repeating word-for-word what the person is saying. This can be experienced as taunting or mocking.
- As for active listening, this term often carries a certain ideological baggage—many counselors, following a particular theory of healing, try to establish a nurturing relationship with their client, thereby either making them "feel better," or in the safety of such "validation," allowing them to emote freely. This is subtly manipulative. By talking to another person as if they were fragile, they may either feel so, or may feel that you are *trying* to make them feel fragile. In either event, this can elicit "contact regression," where the person becomes childish or further angry or even enraged. Unfortunately, this mode of communication has spread far beyond that one sector of counseling theory. We have both heard police officers try to use this with mentally ill subjects, and it hasn't gone well at all!

Returning to our image of an onion, as you peel off each layer, they get to the next layer that is driving them. They might start out complaining about a traffic ticket at the front desk and that paraphrased, begin to tell you that their wife left, and that paraphrased, start talking about suicide.

Paraphrasing establishes that you're truly listening and have understood what they have said. There is another component however where we also take a slightly activist approach. We select what we will paraphrase, choosing the healthiest aspect of what the angry person has just said.

This method is "self-correcting," whereas passive summation can make things worse. If you sum up an angry person's worst impulses, they may find themselves in full agreement with you. You have lined up with the part of them that desires destruction. If you sum up an aspect of what they have said that is in the direction of conflict resolution, you will draw out of them that which *does* wish to resolve the conflict. On the other hand, if they're, in fact, bent on mayhem, they will correct you by escalating what they're saying, believing that you aren't getting the message. Remember, they're trying to communicate! All you have to do is sum up what you understand from what they said. When you get it right, they go to the next layer.

Figure 48.2 Example of Correct and Incorrect Paraphrasing

Angry Father. I'm so mad at my daughter that I could just wring her neck!"

Incorrect paraphrase: "You want to murder your daughter."

Correct paraphrase: "You are *really* furious with her!"

If you have, in the second example, accurately paraphrased the meaning of the angry father's intention, you will naturally go on to the next layer of his complaint.

Angry Father. "You won't believe what she did. I come home and find her on the couch lip-locking that punk from down the street. You know, the kid who epoxies his hair in corkscrew spikes?"

If, however, the second example is *inaccurate*, the angry father will correct you with more vehemence.

Angry Father. "No, not 'really furious.' I honestly want to loop a belt around her neck and slowly strangle her. Seriously! She better not be home when I get back from the police station."

Why not simply ask the person what's going on? If they want to tell me, why don't they just answer the questions?

Asking questions is usually not a good idea with really angry people. They already believe you have to "get" what they're saying, and a question shows that you don't. Still angry and now frustrated at their failure, this makes them try harder, albeit with less organization and coherence than before. Over and over, they experience failure—they can't get through to you! When anger is combined with a sense of powerlessness, the person feels like he/she is "losing" to a more powerful other. In essence, they experience a question, a demand for an answer, as putting you in a dominant position in regard to them.

Figure 48.3 Example of How Irritating Questions Can Be

Imagine coming home after a bad day. You're hot, tired, and frustrated. You walk into your house, drop your gear on the floor, sigh loudly, and walk toward the shower. Your spouse says, "Did you have a bad day?" Isn't this irritating? Isn't it *obvious* you've had a bad day? After all these years together, and he/she doesn't know when a bad day just walked into the house! On the other hand, imagine your spouse observing you and saying, "Bad day, huh?" You continue walking towards the shower, and say, "I don't want to talk now. I just want a shower. I'll talk to you later." You aren't "forced" to explain yourself.

How to Use Paraphrasing Successfully

- It is very important that your voice is strong. You speak to the individual as someone who has the power within to take care of himself/herself and their problem, not as someone who is fragile or volatile (even if he/she is).
- You must contact the strong aspect of the individual, the future looking side, that which is striving for strength, looking for integrity. If you contact the weak, or the insecure, you may foster regression to a less mature level of action. Childish action is often impulsive or violent.
- Sometimes, you can use a dramatic summation, "You're really ticked off!" Here, you sum up the individual's mood with your voice and posture, in addition to what is being said.

Figure 48.4 Example of Successful Use of Paraphrasing With a Mentally Ill Woman (Who often becomes suicidal when frustrated)

Shoshona. "I can't believe it. He is so stupid!"

Officer. "You're really upset!"

Shoshona. "No! I'm really furious!"

Note: When you sum up imprecisely, the other usually corrects you. This is as if she were tuning up the signal rather than arguing with you.

Officer. "I haven't seen you this mad in a long time."

Note: You can include extra information ("in a long time," for example). This is for the purpose of steering the person in a positive direction slightly. It also helps to assess how responsive she is to you. In other words, if you add a little something, is she even able to hear it? In this case, you're validating that she hasn't been angry in a long time: in essence, that she has shown that she is able to maintain control of herself.

Shoshona. "I know. But nobody's ever done anything like this to me!"

Officer. "This is something new, huh?"

Shoshona. "Yeah, I asked him out last week, after my NA meeting, and he said "yes," and then, in front of everybody, he said he was just joking."

Officer. "You must have been really embarrassed!"

Shoshona. "I was ashamed. It was just like when my mom left. I felt like I wasn't good enough for anybody."

You just got the story without a single question. She even trusts you enough to tell you something real about her past. Now you're in a position to do a threat assessment, to determine if she is either suicidal or has aggressive intentions towards the guy who shamed her.

Using Paraphrasing to Communicate with Severely Mentally Ill Individuals

Paraphrasing can be remarkably effective for communication with severely mentally ill individuals. Given the internal chaos that people experience when psychotic, manic or disorganized, it is essential that we don't add to their sense of confusion by barraging them with questions or attempting to solve their problems by taking over and telling them what they should feel or do. When the mentally ill person gets confused, losing track of what he was saying, or drifts off into a tangent, just paraphrase the last thing they said – this will help them reorient to the subject of concern.

Figure 48.5 Example #1 of Tactical Paraphrasing With a Psychotic Individual

After neighbors complained about Murray's "strange behavior," law enforcement officers visit his home for a welfare check, and find him in a decompensated state. Disheveled and staring in the officers' direction he says, "There are pink rose petals, rose petals flying all around my head, clouds and clouds of roses!"

The officer could ask him lots of questions in order to have him explain what he meant, but instead, he paraphrases the only thing he does grasp. (Notice the progression from one layer to another).
- **Officer.** "Pretty confusing, huh?"
- **Murray.** "You're darn right it's confusing. How'd you like to be in my head?"
- **Officer.** "I wouldn't want to be in a confused head. It must be hard to think."
- **Murray.** "Hard to think and scary. The roses turn bloody red, and I fly apart."
- **Officer.** "You can't keep things together."

- **Murray.** *(nodding)* "In the fear, it feels like blood."
- **Officer.** "Feels like blood, huh? I don't see any blood out here though."
- **Murray.** "In my head, only. Where the fear is."

Notice the officer's last sentence. Realizing that they have reached a "core point" of Murray's concern, he intervenes more actively to validate his perception ("I don't see any blood out here, though….") and, at the same time, base him in reality. If, near the end, the officer had asked, "Is anybody hurt?" Murray might have been overwhelmed. Murray might think that the officer seemed worried, and he could start thinking of all the people whose feelings he has hurt over the years, and wondering if he hurt someone and can't remember, etc. By making a matter-of-fact statement, the officer takes a lot of psychological pressure off him, and it is easier to re-organize enough to be able to communicate.

Remember, though, that paraphrasing is self-correcting. Murray might have replied, "There's no blood out here. She's lying in the back. That's where the blood is."

Figure 48.6 Example #2 of Tactical Paraphrasing With a Manic Individual

Johnny. "I never get enough sleep."

LEO. "You look really tired."

Johnny. "I don't know how I look, but I feel exhausted!"

When you're inaccurate in your summation, the other usually corrects you. He isn't arguing with you, just tuning up the signal.

LEO. "You've been up late the last couple days, waking early, and now you're really tired, aren't you?"

You can include extra information that sums up the experience the other is having. This is for the purpose of steering the individual toward problem-solving while not giving advice. It also allows you to assess how responsive he is to you. In other words, if you add a little something, is he even able to hear it?

Johnny. "I'm not tired at night."

LEO. "You can't fall asleep when you go to bed, huh?"

Notice the tag lines like, "huh?" or "aren't you?" These are not really questions. They follow statements and give the other an <u>invitation</u> to correct you or give you more information.

Johnny. "I don't even bother going to bed. I just lie there looking at the ceiling if I do."

LEO. "It seems like a waste of time, and then you wake up early anyway. It'd be fine if you weren't tired."

The second sentence by the officer is an attempt to sum up what he believes are Johnny's feelings about his sleep cycle. It is also another assessment—he offers Johnny something to agree with or correct.

Johnny. "Yeah, I'd be fine if I wasn't tired. I'd just sleepless and do more. But I'm too tired for that. I wonder if I need to talk to Dr. Montour about my medications. I think I need something to help me sleep."

Imagine that Johnny is a young man who is very resistant to talking about his medications and one who usually gets in lots of trouble when he doesn't take them. If the officer had responded to his initial statement about being tired by suggesting he go to the doctor immediately ("problem-solving"), Johnny might have angrily stopped talking or argued with him. By listening and showing step-by-step that he understood him, the law enforcement officer got Johnny to find the "deeper layer" of his concern by himself.

Core

We know we have reached the core level when there is no more "progress." The person *spins his wheels.* They may use different words, but they say essentially the same thing over and over again. Some express relief at being finally understood. Some exhibit an intensification of emotion, because you have reached that which is most distressing. When you reach core, and it is clear that you're on the same wavelength, you can begin problem-solving. This can be:

- Further paraphrasing, where you show greater and greater understanding about what they're upset about.
- A summation of the core problem, followed by a puzzled "why?" For example, "You trusted him, and let him stay in your home. He came on to your daughter and stole money. I can understand why you'd be so furious at him. What I'm confused about is if you do break his arm, he wins. He gets hurt, sure, but you will go to jail, and he'll be out and no one will be home to protect your daughter. We have to figure out a way that you can really win without getting into trouble."
- With some individuals, you have, by paraphrasing them every step of the way, established that you're a person of trust. In some cases, you can now be quite directive, because people are often willing to accept advice or even instruction from those they trust.
- With others, we're ready to engage in a collaborative process of problem-solving, trying to figure out a way to solve the situation that is in the best interest of everyone involved.

Don't Waste It

Paraphrasing is almost a cliché, so much so that we can imagine some of you rolling your eyes when you read the title of this chapter. This technique is too important to abandon, and at the same time, it must be used carefully, i.e., *rarely*. If mentally ill contacts are used to your using paraphrasing as your primary method of discourse, they will cut you off, because you will appear to them to be giving nothing back, except mirroring. It is "cold fare" compared to a rich dialogue, a combustible exchange of views, or a lush conversation. If the individual isn't getting angry and requiring you to use de-escalation tactics, don't use paraphrasing. Simply talk with them.

If there is a crisis, however, and the person *doesn't* believe they're understood, *now* paraphrasing comes into its own. Paraphrasing can have an almost electrifying effect with an angry individual. Imagine the feeling when you try to pull a splinter from under your fingernail, and after 10 long minutes of aggravating struggle, you get a hold of it finally and pull it out of your nail bed. That is the sense you get when, angry and desperate to be heard, you realize that the other person "got it."

Figure 48.7 How to master paraphrasing

As you as you view paraphrasing as a 'specialized,' pseudo-counseling technique, you probably won't want to do it—and you won't be good at it anyway. When you are hit by adrenaline, dealing with an angry, perhaps mentally deranged individual, you will stumble over your words if you try to remember to say things like:

- "So what you are sharing with me is . . ."
- "What I hear you saying is . . ."

Don't do this! Many people will find you irritating, and you will be in your head at a time where you must be aware of what's going on in front of you.

You are, in fact, a master of paraphrasing. You do it all the time simply keeping a conversation going, saying things like:

- "Your kid flunked out, huh?"
- "You're not getting a raise."
- "You hate that guy."
- "She's the one."

In short, the natural statements you intersperse in any conversation are perfect paraphrasing. However, because you do this unconsciously, it's hard to tap into as an *emergency technique*. It's easy to perfect, however. Consider this—how many conversations do you have a day? Twenty? Thirty? Forty? <u>In each and every conversation, at an arbitrary moment of your choosing, decide to paraphrase the next thing they say.</u> Just once. Your conversational partner won't even notice. But because you made a conscious decision to do this, your brain notices. That means you have practiced

---

that skill twenty to forty times a day. Consider how good your shooting skills would be if you do twenty, thirty, forty perfect shots a day—it would become automatic! Similarly, if you do this every day, you will be able to step into crisis oriented paraphrasing without hesitation. It will be so natural to you that you do not even have to think about it.

CHAPTER 49

Some Guidelines for Limit Setting

As soon as you draw a line it will become the main focus of your interchange. Don't ever set a limit that you can't enforce or one that isn't reasonable and simple to understand. When dealing with the mentally ill, limit setting is a kindness rather than oppression. Beleaguered by mental illness, struggling with substance abuse, beaten down by poverty or unemployment, such people experience their lives fragmenting into pieces. When the rules shift, they can become profoundly anxious. Your tone of voice should be matter-of-fact. You shouldn't scold or criticize them. Simply remind them of the rule or set a proper limit (a new rule, so to speak). Only set reasonable limits that the person can do. If you can't explain clearly why the limit is necessary—at least to your peers—then it's not a good limit.

Setting a "Full Stop" Limit
- **Give clear directives with no wiggle room.** For example, you say in a confident, commanding voice, "Billy Jo, lower your voice."
- **If he complies, give him a brief mark of approval**. Continue with the verbal control.
- **If he doesn't comply with the directive, depersonalize the reiteration**. "Billy Jo, you are re-quired to lower your voice." DON'T say, "I expect you to…." The individual should experience what you're saying as the "law," an institutional command or policy, rather than a personal issue between you both.
- **Don't get then caught up in manipulative word games.** Don't respond to professed ignorance, excuses or confusion. You're using this tactic because there is no ambiguity regarding the trans-gression and no ambiguity what the consequence will be.
- **Consequences.** "If you don't immediately lower your voice, then you will be…." Give the indi-vidual the consequence. (Here an individual might be told that they will be physically walked off the property, trespassed, or arrested.
- **The "choice."** This follows almost directly from the previous step. With a detached tone, you will say, something like, "It looks like you've got a decision to make. But if you choose not to lower your voice, you know what will happen." You will follow through on your end based on whether they comply or not.
- **If they escalate.** If they simply escalate further, enforce compliance as needed.

CHAPTER 50

Techniques That Don't Work:
The Big Mistakes That Seemed Like Such Good Ideas

Many of our mistakes are very obvious. As something leaves our mouth, we think, "Uh-oh, I shouldn't have said that!" But some are subtler, and often occur when we think we're doing the right thing.

Don't try to ingratiate yourself with the subject or try to pretend that the aggression isn't happening. _Law enforcement officers don't submit to an aggressive individual!_ We, the authors know that—but some officers fool themselves. They let the individual ramp up, but they try to tell themselves and others that they're letting them get it out of their system as a control tactic. In short, such officers cover their eyes and hope for the best. One of the paradoxes of ingratiation is that people who sell out their integrity often present themselves as having a "special rapport" with the individual who, in fact, intimidates them.

The mistake of mind reading—taking a walk in someone else's head. Sometimes we try to steer people in the direction we want them to go by telling them either what we believe they are, "at heart," or telling them what we (to be honest) wish they were. People may get quite offended by this, because it feels like you're claiming to read their minds. Statements like, "I know you really love your son," or "You don't really want to get into it with your neighbor," are statements that the angry person may not feel at all. When you make such generalized statements, people may feel compelled to prove you wrong by doing or saying exactly the opposite. If you do want to say something positive, praise a specific action and say it like this, "I know you're really mad, so I respect how you're keeping it under control and not going after him." And of course, only praise them for something that is true.

Getting it out of their system: The mistake of allowing venting. Pure venting is an expression of energy, such as going for a run after a difficult day, or chopping wood until fatigued, so that you can let go of a nasty incident at work. However, we also call generalized aggression expressed in front of others (tantrums), or anger expressed about a person, not present, to another as venting.

Many people have a false idea about aggression. They imagine it to be some kind of psychological fluid that builds up pressure inside of us. These people believe that we vent, getting rid of the anger and then become peaceful. Aggression, however, isn't a fluid: it is an arousal state, and just like any other state of arousal—sexuality, happiness, excited interest—stimulus elicits more arousal. When we shout, yell, complain, kick things, or the like, we're escalating ourselves to greater and greater aggression. The longer you let aggression continue, the more "aroused" the aggressor will be, and the harder it will be to control them.

When you let the potential aggressor vent about other people, it seems to them that you're giving covert approval to their complaints and verbal abuse. They believe you're on their side. When they're so angry that they start to become dangerous, and you *finally* object, they turn on you, feeling betrayed. Don't try to help them get it out of their system. It doesn't work.

Head nodding. In Western culture, we generally nod our head once or twice followed by an interval of immobility when we're listening to another person. If we nod our head more than twice, in rapid succession particularly, this means we aren't interested and wish the person would be silent.

In some cultures, Japan being a prominent example, rapid and almost continuous head nodding and brief interjections like, "really, really, imagine that, yes, yes…." denote interest. In other cultures, nodding while someone is talking is considered rude, and people will, instead, hold their head still and look directly at you as a sign of respect. It is examples like these that illustrate the necessity of "cultural information training." Nonetheless, if you wish to be understood as listening with interest to someone in mainstream cultures, nod once or twice, and pause a long moment before nodding again.

Other really obvious mistakes that we shouldn't do, but we do anyway. *Don't!*
- Make promises you can't or don't keep. This will be experienced as betrayal.
- Make threats you can't keep. You will be viewed with contempt.
- Bombard the subject with choices, questions, and solutions. You will overwhelm them.
- Ask "why" to an angry or enraged person. There is usually no more unanswerable question, particularly when you're asking why someone is doing something. A "why" question demands that the person "explain himself/herself," something they may be quite unwilling or even unable to do. (The only exception is the "why" at the end of a paraphrase sequence, as described above).
- Talk down to people as if they're stupid. This can be done, deliberately or inadvertently, when using unfamiliar vocabulary, jargon, or acronyms. It is also done when one sighs while the other is speaking, rolls one's eyes in contempt, or speaks slowly, as if talking to an idiot.
- Use global phrases like "calm down." Specific commands get results. General commands don't.
- Analyze why they do something. Analyzing is "cutting apart to examine." People, upset or angry people in particular, experience being analyzed as a violation.
- Take it personally when they get upset.
- Start making fun of them, teasing or messing with them. They may even laugh along, but you are demeaning them and very possibly creating a life-long enemy for all law enforcement officers.
- Interrupt people as they speak, particularly if you're correcting what they're saying. On the other hand, interruption of aggressive verbalizations or pointless monologues on the part of a person in a law enforcement related contact is the right thing to do.
- Ignore it when they trespass on your boundaries. When we allow others to trespass on us, we're, implicitly giving them permission. Any territory we relinquish is open to whoever chooses to occupy it.

- Suspend boundaries. if we become too familiar, we become "friends." Sharing personal information or not setting limits leads the subject to viewing the relationship between you as eye-to-eye and reciprocal. It is very difficult to accept authority—limit setting, directions, or commands—from a friend or equal. Safety is enhanced when one enforces a strong, decent but real hierarchical relationship.

- Boss them around in a demeaning or authoritarian way, particularly in front of their peers. Authoritarian attitudes and behaviors are among the most common precipitants of assault by mentally ill individuals.

- Expose their private information in front of others.

Figure 50 Concerning Privacy

Warning: Be careful of "hallway consultations" and "curbside debriefing." You may be talking about an individual, either professionally, or just blowing off steam with complaints, jokes, or the like, and another person, perhaps mentally ill, hears you. That you aren't talking about them is irrelevant. They think, "If they talk about that woman like that, they're probably talking about me in the same way. The thought of that cop talking about my family with that smile on his face is makes me want to tear his face off!"

SECTION IX

A Consideration of Communication With
Mentally Ill, Emotionally Disturbed,
and Drug Affected Youth

CHAPTER 51

Working With Potentially Aggressive Youth

Figure 51.1 A Note Concerning Youth

Generally speaking, you will use the same de-escalation strategies with youth as are outlined in the rest of this book. The differences are often more on nuance than on major details. We have, however, "sub-divided" youth in some general categories based on behavior that will help both in understanding young people as well as using the best strategies to help stabilize and calm them when they have become aggressive or are otherwise in crisis. [27]

Youth With Mental Illness: A Law Enforcement Officer's Perspective

Dealing with aggressive children whether in school or home is problematic from several perspectives. Most certainly, you will outweigh and out muscle the child. In many cases, they're small and fragile, and you can easily injure them. Anyone watching you dealing with the child (and their adrenalin won't be pumping) will have their own perspective on how rough and or abusive you were. They may also have their own video phone at hand. We have all read the stories of officers resorting to using a conducted energy device on a child, and the subsequent fallout from schools, parents, witnesses, media, mental health professionals, police administrator, courts, etc. Whatever the necessity, the officers have never looked good.

Many readers may be thinking, "They're kids—how difficult can they be?" Or perhaps worse, maybe the mindset is the school district or the mental health system or the youth detention authority will deal with them. Really? According to the United States Senate's Governmental Affairs Committee, there are many thousands of kids with mental illness in need of community mental health service, while they sit in juvenile detention centers.

A 16-year-old former juvenile detainee was accused of stabbing a high school teacher to death with a butcher knife. Another teen was convicted of killing a roofer during a 30-minute robbery spree. Both were released by the Texas Youth Commission, because the agency wasn't equipped to treat their mental illnesses and had to let them go. It turns out there is a loophole in the law in the way Texas treats under-age individuals with severe psychiatric issues. The Associated Press reported that Texas has released more than two hundred individuals because of mental health issues in the last five years and that more than one-fifth went on to commit new crimes, some of them violent.

Figure 51.2 One Author's Experience

I was working with one of our School Resource Officers (SRO) when he requested my response to his school. He had a 5th grade boy in a state of rage. The boy was small, about four feet tall, and weighing just a bit more than a wet towel. The SRO was 5'6" and a solid 160lbs. He was an avid weight lifter and football coach. It was all he could do to restrain the boy. The school staff present might just as well have been on vacation because, as in many school districts, they're not allowed to touch, much less restrain children.

The boy was face down on the carpet yelling and screaming, and my SRO was sitting on top of him. The SRO moved to a kneeling position ahead of the boy with his knees on either side of the boy's head, attempting to keep him from moving by placing his hands on the boy's shoulders and pushing downward. I straddled the boy's legs, and held his feet to keep him from thrashing and kicking about. The boy had a blood-curdling scream, and unbelievably, he was gripping the carpet with his hands, and slowly, slithering like a snake, moving the two of us along very slowly toward the door. When the ambulance arrived, it took four of us to get this little kid onto a gurney and strap him down. Mom arrived at the same time. Thankfully she was on our side and we did not need to fight her as well!

If a 5th grader can require four grown men to physically control him, it's worth asking:
- What do you do in your jurisdiction when you have a mentally ill juvenile?
- Who is charged with taking care of them? Knowing this in advance could prove critical. Collaborating with them in advance and creating protocols is the wise thing to do.
- What training do you have to have to safely restrain out of control children so that you don't injure them, perhaps severely.

General Concerns

The youth described in this chapter are young *now*, but they will grow up to be adults, perhaps living in your community. Understanding them will aid you in the coming years. Youth today don't just face "coming of age" growing pains. Despite all the prosperity and opportunity in our society, youth face many dangers. Drugs are everywhere, and not only do they affect children directly, but also, far too many have been affected *in utero* by their parents' drug abuse, and not just by their mother; there are questions about genetic changes in the sperm of male drug/alcohol user as well. Furthermore, when one's parents use drugs and alcohol, their attentiveness and caring towards their children is lessened in the "best" of such circumstances; abuse of all kind increases exponentially in drug/alcohol abusing homes.

Gangs metastasize within a community, just like cancer. There is a putrescent vitality to gang life that is both charismatic and compelling. Despite the terrible things one may do, the gang offers solidarity, and a life committed to something bigger than oneself, however damaging that might be. Once initiated, one crosses a line that is hard to cross back over. This charisma, by the way, isn't only attractive to children from broken or abusive homes; the vitality of a warrior culture, no matter how violent and destructive to both its victims and its own members seduces children from loving families as well. It is only when "the good" has a power and charisma greater than that of gang culture that youth find it easy to turn away.

Youth and young adults show mental illness in much the same manner as adults. If a young person is displaying psychosis, mania, latency, or any of the other behaviors described in Section V, the strategies offered there are fully applicable. In this section, we will be describing the character traits that are often related to aggression in youth; you can view these traits as the youth's fundamental attitude towards the world. A reader might reasonably ask when dealing with an aggressive sounding youth, how could one tell what mode they're in?

View each chapter in this section as a quick step-by-step process. If the approach on impulsive youth, Chapter 52, doesn't work, quickly move on to the next. It is quite likely that you will, intuitively, grasp that a youth is in one or another mode, and start with the tactics appropriate to that behavior. Of course, the next time you have to deal with this particular youth, you will know the second time around where best to start. At any rate, this section will take things as a quick (matter of moments) step-by-step process. [28]

CHAPTER 52

No Brake Pads:
A Consideration of the Impulsive Youth

Per orthodox theory, attention disorders come in two major forms. In the first type, the main manifestation is a short attention span (ADD). In the second type, hyperactivity is also present (ADHD). We both believe that the diagnosis of ADD/ADHD, now so astoundingly common, deserves more controversy than it is currently receiving in both media and clinical sources. We strongly recommend that everyone concerned with youth read two contrarian books: one by Leonard Sax and the other by Richard Louv.[29] Whether you end up agreeing with all of what either of the authors proposes, they will require you to think afresh about these issues. And in an era where medications are slung like candy at children, often with little clinical assessment or sound treatment, this is absolutely necessary.

Figure 52.1 Note on ADHD

This type of problem isn't only endemic in America. One of our colleagues wrote to us that in Northern Ireland, "There are various allowances payable to parents of kids diagnosed with ADHD so many parents even lie to their doctor to get the kids on the various drugs, or at least, get the diagnosis."

Let us here consider the impulsive child (ADHD or N.O.T.), as one who tends to act before he/she thinks. Below you will find some examples of actions by impulsive youth.

- He is in a store and sees a video game he wants, and without considering the consequences, shoplifts it right in front of the security camera.
- She gets in an argument with one of her friends and, her feelings get hurt, she assaults her friend right in front of their teacher.
- Another boy bumps him in the hall and he stabs him in the hand with his pencil; he is as surprised as the victim, both of them looking at the bloody pencil tip with their mouths open in shock.

The impulsive young person gets angry or aggressive for the same reasons as any other person, but they get particularly upset and frustrated when someone interferes with the gratification of an impulse. Paraphrasing (Chapter 48) can be particularly valuable with these kids because you demonstrate that you "get" their desire and frustration, rather than argue with them. (NOTE: This is a tactic, just as is done in crisis negotiation, NOT approval for their outburst.)

Impulsive youth track very little of what you say, particularly when they're angry. If they're too escalated for paraphrasing, it isn't the time for explanations, attempts to elicit empathy for the other person, or moral preachments. **What usually works best is a calm demeanor and simple short commands.**

How would you know that they're not merely impulsive or upset? If the following strategy doesn't work, go on to the next strategy. Remember, we're talking about an approach that takes only a few moments—this is NOT a counseling session!

Figure 52.2 Review: Dealing with Impulsive Youth

Until proven otherwise, when dealing with an upset or aggressive youth, assume that he/she is in "impulsive" mode.

- Paraphrase;
- Give them firm, brief commands;
- Help them regain control by directly telling them what to do.

CHAPTER 53

Conduct Disorder:
Fierce Youth

Figuro 53.1 Definition of Conduct Disorder

Conduct disorder is a term that delineates behaviors in children and youth that, in someone over the age of eighteen would merit the diagnosis of anti-social personality disorder, or even psychopathy. Because the child/adolescent brain is still so changeable, we <u>properly</u> don't give them a diagnosis that would suggest that change is unlikely, if not impossible. **The majority of children who fully merit the diagnosis of conduct disorder don't grow up to be psychopaths.** Nonetheless, Chapters 22 & 23 on manipulation and psychopathy are essential in considering any youth who is conduct disordered, because a law enforcement officer must deal with the behaviors that the conduct disordered youth is showing now. This section focuses specifically on youth who display ferocious, manipulative, or predatory behaviors, whatever the cause may be.

The fierce youth typically displays rages in three major categories: fury, manipulation, and predatory behavior (See Section X). Conduct disordered character traits can develop from myriad reasons, some of them heart-rending. This may be relevant for psychological treatment, but not in de-escalation and control of their potential violence. If you contextualize or excuse their behavior, someone will be seriously hurt.

It is almost always a mistake to try to establish a "sympathetic" or "nurturing" connection with such youth at any time, much less during a rage state. They experience these gestures as an attempt to soften their defenses, and/or a sign of weakness on your part. Fierce youth children/teenagers lay extreme importance on protecting themselves from "invasion." In other words, sympathy is experienced as manipulation or an attack.

They strive to defend themselves against any need for other people, as well as building up a callous attitude in which they extinguish caring for other people's pain. In the most basic sense, such youth are profoundly isolated. Without human ties, pride and respect are their most important "possessions," something they will live and die for. This pride can be considered an access route for communication and de-escalation. For tactical reasons, meet such pride with "respect." This is NOT, by any means, approval for what they're doing, or even what they "are." It simply means that you're letting them know where they stand, that they're in violation of the rules of our society, and you, as the agent to enforce those rules will, with no personal agenda, make sure that they aren't allowed to transgress. You're saying, in essence,

"Your job, at least right now, seems to be breaking the rules, and my job is to stop you." **The formula for communication with such fierce youth is "Respect outweighs sympathy."**

In other words, one enforces the rules with calm gravity and strength. Never try to ingratiate yourself, or prove you're a "good guy," because all you will get back is contempt. However, if you manifest yourself as a strong and dignified individual who doesn't make it "personal" when you do your job, you will, sometimes in the most quiet and subtle way, draw their attention and curiosity.

If there is hope for such youth, it lies in their fascination with power. You present to them a world unimaginable—that power and decency can exist within the same body, and that one actually acquires more power through treating others with respect. If you don't manifest this yourself, such a young person will be unreachable.

Figure 53.2 Review: Dealing with Fierce Youth

You first approached the youth as if their aggression is impulsive and you tried to exert authority over them. That didn't work—instead, the youth becomes more focused and directed in his/her aggression towards you. In this case do the following:

- Let them know where they stand—that anything you're enforcing isn't "personal," that you're doing your job and dispassionately enforce your authority.
- Respect before sympathy! Don't try to prove you care.
- Deal with them on a professional, slightly disinterested basis.

CHAPTER 54

Dynamite Under a Rock:
Explosive Kids

The hallmark quality of these kids is that once their fiery tempers are unleashed, it is very hard for them to stop. They rage and rage. Many of these young people can pay attention just fine *until* they lose their temper. Others, such as the child with Fetal Alcohol Disorder or a history of head injury, have learning disabilities, including problems of attention in addition to explosive tempers. Regardless, they're the kids of whom one says, "Billy lost it again today," and everyone nods, imagining the explosion at the judge, along with slung chairs and thrown fits, the young person raging for over an hour *after* they were restrained in hand cuffs.

If you're trying to verbally control them, loud orders and other shouted commands don't work well. They can be unbelievably violent, and they react to commands as further provocation. They flame up at the sound of your voice, particularly if you're yelling. The watchword, instead, is **containment**.

Give commands, but your voice must be very firm and calm. The command is to get their attention. It is to focus everything on one being—you. In favorable circumstances you, and however many others are necessary, escort (or convey) this young person to a quiet area where they calm down on their own. Your task is to stay nearby so that they don't injure themselves or damage property. You can't however, problem-solve or otherwise work things out while they're still on fire. If you're unable to accomplish this, you should avail yourself of the strategies in Section X on rage and violence.

School Resource Officers (Who Have Regular Contact With the Same Kids)

Some explosive youth, particularly those with neurological damage, suddenly shift into an "organic rage," apparently unmediated by any thought processes. However, these kids often show small micro-changes of behavior right before assaults. You should definitely learn these signs to help the youth shift gears into another activity or process, thereby heading off the explosion. Two examples come to mind:

- A girl in a group home had enacted a number of apparently sudden severe attacks against other residents. We found that when she focused on an intellectual task too long, she would begin scratching at her forearm. The "sudden" explosion of aggression followed a few minutes after this "tell."
- Another youth would knit his brows and glower in a stubborn manner when he didn't understand a conversation. He interpreted this as people "making me feel stupid," an attack in his view. This facial expression was a clear sign to the officer to slow down, lighten up, or change the subject.

Figure 54 Review: Dealing With Explosive Youth

You're dealing with a young person and attempt to exert authority, and then, when that doesn't work, you try the professional respect, command presence, and distance that you use with the fierce youth. If such a youth continues to ramp upwards into further aggression, assume you're dealing with an explosive youth. They get more and more aggressive as if they don't have a "circuit breaker" that helps them turn off. They become very reactive to just about anything you say or do.

- Rage is usually explosive. They often have no fear of harm when in an explosive rage state.
- Don't get flamed up yourself, no matter what they say (which will frequently be pretty bad!).
- If you speak at all, use paraphrasing (See Chapter 48).
- Silently, implacably, take them somewhere safe, where they're contained and unable to harm anything. Wait them out, so to speak.
- Containment is the watchword. Thus, the back of a patrol car is often a great "quiet room."

The behavior of "explosive youth," in particular, may necessitate physical control.

CHAPTER 55

Opposition-Defiant Kids: "Even If You Make Me, I'll Still Make You Miserable"

Oppositional-defiant (OD) disorder is considered a behavioral disorder of childhood. These young people, before their behavior was "made" into a mental health diagnosis, were often referred to by such terms as 'brats." It usually develops with upbringing typified by poor boundaries (too invasive and/or too lax). Aggression is typically against "family;" those familiar to the child. Dictatorial parents, who try to break the child, often "create" OD kids among those who are too strong-willed to crumble. The motto of such kids seems to be, "You won't break me. Furthermore, even if you make me do it, I still say 'no,' and ruin your day in the process." Other parents who aren't consistent nor enforce coherent reasonable discipline (overly permissive or chaotic) also elicit such behaviors. In this case, the child is implicitly saying, "I will act out until you're forced to give me some limits." Not every such child is a product of ineffective or failed parenting. There are also parents who haven't raised their children poorly, but the kids have bonded with other young people or with an image that they absorbed from some media, either of which encourages defiant behavior. Finally, exacerbated by drug or alcohol abuse, many previously loving young people turn nasty indeed.

Negative reinforcement, only giving attention for negative behavior, will elicit more negative behavior. Reinforcement through punishment that is both out of proportion or inconsistent teaches the child that discipline is an attack, that the parent is unpredictable, and that acting out at least gets the parent's focus on them. The child experiences a kind of "social power" when punished. They see the punisher as having the right to define good and bad, but at the same time, they see themselves as having impact (if they aren't utterly broken in spirit or body by the punishment).

Unfortunately, once power is acquired in this manner, the youth gets a grandiose sense of his/her own importance, and frustrating and defying adults becomes its own reward. Sometimes oppositional-defiant kids are surpassingly argumentative, fighting over fine-points, claiming to not be understood. They apparently thrive on argument; they look for any pretext to continue the argument, trying to knock the adult off center. This is often not a search for truth; it is simply a power tactic. <u>If you're losing your temper, they're winning, and they hold you in contempt for it.</u> This need to argue, *at its extreme end*, seems related to Obsessive-Compulsive Disorder. Their brain, apparently, won't let go of their place in the argument. Right-and-wrong don't matter; only what they want, right now.

Although the behavior of OD youth can be violent, it seems engendered by the contradiction of resistance to authority, against an implicit plea that a clear, trustworthy, consistent authority be exerted over them so that their place in the world is truly defined. Perhaps the most important recommendation we can make is that all people involved with such youth must maintain consistent boundaries with NO deviations. The oppositional youth will test these boundaries over and over again to see if the limits have changed.

The watchword in dealing with these kids is to pick your battles. Don't waste energy arguing about anything that isn't important. When it is important, become implacable. They put energy in their argument; you put quiet steel in yours. You, an adult, don't argue with such a youth as an "equal." You tell them what will be, with no negotiation whatsoever. If you're correct in what you require, it should be experienced as a force like gravity: not a debate.

These youth are used to a lot of attention for negative behavior. This drains the adults responsible for them and they're often ignored when they aren't making trouble, much less acting positively. Therefore, be sure to notice when they're acting with integrity, agreeableness, and/or respect, so that they experience positive attention for these actions.

Figure 55 Review: Dealing With Oppositional-Defiant Youths

These young people argue for argument's sake. Their reward is the negative attention they require from adults, and the sense that they have you—at least your moods—under their control. They believe they've won if they anger you or get you upset. Pick your battles—those not worth arguing, disengage, change the subject, or ignore. Don't argue; require them to follow your instructions. **Be like gravity**—how can you argue with that! Whenever possible, give extra energy (positive attention) when the young person is doing something worthwhile or worth respecting.

CHAPTER 56

Post-traumatic Stress Disorder in Youth

For both children and young adults, post traumatic stress disorder, includes either the experiencing or witnessing acts of severe violence, is often physically enacted rather than verbalized. Many males in particular, would adamantly deny ever experiencing trauma claiming to live by Nietzsche's adage of, "that which doesn't kill me makes me stronger."

There isn't a unique de-escalation method for use with traumatized youth. They can display aggression and violence in a variety of modes, from terrified and chaotic rage to purposeful predation. If you were to take apart any aggressive or violent episode by such a youth, you would have, in symbolic form, the story of their own trauma, not only what happened to them, but also what was created *within* them in response. Traumatized children, in particular, often display **Terrified Rage**. The de-escalation of this state is described in detail in Chapter 60. The predatory or furious rage states that some traumatized children and teenagers display is a kind of reaction formation. They have found through violence a way to cease experiencing the pervasive dread of the victim. It's only as a victimizer that they feel safe.

One mistake that even seasoned officers may make is to be "disarmed" by the horror that some children have suffered. When we understand that they have already been to hell and barely made it back, we sometimes let our "understanding" direct our response to the youth. The kindest, most respectful thing that you can do is to hold them to the highest standard of behavior. If you allow a traumatized youth "off the hook" because of what may be, admittedly, a horrible history of abuse, they will begin to use their "abuse excuse" to license violence and predation on others.

Figure 56 Review: Dealing With Traumatized Kids
- Whatever their history, de-escalate based on their behavior at the moment.
- Don't let them "off the hook." Hold them to the highest standard of behavior.

CHAPTER 57

Pseudo-Nihilism

Such a youth, who may affect a posture that includes boredom, self-destructive behaviors, or disinterest, is, in fact, striving for power. Their sense of power increases when they can horrify, disgust, or offend others. Taken further, they achieve power when they experience themselves as untouched by other people.

You shouldn't be emotionally bland with such youth. If you try to show that their provocative behaviors don't affect you, they will escalate until they do evoke a reaction. However, beyond a "human reaction," you must demonstrate that you don't *need* them to change. Your ability to be at ease with what they are, embodies what they profess they desire. In particular, don't follow the "self-esteem" model, the fantasy that all they need is someone telling them how special they are. These youth, often, are cynical precisely because people have confused the good feelings that might be elicited from praise with genuine success in life. These young people, however, twisted some of their own values may be, know better.

One is most concerned about youth of this type by what they hide inside. These kids, in particular, need an adult who is able to provide feedback in a way that he/she doesn't feel compelled to resist. They need someone with more life experience to talk with. Without this, their fantasies and unhappiness festering inside, they become more and more destructive, either to themselves or others. Therefore, community safety is served when such youth have someone that they can respect and check in with to provide an alternative viewpoint to the one they, alone and isolated, came up with.

Figure 57 Review: Dealing With Pseudo-Nihilism

This youth is cut-off. They may be aggressive, but their primary goal seems to **NOT** make a link communicating with you. They may be very much at odds with you; they may even rage or curse at you or treat you with contempt. One way or another, these kids try to cut themselves off from you.

- Don't try to make them change or feel better. "No put ups." They may try to repel you with what they say, or what they say they have done. Give them a human reaction, but not an over-reaction. In other words, a Great Dane doesn't get off the porch when a little dog is yapping at him/her.

- They're most dangerous when left alone to stew in their own juices. Be the adult that they almost surely don't have in their life, so they have a moral touchstone. Of course, a law enforcement officer can only do this in brief contacts (with the exception of a school resource officer). Nonetheless, your impact can be profound.

SECTION X

Managing Rage
and Violence

CHAPTER 58

Preface to Rage

Rage and anger aren't merely different in degree. They're different modes of being, just as water, once past the boiling point, becomes steam Angry people, frustrated, posture to establish dominance or to force compliance. If nothing else, their goal is to communicate how angry they are. Enraged people, on the other hand, are in a "threshold" state, trying to unleash themselves from whatever is holding them back from the violence they desire to commit. Therefore, **all the strategies described in the previous section in dealing with the angry individual are more or less useless against the truly enraged.** Let us note however, that we assigned anger arbitrarily within a scale of 20 to 95. This is a very broad range of arousal, ranging from mildly irritated to truly irate. Rage is 95 to 100, that peak being violence. Taking into account, then, that these numbers are images rather than scientific measurements, we still may use some of the de-escalation strategies for anger when, for instance, the angry individual is at "93." For example, we have both used the tactic of "Breaking the Pattern" (Chapter 47) at just these moments, saying something so unexpected that it "takes the fight out of the person."

Past a certain point, however, the enraged individual is intent on committing mayhem. They only focus on how to overcome what is holding them back: fear of consequences, damage to their self-image, or innate morality. Their internal restraints are "fighting" a battle inside them with their primitive desire to maim and destroy.

There are various types of rage. It is very important to recognize what type of rage the aggressor is expressing, because there are different strategies to deal with each type. At the same time, don't worry that you will have a lot to remember. Enraged people's behavior is quite obvious. After reading this section, you will easily be able to tell what type of rage people are in, and will therefore know the best strategies to control them. Finally, although it is true that an individual can manifest a combination of several modes of rage, one mode will predominate, and THAT will be reflected in their behavior.[30]

Figure 58 IMPORTANT CAUTION

Here, and in several other areas of this book, we have used animal symbols to aid in the understanding of various types of rage or other behavior. For example, we use the image of a leopard or a shark in describing predatory rage. These are thought devices, and are not intended to be used in either paperwork or communication to describe such individuals. In our hypersensitive times, such a reference to a specific individual may be misconstrued as stigmatizing them as "being an animal." Nothing could be further than the truth – the images are to assist in understanding modes of behavior, not character. Nonetheless, such images should remain aids of understanding, not terms of reference.

CHAPTER 59

Chaotic Rage: A Consideration of Rage Emerging From Various Disorganized States

Individuals who go into a chaotic rage are usually suffering from a confusion of thoughts and perceptions. They're disoriented, often experiencing severe hallucinations, illusions, and/or delusional thinking. Chaotic rage is common as part of a variety of syndromes, typified by profound disorganization of cognitive and perceptual processes, including severe psychosis that has "crossed over" into a delirium state, mania, drunkenness, intoxication of various drugs, drug withdrawal, severe intellectual/developmental disabilities, senile dementia, and a variety of inflammations or lesions of the brain. **Unlike a classic psychosis, the most salient characteristic is that it is almost impossible to establish *any* lines of communication with the person.**

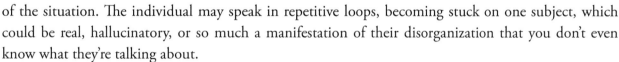

These individuals often can't string their thoughts together logically: uttering cascades of words making no sense whatsoever, or grunts, moans, or mumbling. Others make sentences based on rhymes, puns, or cross-meanings. They may laugh or babble, without any clear object, or completely out of proportion to the possible humor of the situation. The individual may speak in repetitive loops, becoming stuck on one subject, which could be real, hallucinatory, or so much a manifestation of their disorganization that you don't even know what they're talking about.

People in chaotic rage states can become quite frightened or irritable. They may begin yelling; screaming, lashing out physically, and engaging in such self-injurious acts as scratching and gouging their own flesh or head banging. **Any state of chaotic rage should be considered a potential medical emergency.** De-escalation, in whatever form it takes, must be followed by medical attention as soon as possible. Try to get EMS on scene, staged, while you are trying to stabilize the person or take them into custody – not afterwards. The delirium state, in particular, can be a sign of a life-threatening emergency.

Disorganized individuals enter into chaotic rage states when they're frustrated, confused (too much stimulation), or feel invaded (for example, when you must carry out a necessary task, like detaining them and transporting them to a hospital to be evaluated and stabilized). They can be simultaneously enraged and terribly frightened. Impulsive and unpredictable, their rage sometimes explodes, seemingly out of nowhere. **Think of TAZ, the cartoon character in the Bugs Bunny cartoons.**

People in a chaotic rage state strike out in all directions; they aren't coordinated, but they're fully committed. What this means is that nothing—no fear of injury or consequences—holds them back from their attack. They may grab, scratch, bite, kick, and strike in flailing blows. They're often indifferent to or unaware of pain or injury to themselves. Some individuals in chaotic rage actually target people to harm; combat with them is like fighting a tornado of arms and legs. Others are so "lost" that they aren't fighting, per se. They're "swimming through people." It is as if they're drowning, trying to struggle though a river, choked with wreckage, the people and objects around them the debris they're trying to swim through forcefully. **However, some people in chaotic rage states, particularly trained fighters, retain their coordination even though they're completely "gone" on a cognitive level.**

De-Escalation of Chaotic Rage

- If possible, try to work out the arrest process before hand, even if it is just a last minute alert from someone else that the individual appears to be in a disorganized or chaotic state. You can tell a lot about the person's mood/demeanor/behaviors from witnesses. Disorganized people are both impulsive and unpredictable. Therefore, knowledge of any triggers that might have set them off in the past is essential.

- Use calm movements, and a firm but reassuring voice. Delirious people often experience poor motor control, experienced as vertigo, disorientation, etc. Your voice and slow movements helps them orient, not only physically, but as an emotional touchstone as well.

Figure 59.1 Importance of Communication With Cover Officers

This is where communication with cover officers is a must. Some cops get impatient watching another cop take their time. The impatient cop then jumps in to end the situation. Just as the lead officer is achieving verbal control, an impatient officer jumps in, and then all hell breaks loose.

- Disorganized people are sometimes susceptible to being deflected to another topic. They often use *confabulation*, the concoction of spurious memories, as a means of trying to appear normal and stable. You can sometimes "confabulate" a theme yourself that catches their attention and seems to engage higher thought processes, delaying their outburst of rage until help can arrive.

Figure 59.2 Example of Deflection: Dealing With a Person in a Chaotic Rage State

A paramedic approached a delirious man who was standing on the edge of a highway, and said, "Ike, what are you doing here. I haven't seen you since high school." As he kept rattling off spurious memories to the man, whose name *wasn't* Ike and whom he had never seen before, the delirious man gazed into his eyes in confusion, rocking back and forth in rhythm with the paramedic's words. The paramedic was successful in capturing the man's attention, which kept him from dashing into traffic, until police could arrive. To illustrate how dangerous this situation was, the moment the police tried to physically ease him back from the highway, the man exploded into a violent attack, requiring a number of police officers to subdue him.

- One of the last things we "retain" is our name, so use their name, repetitively, interspersing it frequently in your commands in order to get their attention before initiating attempts to redirect them to another activity. This can be very helpful with combat veterans experiencing a "flashback."[31]
- Be very cautious about touching them, as this may be experienced as invasive or even as an attack. If you do have to lay hands on them, make sure you have enough hands and bodies to totally control them.
- Use simple, concrete commands with no more than a single "subject" in each sentence. Repetition several times is almost always helpful. Use only one thought at a time, as complex sentences will be confusing, and thus threatening or irritating. For example, say *slowly*, "Sit down, William. Sit down. Sit down. William, sit down."
- Minimize such distracting behaviors on your part as extraneous body movements. Your movements should be calming and also only be those useful in helping the person understand what is going on.
- Be cognizant of the volume on your police radio. It can be very distracting and it may overshadow what either of you are saying.
- Use tactical paraphrasing (Chapter 48). You can sometimes help by validating and acknowledging their confusion or fear. For example, "Really scary, huh?" or "You're really worried, aren't you?"
- Because of their difficulty in attending to what you say, non-verbal communication is a paramount concern. A calm reassuring presence, manifesting both strength and assurance is your best hope of helping to stabilize an individual in chaotic rage.

Figure 59.3 WARNING

Disorganized individuals are among the most difficult to de-escalate verbally because words and coherent cognitive processes are the first thing that they lose. You must, therefore, be prepared to evade a sudden attack, and further, be prepared, **throughout**, to use physical control tactics to ensure your safety as well as that of others.

Excited Delirium Syndrome (See Appendix E. for Specific Protocols)

Excited delirium is a rare condition at the extreme end of the hyper-aroused wing of the delirium spectrum. Etiology can be varied, but it is most commonly associated with long-term use of stimulants; particularly cocaine and methamphetamine. Single doses of such drugs as PCP, Ketamine, pyrovalerones such as methylenedioxypyrovalerone (so called "bath salts"), and very rarely, psychedelic drugs such as "magic mushrooms," can cause chaotic rage states. It is also associated with extreme manic or psychotic excitement, and can be precipitated by a variety of purely medical conditions. It is typified by some, if not all of the following: a sudden onset of extreme agitation; pervasive terror, often without object; chaotic, sudden shifts in emotions and disorientation; communication difficulties, including screaming, pressured incoherent speech, grunting, and irrational statements; aggression to inanimate objects, particularly shiny objects like glass and mirrors; hyper-arousal with unbelievable strength, endurance, and insensitivity to pain; hyperthermia accompanied by stripping off clothes; and most notably, violent resistance to others, before, during, and after arrest or restraint.

Accompanying their almost unbelievable level of physical arousal and resistance to both physical and mechanical restraints is possible respiratory and cardiac arrest. **These people die!** The usual pattern is that they struggle with incredible power and then, suddenly, they stop moving. Or sometime after becoming quiet, either in a stupor or in seeming normality, they die, usually from cardiac arrest. This can look remarkably similar to a seizure, also a very dangerous syndrome.

If they haven't been already called, get an emergency medical team on the scene now! Correct protocol demands that EMS should be staged, and ready to intervene medically the *instant* the subject is physically subdued. Furthermore, police **shouldn't transport** the person either to the hospital or jail, unless there is no other option. Ensure that EMS transport. If the individual dies in your car, YOU will be deemed responsible! The only time you should transport such a person is when it is proven and documented that EMS wasn't available, and law enforcement had to do the transport.

Such individuals can be appallingly dangerous both to others and to themselves. **We can't emphasize strongly enough that this is a medical emergency manifesting as physical danger, and usually requiring police and emergency medical intervention to secure the person so that they can be treated.** You will, almost surely, be unable to verbally de-escalate the person in excited delirium, but if they aren't presenting an immediate assault risk, make the attempt using the principles delineated above. You may be able to gain partial compliance that makes it easier to take them into physical custody. You may be able to, at least, "buy time" allowing sufficient emergency personnel to muster, making possible the restraint that will most likely be necessary to get them help. If nothing else, getting the subject focused on you will cause them to stop moving. This will make it substantially easier to deploy less-lethal means than if they're running amok.

Figure 59.4 Excited Delirium or Chaotic Rage

Most individuals who go into chaotic rage aren't in an excited delirium, but given the ever-increasing abuse of stimulants (methamphetamine, cocaine, etc.) that are the most common precipitants of this condition, it is important that you are familiar with the signs, symptoms, and "best-practice" interventions. Furthermore, we strongly urge local law enforcement, emergency rooms, paramedic organizations, and emergency dispatch (9-1-1) to become fully familiar and trained to deal with individuals suffering from this syndrome. A joint training of all who may be involved in the restraint and treatment of such individuals is imperative. You need to have an established protocol to ensure public safety, law enforcement safety, and the safety, as best as you can accomplish it, of the delirious subject.

Greater knowledge about this syndrome has led to several new problems:

a. The protocol for Excited Delirium is to subdue the individual as quickly as possible to get them the medical attention they need, as well as protecting everyone from the appalling violence they may enact. As most mentally ill individuals, including severely disorganized people, are NOT in excited delirium states, this protocol can seem to directly contradict the model of verbal de-escalation we have offered in this book. In brief, with most mentally ill individuals, take extra time to talk them into compliance; but with individuals manifesting excited delirium, subdue them as quickly as possible. However, a careful reading of this text reveals a graduated set of interventions, including how to approach a disorganized individual, even one manifesting chaotic rage. As we have emphasized throughout the text that assessment is behaviorally based, any dangerous behavior on the part of the person of concern should elicit a well-practiced physical response.

b. Because Excited Delirium has finally begun to be recognized by the medical community as a genuine medical syndrome, this complicates things for officers. Psychosis, unlike schizophrenia, is a general term. Therefore, it is usable. However, if an officer uses the term Excited Delirium, he/she might be accused of diagnosing the person. Therefore, we recommend the use of the terms **Chaotic Rage** to describe such individuals, because it is fully descriptive, encompassing both the disorganization AND the agitation that such individuals display. Furthermore, the officer isn't required to make a distinction between a person with genuine excited delirium, from a mushroom intoxicated naked man running down the street, or a distraught grief-stricken individual in a chaotic state. All parties, from police, corrections, EMS, and dispatch can use this descriptive term without running the risk of being either over-specific or diagnosing in the street.

c. These terms will help officers, on a behavioral basis, to distinguish Chaotic Rage from lower levels of disorganization or psychosis so that best practice interventions can be used.

d. Refer to Appendix E for specific protocols for law enforcement in dealing with Excited Delirium Episodes

Catatonia: Special Considerations

People may be immobile for many reasons, among them being a variety of medical concerns. Catatonia however, is a very rare, very bizarre condition in which an individual stays in a fixed posture, not congruent with injury or seizure. Catatonia is caused either by mental illness (schizophrenia) or an organic condition, for example, drug toxicity. The catatonic person's posture may be quite awkward or twisted, seeming to require great flexibility. A classic symptom of true catatonia is "waxy immobility," whereby if someone else moves the catatonic's body or limbs, he/she maintains the posture into which they were moved. There seems to be no way to establish any communication link with them.

Considerable caution is needed in dealing with immobile individuals for several reasons. First, they may be injured or having a seizure and at medical risk. For this reason a medical evaluation is *always* indicated. A second consideration is safety. One way to regard catatonia is to view the individual as exerting 100 percent of their will to *not* interact with the outside world. You may be tempted to get them to respond when they're unsecured. This is a disastrous mistake. Image the incredible exertion of will required to maintain immobility for hours, even days, without movement, without response, without even blinking in some cases. Now imagine disturbing this equilibrium. The result is what is clinically called "catatonic rage," a state that really can be considered one form of excited delirium (below). The individual shifts from 100 percent stillness to 100 percent explosive motion. One of the authors can recall an incident where a law enforcement officer's career was ended by such an individual who, all of 110 pounds, grabbed hold of his arm and yanking as if he was cracking a whip, ripping through all the ligaments of his shoulder and shoulder blade.

You would be wrong to think the catatonic is unaware; they *can* hear you. Therefore, speak calmly and respectfully. An individual can have a very long memory of being shamed, and if you speak about or treat the catatonic as an object rather than as a person, you may evoke a terrible sense of humiliation. In their frozen state, they may not be able to do anything about it now, but months or years later, another police officer may be hurt, having no idea that the mentally ill person they're dealing with has been waiting for years for an opportunity to avenge his/her humiliation. Beyond all that, everyone—even a person in a coma—deserves to be treated with respect. Even if it seems that the catatonic person can't hear a word that you're saying, act as if they're listening to every word.

Whenever an individual is immobile and unresponsive, you will of course summons medical attention. If you have any suspicion that they may be catatonic, have them placed in restraints and transported to a hospital where they can be evaluated safely. To be sure, there are protocols in handing over care of an individual to emergency response personnel. Nonetheless, do everything in your power to ensure that EMS are aware that they're dealing with someone who is very likely catatonic and that they shouldn't disturb them any more than is necessary when they're, as yet, unsecured. Testing reactivity to pain, light or noise, for example, shouldn't occur until the individual is safely in restraints. When you move them to a gurney, make sure you have sufficient numbers to safely manage them, just encase they were to explode suddenly while being moved.

De-escalation of Developmentally Disabled Individuals: Special Considerations

De-escalation tactics aren't remarkably different with developmentally disabled folks, but one must be aware of their cognitive deficits. If you use language that is too sophisticated, either in terms of meaning or nuance, you may elicit more frustration and anger, because you will be making them "feel stupid." Many developmentally disabled people are subject to "magical thinking." Their beliefs about the material world and their own powers and vulnerability often don't conform to reality. Sometimes one can use these beliefs to help calm them, as you would with a child. On other occasions, one must be aware of these beliefs to keep the situation from escalating out of control.

If you try to control a developmentally disabled individual based on their physical age (a 250 pound, 35-year-old adult, for example), things usually go very wrong very fast. Most of our associates have found that once we make eye-contact, we can estimate the emotional age of the developmentally disabled person very quickly. **Speak to them at their emotional age: small child, young kid, or teen.** This may seem very abstract, but it is really simple. You look in their eyes, and if you see a childish expression just like the one of your own five year old, ten year old, or thirteen year old, interact with them at that level. If you don't "catch" such an intuition, then just follow standard de-escalation procedures. To be very clear: **Safety considerations are unchanged—what is different is the way you verbally interact with them.**

Here are two examples that show things going right and going wrong:

Figure 59.5 Examples of Incidents With Developmentally Disabled Individuals
Incident #1

A few years ago, a developmentally disabled 32 year-old man was continually bothering store clerks at a local market. The police were called, and an officer trespassed the man from the store. The same officer was repeatedly called for the same individual a few more times as the man aimlessly made his way along the downtown corridor. On about the 4th call, a hotel clerk called to report the man was urinating in the front-door planter in front of guests.

The officer by now had lost a bit of his calm demeanor and patience. He contacted the 5'6", 250 pound man and told him he was under arrest, and to turn around and put his hands behind his back. The officer placed his handcuffs on one of the man's wrists, but he spun around, not in attack but out of fright, and he put his hands up as he yelled out of fear. Of course, that cuffed hand was now a weapon. The officer gave commands for him to turn around, yet he refused (or couldn't). The officer applied a dose of OC-10 pepper spray. In full panic mode, the man took off running. He was tackled in the parking lot of the hotel, and it took 3 officers to get him down, and properly handcuff him for transport to the jail.

As supervising sergeant, I contacted this individual in the jail. He was crying like a little kid. He said he was sorry about running from the officer, but that he was scared. He had the mental capacity of a 5 year-old, and I had him released from jail immediately and returned to the custody of his group home. In a debriefing later, the officer said that he knew something was wrong, but because of the guy's size, he didn't think of him as childlike until it was pointed out.

Incident #2

A developmentally disabled woman once grabbed my finger, trying to break it. I neutralized her attempt by shifting the angle of my hand as she yanked, and as she was at the emotional age of about 8 years-old, rather than commanding her to "let go!" I said, "I know you want to hold my hand. You don't have to twist my finger. We can hold hands as much as you like. Sure, we can hold hands." She suddenly let go and dropped to the floor, crying.

We're NOT asserting that things will always go well! One of the writers recalls another incident where officers tried to arrest a 225 pound, 35 year-old man who was sitting quietly in one of the group home chairs. He talked with the man gently, at his emotional age of about eight or nine years old. As they attempted to handcuff him, without any warning, he slugged one of the officers in the head and knocked the other one over. The officers eventually won, but not without minor injuries and damage to their uniforms.

Don't let down your guard, just because the person does have a childlike presentation. You can talk to them at their age, without suspending, in the slightest, a combative mindset. There are many occasions when you can use tactical paraphrasing (Chapter 48) with an enraged developmentally disabled subject. Don't just sum things up calmly. Use an almost dramatic voice, over-emphasizing words. "YOU'RE REALLLLLY upset. You're SO upset about this! I GOT IT!!!" Your voice is a combination of drama and enthusiasm. In essence, you're trying to catch their attention with charisma, a kind of energy in which you change the dynamics of your relationship through your voice and demeanor. The angry or enraged developmentally disabled aggressor finds himself/herself in an interaction where there is no "fight" coming from you. Your dramatic voice validates how important the situation is to the person. It is the voice, here, more than the words that provide that validation.

Figure 59.6 Using a Dramatic Voice to De-escalate a Potentially Assaultive 300 lb., Developmentally Disabled Man

Man (brandishing a fist): "I'll sock you right in the nose all the way to the swing set!"

LEO: "Wow, that is a huge fist! What do you eat to make your fist that big?!!"

Man: "I eat rocks! I eat rocks and cereal!"

LEO: "I gotta try that. What kind of rocks? That is a huge fist. Thanks for showing me!"

Man: "I eat rocks from the moon. (giggles)"

LEO: "That's pretty funny, isn't it."

The man is calmed down. And this is neither a fight you'd want to have, nor is it one you'd feel good winning.

Talking With a Disorganized Person After a Crisis

With the disorganized person (one who has at least a little cognitive faculties), it is tactically sound to validate feelings, both for yourself and for them. Remember, this aids in controlling them—it isn't for the purpose of therapy! For example: *"Marc that was really scary. I'm glad that's over! I want you to sit on this chair now. Yeah, I know you were scared."*

A detailed critique of what they did, however, is a mistake. People who are disorganized are often cognitively impaired, and this affects their memory. Their feelings, also, aren't under their control, and they will react to your debriefing as if it is a new attack, especially if you put feelings into what you say. Your primary concerns should be behavioral stability (no new attack) and reassurance, because they're very likely to be afraid that you may want to get back at them.

CHAPTER 60

Terrified Rage

Figure 60.1 Concerning Terrified Rage and Chaotic Rage

Be aware that the line between terrified rage and chaotic rage can be very fine. The terrified person, overwhelmed, can shift into chaotic rage. When facing an individual in a state of either pure terror or terrified rage, be prepared, therefore, to shift to protocols suitable to assisting individuals in chaotic states (Chapter 59).

Terrified individuals believe that they will be violated or abused. They look halfway ready to run, halfway ready to strike. Their voice can be pleading, whiny, or fearful, and their eyes are often wide-open or darting from place to place.

The mouth of a terrified person often gapes slightly as they breathe in panicky, short gasps. Other frightened people press their lips together in a quivering pucker. Their breathing is often panicky, fast and high in the chest. Their skin tone is often ashen or pale. They make threat gestures with a flailing overhand blow or a fending off gesture. Their body posture is concave, and they pull away from you and cower.

Figure 60.2 Caution

Wide-open eyes don't always indicate fear. In the case of fear, the muscles <u>under</u> the eyes are also slack, giving the face a pleading look. Even though the terrified person may be looking in your direction, they usually don't look *into* your eyes, nor do they want you to look into theirs. The enraged, aggressive individual with wide-open eyes, on the other hand, displays tension around the eyes. Furthermore, they often look penetratingly into your eyes, or *through* you.

When they yell, there is a hollow quality, as if their voice has no foundation. This is due to the tightening of their abdomen and diaphragm, so that not only their breathing, but also their speech, is high in their chest.

There is usually high physical arousal, accompanied by panting, sweating, and trembling. They often back into a wall or corner. Their body is usually tense, preparing to either defend or flee. They may yell, almost screaming in a pleading tone, such phrases as: "Stay back! You get away from me! I will hit you!! I will! You stay back!"

What Causes Terrified Rage?

People who are terrified often suffer from paranoid delusions, a fear of the unknown, or terrifying hallucinations. At other times, they're afraid of a loss of control or of being laughed at or humiliated. Some people are afraid that they're in terrible trouble with some agency, be it police, the courts, or mental health professionals. Finally, for any one of a number of reasons, they're simply terrified of you.

De-Escalation of Terrified Rage

Imagine a snarling wolf cornered, backed up against a cliff face. It is a frightened animal with fangs; do you think that what it really needs right now is a hug? Your goal is to reduce their sense of danger. Move away from them, slowly. Relax your posture. Make sure your movements are unhurried. Your voice is firm, confident, and reassuring.

Notice if their body relaxes or tenses in response to your eye contact. If eye contact is reassuring for the subject, signified by a more relaxed posture, do so; if intimidating, don't. Keep looking in their direction, of course.

Keep up a reassuring litany of phrases, speaking slowly, with pauses: "I know you're scared—that's okay.————Put down the chair.————You don't need that.————**I keep it safe here.** You can put it down now.————I'm way over here.————Go ahead. Sit down. I keep it safe."

DON'T say, "I'll protect you" or "I won't hurt you." Many people who go into terrified rage have been hurt before by people who said those kinds of phrases. When you say, "I keep it safe here," you're being the alpha who says, "This is my territory and no one, including you, will be hurt on my territory. I'm taking responsibility now—through me and because of me, this place and you in it—will be safe." Furthermore, by saying something similar to what they expect to hear, but somehow different, you cause a "glitch" in their thought process. "What did he say? He didn't say, 'I won't hurt you.' What's different in what he said?" By getting the terrified person questioning what you said, you cause him to "re-engage" the parts of his brain that actually thinks things through as opposed to just reacting.

You will easily be able to see it in their body language as they calm down. Their breathing will get a little shuddery or be expressed in short high-pitched gasps. Often they will slump into a chair or the floor and even begin to weep. Keep up with your reassuring litany, and approach them slowly. If they show signs of getting frightened again, pause, move back slightly, and continue to speak to them reassuringly.

When you approach, move in "half steps." For example, move the right foot a full step, then bring the left foot *up* to the right foot. Pause. Move either right or left foot forward, and then bring the other foot forward *up* to the lead foot. Pause.

The advantage of moving this way is that you stay balanced, in case the individual attacks suddenly: you don't have too much forward momentum. Additionally, if the person becomes *more* startled or reactive, you can ease backward smoothly, creating more space between you. When you walk normally, one foot in front of the other, changing directions is more "dramatic." You have to make a big movement, maybe even lurching backwards, and this action can contribute to an *increase* in the terrified person's agitation.

Don't Allow the Terrified Subject to Just Walk Away (Leave Your Custody)

We can't, in good conscience, allow someone who is that terrified to leave our custody without at least having some sort of community treatment team come to the scene for an evaluation, transport to the hospital or even home if the subject can be calmed down.

CHAPTER 61

Hot Rage

Figure 61.1 Some Good Advice
"Hot rage explodes when officers can't calm a person down for a variety of reasons: didn't take the time to calm them down or the officers themselves were so pissed off that they got the subject into that stage. One out of three is not our fault. Three out of three become our responsibility." Quote from veteran officer.

When we think of people on the edge of violence, it is hot rage that usually comes to mind. We imagine ourselves faced with someone with muscles writhing, yelling, or screaming, fist brandished and threatening. They throw things, tip over desks, and spit in your face. They want to beat us bloody, stab us, or pound us into a pulp.

We often imagine that hot rage is instinctual, a product of primitive drives: a reflex. However, purely instinctual aggression is uncoordinated and flailing: such rage falls under the category of terrorized or chaotic aggression. Hot rage, however, is coordinated. This makes it a behavior that is learned through modeling, trained through repetition, and reinforced through success.

For example, some people with a long history of abuse lash out in rage whenever frightened, with no ability to evaluate whether or not they're currently in danger. At the same time, they target where best to hit, and frequently choose a time and a place where they believe they have the best chance of success. On a more functional level, a good street fighter, even though he has "lost it," still takes a stance with chin tucked in, shoulder rolled forward, and punches with his entire body lined up, so that the power of the blow is amplified by his body weight and the torque of his hips.

Some claim that hot-rage is an expression of extreme frustration, but frustration alone doesn't usually elicit rage in normal people. It is when frustrated desires are coupled with something "personal, "when one believes oneself to be *impeded* by another person in getting one's desires met, that becomes enraged. There are three subtypes of hot rage: Fury, Bluffing, and Aggressive-Manipulation.

General information About Hot Rage
- This mode is typified by emotional arousal or excitement.
- Bored individuals, bullies, or others who simply need a lot of nervous energy to feel alive will amp up aggression to feel this energy and power.

- Over-arousal leads to a deterioration in judgment, and at higher states of arousal, even deterioration of basic cognitive processes.

Figure 61.2 Example of Hot Rage Escalating Into Violence

A man is walking down the street and sees a father slap his child's face. He intervenes, saying, "That's just a child. Be easy on him." The angry father shoves him and says, "Mind your own business, or I'll give it to you, too."

The man later describes hearing a high-pitched noise, and his vision turning black-and-white. He comes to himself astride the abusive man, pounding his face with his fists.

- Arousal breeds arousal. The more enraged people become, the more comfortable they're with their rage, and the easier it becomes to be violent.
- Hot rage is often a behavior that has led to short-term success in the past, such as scaring and beating a selected victim either for criminal gain, or just for the joy of the beating. In a state of rage, such a person has no concern about longer-term consequences, much less guilt.
- For some people, there is a sense of liberation, even a paradoxical kind of joy when they peak into rage. All one's fears and insecurities disappear, and one is left with only the ecstasy of the pure act. Some individuals desire rage, because that ecstatic state is, to them, the best thing they ever feel.
- Displacement is common: Instead of hitting you (yet), they first hit an available target like a chair, wall, or other objects. This also includes picking things up and slamming them down, or throwing things. Predatory individuals (Chapter 62) also use displacement as a tactic to make their target more fearful. Those in a state of hot rage are simultaneously terrorizing their target, discharging tension and, and at the same time, "warming up" to attack.
- Hot rage can be a "transference" in which the officer is a representative or stand-in for someone else. In their mind, you're the emblem of everyone who ever controlled them or put them down, an agent of an oppressive society, or simply a legitimate target to express hatred and violence.
- There can also be organic contributors: low blood sugar levels, head injury, or the use of intoxicants that lessen the individual's inhibitions.
- Hot rage is also associated with peer group influence and masculine display: "fronting" in front of one's group. It can be a primitive attempt to dominate access to or eliminate perceived competition for women, status within a group, or other objects of desire. Finally, it can have a resonating effect among a group, creating mob violence, one person's rage fueling another.

De-Escalation of Hot Rage: The Ladder

The primary method of de-escalation for hot rage is called "The Ladder." It is used only for rage, that gray zone between anger (even extreme anger) and violence. The individual is no longer trying to communicate with you. They're right on the edge of assault; in a sense, doing a war dance to work out inhibitions to committing violence. Don't hold back from any action to keep yourself and others safe. Protect yourself and/or other! Verbal control is, of course, ideal with people in a state of rage, but if they cross the line into violence, do what you have to, to stay safe.

The technique itself is simple. Use a short sentence with no more than four or five words. Choose the most dangerous behavior and repetitively command that it cease. Use short words. Don't use "psychologese," like "It's not appropriate for you to…." Once dangerous behavior stops, choose the next level down of problematic behavior and use the same technique. Continue until the individual is de-escalated and under control. **This technique is only effective right before, during, and after the peak of the crisis because it is a Control Tactic rather than a "Lining Up" we use for angry people.** Control Tactics will provoke rage in an angry person, someone we might have over-estimated, due to his/her loud tone, or dramatic behaviors. **As described earlier, facing an enraged person causes us to experience fear in a way that anger doesn't.** Remember the image in Chapter 40: is the spider in the box or out on the floor? If the person is in a rage state, the danger is NOW, not merely something possible if the situation continues to deteriorate.

With the ladder technique, you establish a hierarchy of danger. What you need to perceive right now is what action of the enraged person is most dangerous or problematic. The general hierarchy from most to least is as follows:

1. Brandishing an object as a weapon or a weapon itself in a menacing way. (NOTE: If they're too close, or are trying to use the weapon, this is a situation of violence, not rage). All force options should be considered.
2. Approaching or standing too close to you with menacing intent.
3. Kicking objects, punching walls, or throwing things (displacement activity).
4. Pacing, stomping, and inflating the body in an aggressive manner (posturing).
5. Shouting, *or* talking in low, menacing tones.
6. Using language that is intended to violate, demean, or degrade.

Give the aggressor a straightforward command to stop their most dangerous behavior. You shouldn't scream or shout: that won't get through to the person. Instead, they will ramp up on your screaming tone, and this, alone will increase their aggressive energy. Rather, your voice should be strong, low and commanding (Chapter 45).

This isn't the time to be trying to think of something brilliant or life changing to say. By keeping things simple, you use your mind to keep track of your team, other potential aggressors, escape routes, and where weapons might be. In addition, by holding to a demand that the most dangerous behavior cease, you're displaying clarity and strength to the aggressor, as well as helping them focus *his/her* mind on the most problematic thing he/she is doing, something particularly important with a mentally ill subject who may truly have lost it and, among other things, needs help orienting back to this world where it is so profoundly not-a-good-thing to assault an officer.

Figure 61.3 Witnesses

All witnesses will have heard your commands. Because you will have calmly repeated the same order in a strong, non-abusive voice, there is a better chance that they will be **good** witnesses should this situation deteriorate further into a physical confrontation. You will have been heard, repeatedly, commanding the person to comply with an order that they repeatedly ignored or refused.

After a couple of repetitions, always add, "We'll talk about it when you...." Once that behavior is stopped, pick the next most problematic behavior, and command/require that it stop. If the aggressor does calm down and stops all the aggressive behaviors, including assaultive language, THEN set a firm and direct limit. You should frequently intersperse your sentences with their name, using this to pace and break the rhythm of your commands, as well as "calling them back" to a human relationship, name to name.

The Ladder isn't merely a verbal intervention. Like any other control tactic with an aggressive individual, but particularly with hot rage, you must move as needed to maintain the optimum space to both defend yourself and exert maximum influence upon them. If they're very close, or threatening, depending on the situation, your hands should be:

- on your weapon;
- up in the fence position, prepared to fight as well as ward off any attack, but also as a gesture that is both calming and dominant;
- clasping the wrist of one hand with the other hand.

You continue to work your way down the "rungs" until the aggressor is no longer in a state of fury. **If the individual re-escalates to a higher and more dangerous activity, simply go up to that "rung" of the ladder and begin repeating again.** Remember to stand and use your voice as described in the previous sections. Usually, the last rung is either shouting, or even further down: swearing, and using demeaning, ugly language.

Figure 61.4 Example of the Ladder

Your voice is firm, low pitched and commanding, as you "descend" down the rungs. You should imagine that there are pauses, sometime of several seconds or more, between each phrase below. In the following scenario, each statement is, of course, in response to something the aggressor has done or said. Don't talk too fast. Command presence, not hysteria!

1. "Step back. Step back. Robert. We'll talk about it when you step back. Robert. Step back. Step back, Robert. We will talk about it when you step back."
2. "Stop kicking things. Robert. Stop kicking things. We'll talk about it when you stop kicking things."
3. "Robert, I can't follow you when you pace around. Sit down and we can talk. Sit down, Robert."

Notice the paradoxical message, that you can't "follow" him. Of course you could, if you wanted to. This is another example of what we call a "brain glitch," the same as we do with the individual in Terrified Rage, when we say, "I keep it safe here." You are trying to catch their attention as they try to make sense of what you said. We want them thinking again, trying to figure out what you said and why you said it. We want the part of the brain that thinks things through taking over from the part that is driving them towards violence.

Imagine they have stepped forward again, thus ascending to a higher "rung" on the ladder

1. "Step back! Robert! Step back and we'll talk. We will TALK about it when you step back, Robert. Step——back."
2. "Sit down Robert. We will talk about it when you sit down. We can't talk when you are walking around. We will talk about it when you sit down."
3. "Lower your voice. I can't hear you when you yell that loud. Lower you voice and we will talk."

Here is a second paradoxical communication; of course, you can hear an aggressor who is shouting loudly. Once again, you are trying to create a "glitch" where he tries to figure out what you mean when you say you can't hear him when he is yelling.

"Talk to me with the same respect that I talk to you. We will talk about it when you stop swearing. Stop swearing. Robert. We will talk when you talk to me with respect, the same way I talk to you."

Remember, people often swear as punctuation. They have no hostile intent whatsoever. If the individual is swearing in this manner, it isn't a problem. For example, "Officer, I'm sorry, I was just mad at my f**king daughter, and s**t, you happened to arrive at just the wrong damn moment."

*However, if the swearing is an attempt to violate you, it **must** be dealt with in proper order. However, **don't** focus on the language, no matter how vile, if the aggressor is doing something dangerous. Remember that predatory individuals will use language to shock, distract, immobilize or terrorize. What they're **doing** is far more dangerous than anything they're saying.*

Figure 61.5 Caution

Remember, the Ladder should only be used with an enraged individual. Using this technique with an angry individual will cause them to escalate into rage. In most cases, de-escalation tactics suitable to dealing with angry individuals are sufficient.

Hot Rage Subtype #1: Fury
Take control until the individual can achieve it on his own

What does fury look like? Furious people look as if they're about to explode. *If they're of big stature, think of a grizzly bear. If they're smaller, think of a wolverine.* In either case, the image suggests an animal that will tear you to pieces to get what it wants. Many people, both with a mental health diagnoses and without, show hot rage. It is common particularly among people who have suffered head injuries. The following are physical manifestations of hot rage:

- Their skin tone is flushed as they're angered, becoming red or purple. As they become even more enraged their skin blanches, as the blood pools in the internal organs. They turn pale or gray, depending on whether their skin is light or dark.
- Their voice, be it loud or low and quiet, has a menacing and belligerent tone.
- They often pace, inflate their upper body, and hit things or smash their hands together, often one fist in the other hand.
- They tend to stare into your eyes directly. The eyes may be wide open, but definitely NOT in the same manner as the terrified person. There will be tension all around the eyes, and they stare directly into yours. Others, however, look out under their brows. In either event the face is furious and hostile.
- Their eyes will appear red or inflamed.
- Physical arousal, blood pressure, and muscular tension all increase. You will sometimes see veins pop out of the skin, particularly around the neck.
- Sometimes they will have a smile that shows no humor or joy. Others snarl, or compress their lips with a twist, as if they have a foul taste in their mouth. Still others bare their teeth, sometimes edge-to-edge, or clench their jaws so tightly that the muscles stand out in bunches.
- They're very impulsive, and unconcerned with possible consequences.
- Depending on their emotions, which include how comfortable they're with the rage they're experiencing, their breathing is either strained or easy. The person usually breathes deeply, from the chest into the belly. They often draw the belly inward on the inhale as their chest inflates.
- They may claim to be disrespected, humiliated, or shamed. Others will allege that they aren't getting their questions answered or their problem solved, or that no one listened or cared. They may rant about some person or system or claim that these are their enemy.
- At their most dangerous point, they may become calm, breaking off eye-contact, or go into a thousand-yard stare.

Control of Fury
- Your posture and tone should be confident, commanding, even imposing.
- Stand out of range of an immediate blow, but directly in front of them. If you're too close, it is a challenge; too far away, you will be seen as afraid, and you will be a juicy target to vent

their frustration. You may have to move forward and back to maintain this spacing. Try to move smoothly, without flinching. When you move with a relaxed body, you're more ready to protect yourself, yet you don't appear as if you're trying to initiate a fight.

- Stand with your feet in a "blade" stance, with one foot advanced, and the other behind at about a forty-five degree angle. (If you drew the back foot forward, there would be one or two fist's space between the heels—don't line-up the feet, one behind the other.) This best prepares you to slip along tangents to his attack, to ward off blows, or to fight back if necessary. It also keeps your weapon out of reach, as far away as possible from him. Don't square your feet so that you're confronting him/her in full frontal fashion. Not only are the most vulnerable areas of your body exposed to attack, you're "double-weighted." To avoid an attack or to fight back, you must first shift your weight to one foot or the other before you can move. With the blade stance, you're already "chambered" to do this.

- As described earlier, your hands are either up in a fence, the wrist of one arm is clasped in the hand of the other in front of you at waist level, or in high threat situations, either on your weapon or holding your weapon.

- Your voice is strong and forceful. Don't, however, shout. Instead, keep your voice low- pitched and calm, dropping it into your chest where it resonates, as enraged people, in particular, react violently to threatening or angry vocal tones. The only time you should shout is a "battle cry," the lion's roar that you use only when you're trying to stop an actual attack.

- Use direct eye contact, and say their name frequently, interspersing it among your commands.

- Use the Ladder in its most orthodox form with your voice pitched low and powerful. You should feel it vibrate in your chest.

The individual will exhibit one of only three actions:
1. They keep on coming; in this case you will do whatever you have to do to ensure safety.
2. They get close and when you tell them to step back, they say, "make me." You will do whatever you have to do to ensure safety.
3. They comply. When individuals in hot rage comply with the command to step back, they usually do so yelling and screaming: "You can't tell me what to do." Then continue the Ladder and expect compliance at each "rung."

Once you have them de-escalated, you must maintain control. This can mean anything from an arrest to simply "reading them the riot act" and putting them on notice that they came dangerously close to either being hurt or arrested. Only after setting very strong limits would you shift into problem-solving, even with a mentally ill individual. Otherwise, they will assume that the best way to get a reward— your attention or help—is to abuse you.

Hot Rage Subtype #2: Bluff-Rage
Taking Control of Them Includes "Face Saving"

What Does bluff-aggression Look Like? These individuals, like gorillas beating their chests, display aggression to keep you at a distance, or otherwise make an impression. They're like a wind blowing against a stone-wall rather than like the pent-up explosiveness of dynamite under a rock.

Nonetheless, their manifest behavior appears much the same as the individual displaying fury, hence the terrifying image of the enraged gorilla. At 50 yards, could you tell the difference between a charging gorilla and a charging grizzly bear? Both are huge, hairy beasts that apparently mean you harm. The gorilla, however, would prefer to be left alone, rather than engaging in combat. But he postures as if he wants nothing more than to tear you to pieces. And if he perceives no other alternative, he will.

Figure 61.6 Difference Between a Furious Aggressor and a Bluffer

How do you know the difference between a furious aggressor and a bluffer, if their behavior is so close? When you are facing a furious person, fear is your natural and likely response. Your animal mind—that part of you that puts survival above all else—demands your attention now, and it uses fear to accomplish this. A bluffer, in a state of hot rage, will also elicit fear, but this will be accompanied by another emotion: irritation. You will be, to use the vernacular, "pissed off," thinking how stupid this incident has become, and that if the bluffer hadn't chosen to bring his friends, or if his wife hadn't chosen to taunt him as being less than a man, this dangerous situation would never have developed.

Those showing bluff-rage are often displaying aggression for the benefit of friends or family. *They're frightened that they will be found out as frightened.* They may be trying to impress others or convince them that they're someone to take seriously. Their friends or family members have, on many occasions, provoked them to "prove" they're tough.

Warning: you still must take bluff-rage very seriously! If they do succeed in working themselves up, they will become violent. Such people can be quite dangerous for another reason. Because they're performing in front of an audience and afraid that those watching will realize that they're afraid, they will often attack if they feel found out for what they are. Many bullies, who have a long record of serious violence, actually function in bluff mode. They're in a perpetual quest to prove to others—and even more insidiously, to themselves—that they aren't frightened. They repetitively solicit situations where they must either intimidate or beat someone bloody. Therefore, it is essential to short-circuit this behavior before it escalates into violence.

Sometimes bluffers are alone, but they still have an audience, the one inside their own head. They have an image inside their own mind to which they believe they must conform.

When the bluffer is frightened, he moves forward, not back, so that no one will see how scared he is.

Figure 61.7 Concerning an Individual in Bluff-rage

It isn't helpful to empathize with them that you understand that they're scared underneath. You must take them seriously, just like you would a very big, threatening gorilla.

Control of Bluff-Rage

These individuals aren't really in confrontation with you. They're *pretending* that they are. But this is a pretense that can kill. Use the Ladder, the same verbal control tactic you use with an enraged individual. Your tone, however, should be much more matter-of-fact and relaxed. Your eye-contact, too, is matter-of-fact, as if you're having a conversation rather than a confrontation. Rather than having your hands in front of you (clasped or in a "fence"), open your hands, slightly to the sides, palm up. You're definitely prepared and able to protect yourself, if you need to, but at the same time, you aren't trying to frighten or intimidate them. You're, in essence, saying, "There is no fight here. But I'm so confident and in control that I certainly could handle myself if there was." Remember, they will attack out of fear. Your task is, paradoxically, to help them save face so that they willingly step-back rather than *forcing* them to do so.

Figure 61.8 The Bluffer's strut

When you have done things well, they often strut back with a smirk, sometimes glancing around and making eye-contact with their audience; this is for the benefit of the audience, and their own self-image. They're trying to show that they aren't afraid, and in control of the situation.

In some situations, you can short circuit things before they become too intense by helping them save face. Include in your strategy some information and re-assurance. For example, you can say, "Look, Frank. I know you thought I was making fun of you, but that wasn't the case at all. I was just pointing out that you forgot your meds, so you wouldn't have to come back for them later." **Be careful that in doing so, you don't make the bluffer out to be a winner! Helping them save face must not mean that you have "backed down" that compromises your lawful authority.** Furthermore, if they have ramped themselves into true "bluff-rage," they may view conceding a point with you as giving up. In these cases, only by taking total control will you be able to ensure your own and other's safety.

- Don't point out their fears in front of others. They will feel the need to defend their honor.
- If they aren't responsive to a more low-key approach and continue to escalate, you may have a furious aggressor who happens to be in front of other people or a bluffer who has shifted into

fury. In this case, you "turn up the dial," and drop your voice to be low and powerful, shift into the Ladder technique for the furious individual. In essence, you would say, "Move back, Stephen. We will talk about it————<then amp up> MOVE BACK!, etc."

Just as with the furious aggressor, you must set limits at the end of the confrontation. However, you should also include some "ego building." These individuals are most dangerous when they're depending on others to feel strong. Therefore, draw them aside, perhaps already in handcuffs, and say something like what is stated in the figure below:

Figure 61.9 Example of Communicating With a Person Under Control After Being in a Bluff-rage

"Bernard, I'm glad this worked out with no one getting hurt. Had you not chosen to sit down and talk, you very likely would have ended up being face down on the floor. No. Listen to me for a minute. I'm not disrespecting you—that's why you and I are over here talking instead of in front of them <indicating the onlookers>. I'm telling you, it was a very near thing. Again, I'm glad this has worked out that you and I are standing here talking."

"Next time, though, don't do this in front of them" (referring to his friends or family for whom he was on display, and actually put a little *contempt* in your voice when you say the word 'them' as if to indicate that Bernard is better/cooler/stronger than those people he is trying to impress.)

"Come to me and talk to me one man to another" OR "one woman to another" ("one adult to another" in male-female conversations). "You shouldn't put your personal business in front of them." You will observe him "puff up," feeling flattered. You then continue, "Okay. Are we clear for next time? Good. Now as for this time...." Then set the same types of limits as you did with the individual in a state of FURY, which will often include the phrase, "You are under arrest."

Remember, it is the audience that makes this individual most dangerous. If they feel that they will get "respect" by themselves, if they believe their status will improve if they come in alone rather than with their crew of friends or family, they will be far less dangerous next time. This technique is advised when dealing with gangs. Face-saving is extremely important and by removing the subject of your attention away from the others will benefit your investigation. Though we don't care about them respecting us, they, paradoxically, care more about such respect, even from us, than they care for their lives or their friends.

Hot Rage Subtype #3: Aggressive-Manipulation
Taking Control Means Not "Buying In" to the Game

What does aggressive-manipulation look like? Aggressive-manipulation is a *strategy*, not a symptom of illness. People displaying this type of behavior can have any one of a number of mental illnesses. Aggressive-manipulators are calculating, trying to monitor the effect of what they're doing. They don't care about honor, integrity, or pride. All they want to do is win anyway they can. You can sometimes tell when you're being manipulated ("played") because you're confused about why the person is upset, or what is the purpose of the argument. The aggressive-manipulator frequently changes either his/her mood or the subject of the complaint. Such individuals often display some or all of the behaviors described in Chapter 22 and 23, on manipulative and psychopathic behaviors.

Aggressive manipulative people may have a long history of losing control, particularly when their desires are frustrated, or when they believe they aren't given what they believe they're entitled to. Very frequently they have a history of personality disorder (particularly psychopathic, anti-social, paranoid, narcissistic, borderline or histrionic).

They might start with a plea for something, talking about how they're suffering, but once refused, they blame or criticize you. They may try to seduce you, "C'mon, it's just a pipe. You aren't going to arrest me for a glass pipe, are you, officer? C'mon, you know me!" They might try to make you feel guilty and then start demeaning you verbally. This may shift to allusions or threats of violence. They may talk in an arrogant manner, trying to make you look incompetent or stupid. They often claim to be a victim, basing this on either real or imaginary issues. Furthermore, they may use their "status" as a member of an oppressed or victimized class of people as a means of intimidating others or making them feel off-balance. They may make their demands in a whiny, accusatory voice. They will footnote old grievances, bringing up trivia, accusations and old history. They will tell you how you're just like someone else who "did them wrong." They ask frequent and repetitive questions, and try to frighten you or make you feel uncertain of yourself.

We often use the image of a large rat, because rats are the ultimate survivors. They will do whatever it takes to win. This image is not intended to be demeaning. It merely underscores that aggressive-manipulators, like our furry, long-tailed cousins, are infinitely adaptable and whatever the conditions, will attempt to find a way to endure or win.

Manipulation doesn't mean false threat. Manipulative people will often harm others; some will even kill. The difference between such an aggressive-manipulator and those in a state of pure fury is that the furious are swept by their rage. We say, "They lost it." The aggressive-manipulator attempts to monitor your responses and the situation as a whole to assess if what he/she is doing is the best way to get what they want. He/she is, therefore, calculating. However, that doesn't mean that he/she is in control. As they gets more and more agitated, their judgment deteriorates, and they may concoct a rationalization for violence that makes sense to them in the moment—even when it would to no one else

The idea of "intimidation for next time," as stupid as it sounds, is the driver of some aggressive-manipulators. Imagine someone the size of the authors, 6'4" and 6'6" respectively, facing a young 5 foot 3 inch female police officer. Such an individual thinks either, he/she might get away, or at least, they will be able to put some significant damage on this officer before subdued. He/she may take it further and imagine that "next time," officers will leave them alone as being too much trouble. That is NOT going to happen doesn't necessarily make it unreal to such a person.

Another example would be the guy who knows he is going to be arrested. In previous arrests and bookings into jail, he's been at the bottom of the jail "pecking order." He begins to arrive at the idea that if he assaults this cop, that will move him up higher in the social hierarchy inside.

Control Tactics for Aggressive-manipulators

People who use this strategy of attack are, by definition, acting in a degraded manner because they're trying to twist your feelings (making you feel guilty, ashamed, off-balance, or scared), or trying to trick you to get what they want. Don't buy in to it: **If you catch them using this strategy early, cut it off at the onset. Verbally suppress any and all verbal gambits.**

If however, the manipulative-aggressor begins to escalate his/her strategies, you may have to use the Ladder as you put them under control. With these people, you can and should use the Ladder *even before* they shift into rage: view their manipulative verbal games as the first initiation of their attack.

Rather than making eye contact, look past one ear. Making eye contact allows them to get information from you. Aggressive-manipulative people don't care about you; they use eye contact to "read" you and control you. They're interested in what they can use when you reveal yourself to them. Similarly, they will use their own eyes to create a false intimacy; they "reveal" both truth and falsehood, as it suits them to confuse you, misdirect your attention, or dominate you. Your disinterested look conveys, "I'm not in your game," and also shows a kind of strong dominance, indicating you won't lower yourself to their currently degraded level. Such disinterest is also revealed in your vocal tone, which should be matter-of-fact and slightly detached.

Figure 61.10 Don't Look Away

Don't look away. While looking past an ear, you can still see what they're doing. If you look away, you will be assaulted and not even know it is coming. This disengaged look, done properly, indicates that you won't participate in the degradation that manipulation creates.

Aggressive-manipulative rage is distinguished from pure fury in that, even now, they're attempting to read and monitor you for advantage; are they intimidating you; have they succeeded in distracting or throwing you off balance so that you're open to an attack; have they got you trying to "bargain" your way to safety? At the same time, they will begin to "lose it," as their strategic application of intimidation is unsuccessful. They get frustrated because they believe their manipulation *should* be working. In essence, aggressive-manipulative rage is a merger of hot rage and predatory rage (Chapters 61 and 62).

- Stand relaxed and ready to evade a blow and counter the attack.
- Express flat disinterest in their demands, accusations, and complaints.
- Use the repetitive commands of the Ladder technique. Your vocal tone is flat. Don't negotiate. Don't discuss anything as long as they're using this kind of degraded behavior.

Figure 61.11 Important: Locking Eyes—The Loop

If they flare into *fury* or if they continue to be non-compliant, turn from looking past the ear to looking right in their eyes with a firm command to stop what they're doing. When you turn you head to look directly in their eyes, roll it slightly up and then down as if sighting a weapon. Speak powerfully and directly, just as you do with the individual who is in a state of fury. If they don't stop immediately upon being "hit" with your eyes, this means that an attack is imminent. You will shift into the de-escalation for fury or even further, take action to ensure your safety in the event of violence.

With the aggressive-manipulative individual, several things can happen when you attempt to control their escalation:

- Your flat disinterest means to them that they can't "get to you." After trying several different avenues, they shift to another strategy, or give up in defeat.
- In more heated situations, they will flare into a fury or pseudo-fury.
- When you "lock in" eye-contact, they may "bounce" off into another tactic: sudden tears, for example.
- As described above, the flare into pure fury, you will manage their behavior just like any other subject in a state of fury.

CHAPTER 62

Predatory or Cool Rage

Thankfully, this type is rather rare. Such individuals are like a panther or a shark. They're intimidators who threaten either with vague innuendoes or explicit threats. Their behavior is calculated, but unlike the aggressive-manipulator, violence is often their first choice rather than one of many options. The predator delivers threats in cool, dangerous tones, often *after* a clear and strongly stated demand. Then they offer you a chance not to be injured if you comply with their demand. A variant tactic is to pretend being out of control. (This is in contrast to a genuine attack, an action that they're eminently capable, and willing, to carry out).

These individuals seethe with hostility and/or contempt for other people, but they have developed the application of these emotions as a deliberate weapon of terror, or even enjoyment. Paradoxically, many experience low levels of anxiety in situations that would frighten ordinary people. Their heart rate can actually go down as they prepare to commit violence. They can be charming and attractive, as fictional pirates are when not being aggressive. Therefore, in trial, some members of the jury may have a hard time believing that they're so capable of terrorizing others psychologically, or hurting them physically, because they can act like such nice people. These people, either situationally (the "professional" criminal) or pervasively (the psychopath) lack a moral sensibility or conscience. Nothing inhibits their aggression other than tactical calculation or self-interest: they have no capacity for sympathy or guilt. Every time they intimidate someone, their behavior is reinforced. They take non-action on your part as either the behavior of weak prey or of tacit approval of what they do.

The best response is a combination of overwhelming force and respect.[32] The former is obvious. Never be in a situation where you're vulnerable with such an individual. "Respect" means, simply, that you make your control "institutional," not "personal." When you're dealing with them, they shouldn't have a problem with you, personally; their problem is between themselves and society, whose rules they're breaking. As a law enforcement officer, you're merely society's agent.

There are, however, times, where you have gotten over the "horizon line," and you no longer have the overwhelming force component. Imagine, for example, being accosted at a shopping center, with your children, whom you don't want to expose to the predator in another aisle, and the predator beginning to offer vague innuendoes of potential danger. He/she hasn't seen your kids yet, and you don't want them to.

Your basic task is to demonstrate that you aren't prey, that it would take too much effort on the predator's part to hurt you. It may be that you create an impression that you're another predator. That isn't necessary, however. It is enough that he/she sees you as not "edible," like an animal with quills or one that would taste bad:

- Stand ready to move. Be poised, but not too defensive.
- Be open and strategic in everything you do—the way you position your body, your voice, and your posture. He/she is a professional at reading weakness, at delving out what you're trying to hide. Therefore, protect yourself openly. If he/she says something like, "You think backing up is going to help you," ignore it and act in your best interests. Don't change your actions based on what he/she says.
- He/she will try to use anything you do against you, either deriding you or pretending that you're out of control, paranoid, or acting strangely. Ignore all that and act to keep yourself safe. Keep your head in the game.

Cryptic Consequences: Your Strategic Response to the Predator

Keep your voice matter-of-fact, and give clear and direct statements of *potential* consequences. If you can, smile. **These consequences are of a special type, clear, but cryptic,** e.g., "You know what would happen if you did that." In this case, don't tell them what would happen. Let their imagination take over. These vague consequences are a mirror of their own method of intimidation, and they may react to you as "not prey, not edible, not worth the trouble."

- If they say, "What are you talking about?" you should reply, "You know exactly what I are talking about." When the predator responds to your cryptic consequence with questions or with confusing statements that would make your statement illogical, simply say, "You know what is going on here. You know what is happening."
- You may have to intersperse your vague consequences with Ladder commands if they escalate their behavior.
- Try to minimize eye contact. However, you need to look directly at them, so look between their eyes, or look with an empty stare (imagine turning your eyes to buttons. He/she will look like a cut-out or silhouette). Your eyes are flat, with no attempt to "penetrate" or make contact. (You should make sustained eye-contact only if in a fight for your life. Then, you must shift focus, trying to penetrate his/her eyes as if you were a laser beam).
- Don't over-react to threats, or they will interpret your reaction as a victory.
- Your entire goal is to convince them that it isn't worth it to hurt you. Once you have succeeded and are free, you need to get help.

To reiterate, you don't have to prove that you're bigger, tougher, or more dangerous. You're establishing that you're merely on to their game and aren't, by nature, someone to victimize. Like a leopard who chooses *not* to chase an antelope because it is moving too smoothly, showing that it is healthy and strong, the predator is likely to disengage if you don't give him anything to discount (an attempt to intimidate them with a direct threat) or if you try to negotiate (something they have no interest in).

Figure 62.1 An Explicit Threat Is an Empty Threat

Particularly when you don't have the overwhelming force component **don't** make explicit threats, such as "If you come near my family, I will kill you!" That tells them what you **won't** do. In their mind, if you really meant it, you would do it now. They think, "I'm serious. I mean what I'm going to do. He/she knows it, but all they can do is tell me what they're going to do after I do what I'm going to do." **An explicit threat is an empty threat.**

Figure 62.2 Example of Cryptic Interaction with Predatory Individual

Predator. "Look, this is very simple. I think you and I can agree that you misinterpreted what I said about punishing my child. I don't know where you got the idea that I said I beat her. Look, I understand. You must have been having a bad day, and you over-reacted. This can be fixed very easily. Just call the DA and tell them that you didn't quote me accurately, that you've been overworked lately and misjudged the situation. See, I bet you love your family as much as I do. You've got your child in a good school over at Echo Lake. Actually, it's amazing, that's one of the last schools in this area that still lets the kids out for recess. Oh, sorry, I'm a little off track. What I'm saying is that I bet you would be devastated if anything happened to your family. I'm the same. The problem is that what is happening to my family is you! And this is a problem you could fix, unless you are really sitting there telling me that you want to destroy my life and that of my child. IS THAT WHAT YOU ARE SAYING??!!!!"

You. *(With a little smile and a strong, confident voice)* "I'm really glad we're having this conversation, because it's good that we both understand each other."

Predator. "So you'll make the call."

You. "Oh, you know what's going to happen."

Predator. "Suppose you tell me."

You. "There's no need to do that. You know exactly what's going on."

Predator. *(Getting a little confused)* "Are you threatening me?"

You. "I don't know where you got that idea. In fact, we both know the situation here."

Predator: "Suppose you spell it out for me."

You: "There's no need for spelling lessons. We both know how to spell. We both can tell time too." (*This last phrase is a little nonsensical, deliberately. You are deliberately making the communication a little more confusing*).

Predator. (*Walking away after a hard stare*) "You think this is over. You better watch your back."

Please note that this exchange could conceivably go on for a longer period of time. We are here presenting enough back-and-forth that you should clearly understand the principle. And of course, it is NOT "over," as discussed below.

As soon as you have achieved your goal of separating yourself from the predator, start establishing safety. Contact the individual's parole or probation officer, and/or get reinforcements and arrest them, if their threats were explicit enough to have violated the law. As you and your family have been threatened (whether the tone is velvet or harsh), you must do everything necessary to keep everyone safe (Chapter 65). You may have to be on your guard for a long time. Such incidents are sometimes just words, or sometimes just a one-time affair, but on other occasions, they can go on for a long time, with further threats, stalking or other dangerous behaviors that require you to muster all professional skills and assistance to ensure that you and your family are safe.

Figure 62.3 CAUTION
You ONLY use this strategy with the openly predatory, that most rare of people, and ONLY when they're escalating into predatory rage, **and only when you don't have sufficient force or backup to place them immediately under arrest.** In other words, it should never happen, but you need to know what to do if it does.

CHAPTER 63

Feeding Frenzy: Mob Rage

Figure 63.1 Rage State and Possibility of Violence
This discussion covers both the rage state and the possibility of violence. Pack behavior can easily escalate and therefore, it is impossible to separate rage from violence in this discussion. The discussion here concerns situations where you don't have sufficient forces to manage the mob.

Pack behavior amplifies hot rage exponentially, one person's arousal ramping up those around. The more people there are, the more likely that one will create an enraged mob, a beast of many heads, but one terrifying, destructive mind. You will have individual people in the mob manifesting any one of the types of rage, including terrified, chaotic, fury, bluff, manipulation and predatory. Sometimes mob frenzy is created and stoked by one predator, who coolly uses the mob as a weapon.

The sum total is frenzy. Whenever possible, make a tactical withdrawal! You will need cover officers, perhaps mutual aid. Most certainly, supervisors of all ranks will be engaged in establishing a command post, and subsequent plan of attack and mass arrest. Your agency policies will gage your actions. At this point, you're talking about multiple applications of less-lethal force and other crowd disbursement options, and conceivably lethal force as well. The bottom line is, if you're caught in such a group, GET OUT QUICKLY. Within a mass, people lose any sense of compassion or guilt and they believe there is anonymity within the mass. Note the grinning faces of people in photos of lynch mobs; all the inhibitors against violation of another melt away within the ecstasy of the group mind.

Figure 63.2 Example of Mob Rage
We recently had an incident at a local college, where an officer attempted to make a simple arrest for assault during a rock concert. In the subsequent mob action, two officers found themselves trapped in their car, which was overturned and set on fire. The officers barely escaped with their lives, and mutual aid was called for throughout the county. After-action review determined that the officers should have driven through the mob, because they were facing a lethal-force situation.

Intervention with a Group or a Mob

Horribly, you might be in a situation where you shouldn't or can't escape Because there is no escape route; you're responsible for the safety of others; were you to escape, you would never be able to live with yourself, much less it would be an abandonment of your professional oath and responsibilities; or if the mob is just coalescing, and you step in now, you may be able to diffuse things.

- **Overwhelming force.** Quite simply, the most powerful method of de-escalation is a demonstration to the mob and its members that they will be stopped. Each member of the mob suddenly feels alone: "the first to go down." There are famous stories of lynch mobs, for example, faced with a sheriff and a shotgun who calmly states that no one will be taken out of his jail.

- **Isolate the leader.** Isolating the leader as the one individual who will face the consequences. All of your psychological energy should be focused on the leader. This is particularly powerful when the leader is hiding behind the power of the mob. If you perceive that the leader is manifesting manipulative, bluff, or predatory rage, make it clear that whatever happens, they won't emerge unscathed. The goal is definitely not to shame them. If you present yourself with calm veiled menace, the mob leader can save face. This is essential if you have any hope of causing him to draw his forces back. Sometimes this strength is veiled behind a smile and a casual mode of communication. At a distance, you would appear as relaxed as in a social outing.

- **Build up the leader's ego.** When it is clear that the leader is trying to puff up his/her ego through the mob, make it clear they are the only one worthy of conferring with you. This is for the purpose of either drawing them away from the group, so he/she can't wield them against you, or to appeal to their grandiose narcissism. If his/her goal is to appear important in the eyes of the mob, you may have given him/her what they really want, without the need for violence.

- **Break the pattern.** As discussed in Chapter 47, you do something so unexpected or outlandish that none of the individuals in the mob knows how to react. One our informants wrote to us that during what was possibly a build up to a riot in Belfast, Northern Ireland, a police officer played ice cream truck music from his I-phone over the public address system in the vehicle. This resulted in the de-escalation of the situation but unfortunately "some senior officers didn't approve and the officer was spoken to about his behavior."

Figure 63.3 One Author's Experience

About 40 years ago, while hitchhiking, I was malevolently dropped off in a very dangerous area of a city during a very volatile period of racial strife. A crowd began to coalesce around me. I grabbed a stick I found on the ground, began cackling and shrieking like I'd lost my mind, and began dancing and whirling down the street, hitting my head and attacking moving cars with my stick. Everyone pulled back. I continued for about 10 blocks until I reached a safer area.

To reiterate, the best option when facing a mob, in most circumstances, is to tactically remove to a safer position and summon assistance. If you do intervene, be aware that you may have to fight for your life. Your best hope, were this terrible situation to develop is "to go berserk." Be like a wolverine in a trap with teeth, claws, and anything else you can use, try to tear your way free; trying to maim your attackers as savagely as you can. The goal is to become so appallingly violent that each member of the group wants to get away from you. As they recoil, hopefully, an escape route may open up.

CHAPTER 64

Deceptive Rage

As you surely know, many criminals spend time in mental hospitals, especially forensic units. Some have concurrent mental illnesses that warrant such a stay; others are placed there for forensic evaluations; still others are there because they were able to fake mental illness so that they could be moved to a hospital either for a more attractive environment, or for the purposes of escape.

What do you think such individuals, particularly the manipulative and sociopathic, do while in the hospital? They victimize more vulnerable patients, either directly, or indirectly. They have an opportunity to play with other people who are comparatively poorly supervised and easily influenced. The opportunities to torment the genuinely mentally ill are endless.

Beyond such predation, they study. Who knows, perhaps the behaviors of a mentally ill individual may prove advantageous some day. Perhaps it will prove useful in convincing an evaluator that they are genuinely mentally ill and of diminished capacity, not responsible for the crime they committed. Furthermore, perhaps it will give such a person an opportunity to catch someone, even a law enforcement officer off guard.

Such an individual obscures his/her behavior behind a screen behavior: the imitation of genuinely mentally ill individuals whom they have observed. They pretend to be psychotic, in a state of terror, distressed or needing your help. All this is for the purpose of either conning you into leaving them alone, or more dangerously, drawing you close enough so they can harm you.

Imagine a snake coiled in the leaves, pattern almost indiscernible from the ground, ready to strike

The "de-escalation" strategy here is simple: deal with the behavior, not the cause! Imagine you have stopped a confused, psychotic appearing person in a residential area. What you don't realize is that a moment earlier, he was easily walking through the neighborhood, casing houses for burglary. Spotting your oncoming car over a rise, he began walking in a gimping fashion, his head lolling. When you pull up, he looks frightened. You ask him for identification, and he tells you, stumblingly, that he was just released from the hospital and is visiting his cousin, and his eyes are a little teary, and he looks so intimidated as he pats his pockets for his wallet, and he slightly turns away to get it from his pocket (!!!!!!!!!). What should you do? Obviously, you get some distance between you, put a hand on your weapon or your weapon in your hand, depending of your best judgment and you order them to show you their hands. One of two things will result:

- A predatory individual, they slowly remove their hand and exercising due caution, you pat them down and find not only a wallet, but a knife.
- They are genuinely mentally ill or developmentally disabled, and at your sharp command, they begin crying in terror. You are now in the position of helping them. Once you ascertain everything is safe, you kindly but firmly tell them that you are going to teach them the rules of how to talk with law enforcement officers.

Figure 64 Teaching the Inadvertently Threatening Person How to Interact with a Law Enforcement Officer in the Future

Imagine in our hypothetical situation, the individual turned aside, and seemed to yank an object suddenly out of his pocket. He is knocked to the ground, cuffed, pinned, searched and then, finally sat-up. He is crying like a little child.

Man: "Why did you sock me? What did I do? You wanted to see my idea, and my hand got stuck and I thought you'd be mad if I didn't show you!!"

LEO: "I'm sorry you were knocked down. But you broke a very important rule. You never turn away and hide your hands from a police officer."

Man: "But I didn't know that rule! I didn't know what you wanted me to do!!!"

LEO: "I will teach you a special sentence to say to a police officer so you don't get in trouble again. Are you ready? Now, repeat after me, "Officer, what do you want me to do?""

Man: "Officer, what . . . . I forgot."

LEO: "Listen carefully. 'Officer, what do you want me to do?"

Man: "Oh, OK. 'Officer, what do you want me to do?"

LEO: "Bobby, listen. Don't pound your fist in your hand when you say that. Just hold your hands together."

Man: "OK, Officer, what do you want me to do?"

It is conceivable that this lesson may keep this man safe in future encounters with police officers. And if, instead, he was a deceptive predator, your actions will have saved your own life.

CHAPTER 65

The Aftermath: What happens Within the Mind of the Individual after an Aggressive incident?

Rage and even more so, violence, are exhausting experiences: both emotionally and physically. Many people get the "shakes" after such an incident. So much blood has "pooled" inside the core of their bodies to prepare for combat that they feel cold and start to tremble. Most individuals have a significantly impaired ability to remember what happened in sequence. They may have a patchy memory of a few events. Much of the rest of the incident is a blur. Although they may be remorseful, they usually don't remember what happened, how it started, or who was responsible. Even more drastically, they can lapse into a state of defensive confusion where they no longer recall what happened at all, or they distort the incident in their memory completely, thereafter taking no responsibility whatsoever.

Others may feel profound guilt. This might be positive, were it to lead them to reflect on their own responsibility, but for most people, this guilt is so noxious that they project responsibility onto the person who "makes" them feel guilty. Thus, they soon shift to resentment and begin to blame the other person.

Humiliation, the feeling of having one's faults or vulnerabilities exposed to others involuntarily or forcibly, is quite common, and here, too, many people become defensive. People describe humiliation like being flayed and exposed. Some people respond to shame by becoming enraged all over again. Their thinking seems to be, "If I feel this bad, someone must be doing it to me." What is almost universal is a post–crisis fatigue, a combination of the depletion of energy stores in the body and the cumulative effect of all the mood and cognitive changes described above.

Managing Risks Post-Crisis

You may have to "take care" of the aggressive, mentally ill person, particularly if they're mentally ill or developmentally disabled. Even if you have successfully controlled them so that they didn't commit an act of violence or other criminal action, you still may have a supervisory or protective role while the person is being seen at a hospital, crisis triage center, or even in the field. Your tasks may include maintaining control, and establish limits and consequences. You may even need to possibly regain rapport and provide reassurance. Beyond that, you will almost surely be seeing them again! If you're able to educate the person in this aftermath how to behave so they don't put themselves in such a dangerous situation in the future, this serves public safety.

Of course, there must be consequences for any criminal actions and quickly. Even here, such education can take place as part of the arresting process. If the individual is someone who can accept feedback and help after the crisis is resolved, your first responsibility is **clarification**—clearly delineating what was abusive, aggressive, or otherwise unacceptable behavior.

If an individual, perhaps severely mentally ill, is really frightened, or devastated by what happened, the first priority is **reassurance and orientation**—letting them know that they aren't going to be punished (this, of course, is different from consequences—in other words, no one is going to take revenge on them, something the more paranoid will expect). In cases with people who are demented, psychotic, or otherwise in fragile mental states, you may have to explain to them what has happened, where they are, what is going to happen now, and who you are, etc. If individuals do have cognitive abilities and are calm enough to understand, **educative follow-up** should include:

- Discussing what other tactics they might have used to get what they desired;
- Assisting them in becoming aware of patterns that led up to the aggression or assault;
- Negotiating agreements on how to avoid such incidents in the future;
- Assisting the individual to return to a sense of dignity and integrity.

Some people aren't suited to have such a debriefing. Developmentally disabled individuals, or others with dementia or cognitive impairments can't really remember what happened, and they may re-escalate thinking they're, once again, under attack. With people who don't have the mental capacity to really understand the details or implications of what happened, it is better to be calming and reassuring, not problem-solving.

CHAPTER 66

Managing Threats to Your Family

More horrifying than any threats to us are threats to our families. The aggressor creates a sense of helplessness, promising to attack when we aren't there. Usually, the threat is empty—words meant to terrify, but not acted upon. However, we must always take any such threats seriously, because it is almost impossible to know when the threats are real or not.

You will have to inform your family of threats and of the need to take protective action. Explain everything your children *need* to know, but no more. Don't over-explain, as this will make them anxious or confused. Furthermore, manage your own fear; you will worry your children much more if they perceive that you're frightened. Remember, a calm, strong individual is best able to evaluate dangerous situations. In addition, such a demeanor makes you and your family members appear less vulnerable to the predator who may be tracking you. It isn't enough to discuss the fact that you or your family has been threatened. You must set up a safety plan, and review it with your family on a regular basis. Below are some elements that should be considered in developing your safety plan:

- Inform the law enforcement agency where you live, and plan with them how best to manage the threat.
- Are you a soft target or a hard target? A soft target is easily accessible, predictable, and unaware of danger. A hard target isn't easily accessible or predictable. Furthermore, such a person is aware and in touch with his/her surroundings. This isn't a task for you alone. This is a task for your family as well. To this end, we strongly recommend that you acquire two books by Gavin de Becker: *The Gift of Fear* and *Protecting the Gift*.[33]
- Watch your back. You and your family must learn to scan your surroundings to become aware if you're being watched or stalked. Remind family to report suspicious people and cars. You can make this a game with your children, but this isn't an "under the radar" trick. The children should understand why they're being asked to do this, but this doesn't preclude making it a challenge or even fun. Ask them if they have ever seen someone—maybe wearing different clothes—on another occasion or at another location. Ask them to count cars while driving or play "slug-bug" (calling out the Volkswagens), but in addition, to tell you if they see any car over and over again.
- Make sure your family's work and school settings are **aware of the identity of the potential assailant.**
- Make clear to those involved with your children **who are allowed to meet or pick-up your children**.
- Both you and your family should **change routines** on a daily basis. Travel by different routes and different times. Don't always go to the same store, the same coffee shop, etc. Be unpredictable.
- Don't be alone. Neither you nor your family should be the last person to lock up or leave a work or school location.

- Enlist co-coworkers, coaches, school personnel, etc., to be part of your team. Establish **safe havens**, places to escape to in the event of danger. If possible, enlist your neighbors in your safety plan, in watching for danger signs associated with your situation. This can include noticing strangers, observing anything unusual happening around your property and acting as safe havens for the family if they suddenly need a place to go.

- Figure out with your family the best ways to **escape** from the home. Rehearse this with them. You can combine this with fire drills, something the children are already familiar with from school.

- Plan how to ask for help if in public and how best to call for help if needed. NOTE: if your children are alone, the best stranger to ask for help is a *woman*, as women are far less likely, *exponentially* less likely, to be a threat. Of course, this isn't the case if a woman is the threatening individual or associated with that individual.

- Teach your children a code word or phrase that any individual must say if they're trying to get your child to go with them. This includes neighbors and even, in some cases, relatives. For example, a person approaches your child after school and says, "Tasha, your mother and father were injured in an automobile accident. The police told me to take you to the hospital! Please come with me now." Your child should have been taught to keep his/her distance, looking for escape routes as he/she asks (if it wasn't said), "What's the word?" If the individual doesn't immediately reply "Edsel," to make up an example, he/she should run to a safe haven and describe the individual as best they can.

- Post emergency numbers near each telephone extension.

- Notify office, school, and family members of travel plans. All of these parties must be forbidden to *reveal* any travel plans or other schedules.

- Be careful about giving out personal information. This can be very tough on kids, as they happily exchange information with their friends or others. You will have to be explicit on what they can say and to whom. Remind them to be careful of strangers who want such information and to be sure to report any such queries. CAUTION: Don't forget Twitter, Facebook, and/or My Space and all the other internet avenues of communication. Many children don't make the same distinction about personal information when it is on-line that they do face-to-face.

CHAPTER 67

Conclusion

Having completed this book, your work has just begun. It is important that you regularly review and practice the safety and de-escalation methods in this book. You should be as familiar with this information as you are with the skills necessary to drive your car or use your firearm. Just as you automatically snatch your hand away from a hot stove or blink your eyes when a small object flies toward them, these skills must become so familiar to you that they seem as reflexive as instincts.

The best way to practice these skills is to integrate them into EVERY "scenario training" when updating defensive tactics skills. In other words, if you're practicing proper conducted energy weapon or baton techniques, every practice confrontation should be an "either-or," with the following options:
- Immediately deploy physical control tactics.
- Attempt to verbally de-escalate and then shift to physical control.
- Verbally de-escalate and control.

Each one of these options can be correct or incorrect. And there should only be one correct choice at each moment of the drill. As you have read, this is far more than just "how to deal with mentally ill" people. We deal with all kinds of people, of any age, shape, or size. Anyone can be dangerous, and we must have a "best practices" response to each. If we have done our work well, this book should cover just about any type of individual you will meet, be they mentally ill, substance abusing, having a bad day, or being a really bad person. We wish you a long and safe career. Thank you for choosing law enforcement.

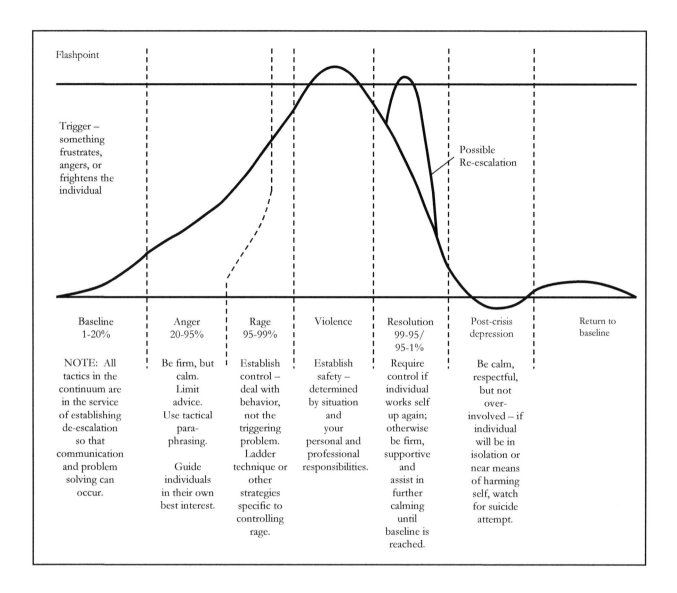

Flashpoint

Trigger –
something
frustrates,
angers, or
frightens the
individual

Possible
Re-escalation

Baseline 1-20%	Anger 20-95%	Rage 95-99%	Violence	Resolution 99-95/ 95-1%	Post-crisis depression	Return to baseline
NOTE: All tactics in the continuum are in the service of establishing de-escalation so that communication and problem solving can occur.	Be firm, but calm. Limit advice. Use tactical para-phrasing. Guide individuals in their own best interest.	Establish control – deal with behavior, not the triggering problem. Ladder technique or other strategies specific to controlling rage.	Establish safety – determined by situation and your personal and professional responsibilities.	Require control if individual works self up again; otherwise be firm, supportive and assist in further calming until baseline is reached.	Be calm, respectful, but not over-involved – if individual will be in isolation or near means of harming self, watch for suicide attempt.	

Recommended Reading List

Blum, L. N. (2000). *Force under pressure: How cops live and why they die.* New York: Lantern Books.

Early, P. (2006). *Crazy: A father's search through America's mental health madness.* New York: Putnam.

Gladwell, M. (2005). *Blink: The power of thinking without thinking.* New York: Back Bay Books.

Hipple, E. (2008). *Real men do cry: A quarterback's inspiring story of tackling depression and surviving suicide loss.* Naples, Florida: Quality of Life.

Jamison, K. R. (1995). *An unquiet mind: A memoir of moods and madness.* New York: Vintage.

Janoff-Bulman, R. (1992). *Shattered assumptions: Toward a new psychology of trauma.* New York: Free Press.

Kirschman, E. (1997). *I love a cop: What police families need to know.* New York: Guilford.

Nasar, S. (1998). *A beautiful mind: The life of mathematician genius and Nobel Laureate John Nash.* New York: Touchstone.

Schiller, L., & Bennett, A. (1994). *The quiet room: A journey out of the torment of madness.* New York: Warner Books.

Appendices

APPENDIX A

Setting up a Crisis Intervention Training (CIT) Program

One rain does not make a crop—
Creole Indian saying

As you know, police work is all about using the right tool to do the right job. One tool can have several applications. So it is with the Crisis Intervention Team (CIT), originally created via collaboration between Dr. Randolph Dupont (professor and clinical psychologist) and Major Sam Cochran (Memphis PD). Memphis is such a large police department that they can afford to exclusively train their own police officers and maintain a "Team" approach, integrating the police, corrections, hospital, court and mental health systems to more effectively handling the mentally ill in crisis. They created the first CIT team in 1988 and it continues there, today. The Memphis Model is considered the core standard, and it has been adopted, with a variety of regional variations throughout the country. Texas has the largest CIT program in the nation with 1,289 CIT officers. They graduate 250-300 officers per year. This is a 40 hour comprehensive training course.

However, there are nearly 600,000 police officers making up the 15,500 different police departments in the United States and 93 percent of all the police departments have less than 50 employees and there are over 1,000 one-person departments. What about the police officers from these agencies? They can't afford a specialized team approach.

The Olympia Police Department (OPD), Washington, created a Crisis Intervention Training program in 2001 modeled after that of the Memphis Police Department. This isn't a one-department "team;" rather it is a multi-jurisdictional approach to this issue. The OPD has graduated officers, dispatchers, chaplains and correction officers through a 40 hour CIT program designed to "fit" the greater Thurston/Mason County areas. To date, nearly 300 personnel have graduated from this National Alliance for the Mentally Ill (NAMI) award winning CIT program. Persons with mental illness live in these smaller communities, as well as the larger ones. We could, each of us, benefit from this training.

The vast majority of these departments have less than 100 officers and most have less than 50. They can afford to send 1-2 officers to the week-long course and over time, every member of the department can receive this valuable training.

Former Sergeant Jon Dowd (formerly of the Northumbria Police in England) researched three CIT programs: Seattle and Olympia, Washington, and Portland, Oregon. He did this for his 2004/05 Fulbright

Police Fellowship. He was the first to show CIT training had significant positive impact on officers immediately after and six months after the training, Jon Dowd is now a clinical psychologist, practicing in the northeast of England.

The Washington State Criminal Justice Training Commission, at the direction of then Governor Gary Locke, created a statewide standard CIT training program modeled after the Olympia Model.

For more information on the creation of your own evidence-based CIT program, contact founding member of the OPD CIT Alliance, John Hutchings at jfhutch@comcast.net He is available for consultation.

APPENDIX B

Example of a Plan Developed to Assist
a Chronically Para-suicidal Individual

Shauna was somewhat developmentally disabled, with borderline personality disorder (Chapter 21). She was in a mental health program that used a "nurturing model." In other words, the counselors believed that if they were supportive and accepting, Shauna and the other women in the program would do best. For that reason, they "encouraged, but never directed." Among the things they encouraged Shauna to do was to have more of a social life.

Shauna lived in a rough area of town, but following her counselors' suggestions in her own way, she began going out to bars near her apartment. Naïve, childish, insecure, and quite overweight, she was perfect prey for predators. A man would approach her, speak nicely to her, and suggest they go somewhere private. She'd invite him back to her apartment, where she would be raped. In each case, after the attacker left, she would cut her wrists deeply and then call 9-1-1 for help. Even though this happened on a number of occasions, no investigation was successful. She couldn't describe her attacker, except in terms such as, "He was a nice man. He had blonde hair. Why did he do this?"

Because of her childlike nature, most people remained kind. The police talked gently to her as did emergency medical technicians. She was taken to the hospital, where the nurses, doctors, and social workers took care of her, followed by a "rape victim advocate," to be followed by a mental health outreach worker. She would have multiple follow-up appointments with her therapist, who comforted and nurtured her.

One day, a coworker and I were discussing the case, and we essentially came to the conclusion that we, in the system, had become part of Shauna's rape cycle. Each time she would go to the bar with high hopes of meeting someone, she would be violated and cut her wrists, *requiring* that a number of kind, strong, wise people would encircle, care for, and comfort her. We couldn't stop her from going out, we couldn't move in with her to stop the rapists, but we could, without violating any ethics, respond differently. Here, in brief, is the plan the team developed:

- **Police response.** Response time and attempt to investigate crime unchanged. However, each officer was to have a flat affect—nearly emotionless, "just the facts," approach to their interview with Shauna. They shouldn't be cold, mean, punitive, or sarcastic. Simply take the information.
- **Emergency medical services.** Emergency medical care unchanged. However, there should be no comforting voice or gesture, no matter how much Shauna was crying or wailing. They should move her to the gurney in a matter-of-fact way, like she was a sack of potatoes.

- **Emergency room.** Medical treatment unchanged. Anesthesia, was, of course, used when stitching her wounds. (Despite any imputation to the contrary, we weren't punishing her. We were also not rewarding her.) The doctors and nurses, however, asked no questions beyond what was needed for medical treatment. The social worker, too, would take just the basic facts. If she needed something to drink, she would receive water, not juice or anything sweet. "Sweet" means nurturance; we didn't want to nurture her into being raped and possibly killing herself.

- **Rape victim's advocate.** As might be imagined, these big hearted people, doing a job that few of us could handle, had the hardest time with the plan. With sufficient discussion, however, they understood. Their approach was to be "distantly kind." In other words, the same kind of approach one uses with a child who skins their knee—you tend to them and send them on their way. If you make a big deal out of it, they will think it is a big deal as well!

- **The emergency evaluator for mental health would do a full evaluation.** If Shauna wasn't immediately suicidal, she was to be sent home. (This, by the way, was always the case. She slashed herself immediately after the sexual assault, as a means to initiate the "help" portion of her cycle of behavior. She wouldn't do it again in relation to the same incident.) This type of plan is individualized to the person. You cannot impose this plan on a similar person in your area. That's why you need to get together with all the "players" involved both in the "frequently-in-crisis person's" treatment and in the emergency response system that is now part of their life, and figure out the best, tactically and humanly sound plan for that person.

- **Welfare check.** Shauna would get a call once daily from the crisis line that was kept brief. She would be reminded to see her therapist and the date and time of her next appointment.

- **Counselor's responsibility.** The counselor, at their meeting, would have Shauna go through everything she did that night in exhaustive detail, including questions as to why she did not call 9-1-1 *before* cutting herself. In a sense, it was an "after-action review," not emotionally rewarding in the least. On the flip side, once this was complete and better safety planning was done, ("Don't go to bars anymore," for example.) they would talk about other things, and Shauna would get *emotionally rewarded* for non-pathological discussions, thoughts, and actions. The idea was that Shauna would get no emotional reward for suicide or dangerous actions and *much more* reward for healthy behaviors.

Several weeks subsequent to the implementation of this plan, Shauna again made a suicide attempt after a sexual assault. Everyone held to the plan, although some later confessed that they felt like brutes, seeing this child in an adult's body, walked out of the ER, sobbing like her heart was broken. Her counselors began to work with her according to the plan. For a period of over 12 years, she had no contact whatsoever with law enforcement or the emergency medical system, nor did she suffer from any more sexual assaults.[34]

APPENDIX C

Support Staff: Managing Aggressive Individuals
in the Lobby and on the Phone

Support staff, particularly those who work at the front desk, are in a difficult position. Some agencies include support staff in both training and safety procedures. In such circumstances, your agency policies and training may supersede some of the recommendations here. In any event, the following will postulate that support staff isn't provided with the necessary level of training in de-escalation to empower them to undertake the management and control of an aggressive individual, from "start to finish." This is certainly a subject of debate. On one side are those who argue that crises situations require specialized training, and that de-escalation and crisis intervention aren't part of support staff's job description. There also may be liability issues if such an important task is delegated to someone without the proper credentials. On the other side is the understanding that many support staff have years of experience in managing aggressive behavior that they have learned, literally, on the front lines of the agency for which they work. Furthermore, there is a legitimate concern that if, supervisory, or professional personnel are delegated to step in on behalf of support staff when encountering a belligerent or aggressive individual, they will soon learn that they can "move up the food chain" by abusing the people at the front desk.

In any event, the discussion that follows will be under the assumption that support staff has a limited but vital role in de-escalation of aggression, but once a certain threshold is met, Law Enforcement Officers (LEO's) and/or supervisors should step in.

Appendix C One Author's Experience
My secretary is well versed in controlling the front of the office, and she often handles all sorts of problems with the public that I never even hear about. She doesn't accept any nonsense from anyone in her area of control, and has no trouble establishing her authority. It is vital that the secretary feels safe and secure within her work space, so locked doors and restricted access to the front desk are a must as a first step in office safety, because everything else can feed off of that first contact and how it is handled.

Systems Issues Regarding Face-to-Face Encounters for Support Staff

NOTE: **What follows in this section are ideal principals. A variety of considerations may make some of these impossible to implement. The decision to or NOT implement, however, should be an informed one:**

- **Lobby layout.** The lobby should be a place where people feel welcome and comfortable. If people are made to feel unwelcome, they will behave accordingly. Therefore, the carpet or floor should be clean, and furniture should be comfortable. A well-kept place is "territory." It is more difficult to behave in an aggressive or disorderly manner when the environment is clearly "owned" and one experiences oneself to be a guest on someone else's territory.

- **Own the environment.** No one owns a sloppy, unkempt, uncomfortable or dirty environment. It is obvious that no one takes ownership of it or cares for it. In such an environment, people have "permission" to act in a more disorderly fashion because no one cares.

- **Make it warm.** On the other hand, if the lobby is too cold, sterile, and impersonal, people experience a sense of isolation. They find themselves facing an apparently uncaring, distant institution, and some will act in all-too-human ways to make sure that they're recognized as "counting for something."

- **Front desk layout.** Some consideration must be made to the placement of the front desk. The secretary should, ideally, be behind some sort of glass barricade/closed in office with only a pass thru window to communicate with the public, and receive report forms or other paperwork.

- **"Support" support staff.** Support staff must have an assurance of immediate response of law enforcement officers, on site, in the event of any danger. Officers may be within earshot in many police stations—others need an emergency button system. **The bottom line is that support staff must have a guaranteed rapid response by law enforcement officers when needed.** There should be occasional, random tests of the system to assure that staff will respond as needed.

- **Empowerment.** Support staff should be encouraged to report anything that appears to be amiss, and their observations must be treated with respect. If their concerns are belittled or ignored, they will, quite understandably, stop reporting. If a particular employee is too reactive or frequently misjudges situations, either seeing danger at too low a threshold or not seeing a threatening situation developing when it is right in front of them, this should be considered a training issue for that specific person, not an indication that support staffs' concerns should be ignored.

- **Alerts.** Support staff should be made aware of: Any individual who present any particular concern or risk; Or, people whose behaviors are odd or eccentric, but don't pose a risk. That way, the front desk individual can recognize something that is out of the ordinary for that particular person, given that their baseline, non-threatening behaviors are always "out of the ordinary."

- **Cultural training relevant to aggression.** Staff need basic training so that they're familiar with styles of behavior that, unfamiliar to them, might be misinterpreted as aggressive, particularly cultural styles that may be unfamiliar to personnel who come from another background. **However, such training shouldn't include "reframing," in which aggressive, intrusive, or sexualized behaviors are "contextualized."** Here, offensive acts are claimed to be acceptable because someone asserts that they're derived culturally. This is almost always not the case. *The basic stan-*

dards of human decency are held in common by almost all cultures. Attempts at cultural relevancy or understanding should never allow abusive or threatening behavior.

Threat Assessment for Support Staff

NOTE: This is the basic information that support staff should know. If they observe any of these behaviors or characteristics, they should call for assistance as soon as possible, to circumvent any potentially dangerous escalation.

Support staff should note:

- **Any weapons.** This includes ordinary objects: canes, bags, books; whatever, if the individual is wielding them in a threatening way.
- **Intimidation towards others in the area in front of the desk or entrance way to the building.** These behaviors may include but aren't limited to: staring with hostility, abusive language, or threatening behaviors towards other people. This includes both staff and other people.
- **Scapegoating**. An individual may vent, pick-on, or otherwise be aggressive to a child, spouse, or others in the front area.
- **Fear.** The individual seems to be quite afraid.
- **Reactivity.** The individual who snaps at support staff with inordinate aggression, particularly when asked reasonable questions.
- **Low frustration tolerance.** The individual who becomes frustrated when requested to wait. This is especially common because many in the world suffer from "instant gratification syndrome."
- **Intoxication.** Law enforcement officers should always be alerted if an individual shows signs of intoxication.
- **Mood swings.** Staff should be alerted if the individual shows rapid changes in affect—from elation to anger to fear to withdrawal.
- **Atypical behaviors.** Staff should be alerted when an individual, familiar to the front-desk personnel, is behaving in a quite different way from their baseline behavior.
- **Trespassing.** The individual who trespasses on support staffs' space and doesn't cease when a limit is set. This includes leaning inside the desk (if there is no protective barrier), waving hands in support staffs' faces, or trying to take paperwork from them.
- **Electric tension.** Information on aggressive behaviors will be presented in other training modules. However, any time support staff feel a shot of adrenaline, a sense that something bad is about to happen, *even when they can't explain why*, they must call for assistance. Better an occasional false alarm than allowing one developing emergency to go unattended until it is too late.

Self-control for Front Office/Support Staff

- **A simple breathing method to calm oneself in crisis situations.** Let the belly expand on an inhale to a moderate four count, hold for a four count, and exhale, letting the belly drop back into the rib cage for a four count. Continue, using this breathing when you anticipate a crisis developing, while enmeshed in the middle of a crisis situation, and to de-compress after the situation.

- **It's not personal!** Staff must be trained that difficulties with people aren't personal issues, no matter what they say or do. The people they're dealing with are troubled individuals, often in desperate situations. Support staff must understand that if they don't take things personally, they will actually have far more control over both their own responses and the aggressive people's behaviors.
- **Professional pride.** It should be a mark of professional pride to be able to move people through screening and waiting procedures expeditiously respectfully so that they're calmer *after* interacting with support staff.
- **Bracketing**. Part of training for support staff should be an awareness of one's own "buttons." A discussion with your staff about the subject of their hot-buttons *isn't* a request for revelation about what their issues are. Rather, they should be educated to maintain a "background" awareness regarding what causes them to lose their temper, so that they're prepared for these events when they occur.

Education
NOTE: Although support staff won't be responsible for full de-escalation, they need to be educated in the following, subjects that are discussed in other sections of this book.

- **Cycle of aggression.** In addition to helping support staff assess when a problem is occurring, we have found that knowledge of the escalation cycle is invaluable in helping people keep themselves calm.
- **Why someone would be aggressive.** Empathy, the understanding of what is going on within others, is one of the primary routes to effective-communication, particularly with the mentally ill. It is very difficult to be understanding when one can't comprehend why other individuals would act the way they do.
- **Recognizing aggressive behaviors.** This is an expanded version of risk assessment. When one isn't surprised by another's behavior, one can anticipate and act, rather than merely react.

What NOT to Do: and What to Do Instead

- **Don't shout.** It is important to keep your voice strong and firm. The only time you should yell is to call for help or to stop an assault in progress. When you're trying to calm down an aggressive or upset person, try to pitch your voice a little lower so that it is "in your chest." This will serve to show your strength and authority and will also help you keep calm.
- **Don't talk down**. Talking down to anyone is demeaning.
- **Don't roll your eyes.**
- **Don't show your frustration by sighing.**
- **Don't ignore someone.** Never ignore someone who is talking to you. It is fine to say, "Please sit down, I'll speak with you in just a moment," for example, or "I've already told you that you have to speak to the investigating officer about this." But don't simply turn your back on people or act as if they aren't there.
- **Don't talk to them "through" the paperwork.** Instead, speak to them as a person with clean, direct, eye contact.

- **Keep your problems to yourself.** Everybody has problems in life. It is important, however, that before you enter the agency, you remind yourself that you will be dealing with some of the most vulnerable members of our society, as well as some of the most difficult. As a professional, leave your problems at the door. If you find you're unable to do this—if things that are worrying you intrude into your work—consult with your supervisor to figure out best how to take the pressure off. This is a safety issue. If you flare up at people, or conversely, are overwhelmed by them, you're at greater risk for possible harm.

- **Ignoring problems.** Don't hope that a problem will go away if it is ignored. It is better for you to address it now when it is a minor situation, perhaps for example, asking for someone to sit down and wait quietly, or to lower their voice. If it is a bigger problem, then you should call officers who can deal with dangerous situations. Don't be embarrassed or otherwise hesitant to disturb the LEO. If you're over-reacting, you will get support through more training. If, however, you aren't taken seriously, then the problem would be the fault of the "designated" staff, not you. A simple discussion with your supervisor should help with that kind of problem.

- **Don't be bossy.** Authoritarian attitudes are one of the biggest precipitants of aggressive behavior—in *reaction* to the authoritarian attitudes.

- **Don't point.** If you want someone to back-up, for example, put BOTH hands up, close to your chest, and request that they move back.

Strategies for Front-Desk Staff

<u>NOTE</u>: **Although not expected to do de-escalation of aggressive behavior, front-desk staff are responsible for trying to help mildly upset individuals calm down. Here are some basic principles:**

- **Don't make things a power struggle.** Whenever possible (most of the time!), make requests rather than give orders.

- **Leave people alone if that's what they want.** There are times that we believe we must get certain information. If the person is resistant or suspicious, don't push it. Simply inform the responsible officer that certain information you need is outstanding.

- **Eye contact.** Calm, direct, and open eye contact is best. If the person is uncomfortable with this, limit your eye contact *without looking downwards.* Instead, detach, moving your eyes to the side, and then return to making eye contact occasionally.

- **Names.** People have different styles, but it is often helpful to use a person's last name rather than their first. Let the person invite you to use their first name.

- **Paraphrasing.** VERY IMPORTANT—When people are upset, it is very hard for them to answer questions. Help them calm down first. With paraphrasing, all we do is sum up what they said in different words. (See Chapter 48). If you sum things up accurately, you've established that you've "gotten" what they said thus far, so the upset person doesn't have to say it again.

- **Get the whole story.** Don't problem-solve until you know what they're trying to tell you. Otherwise, you will be seen as either interrupting, which is rude, or not interested. Paraphrasing will help you get the story in a minimum amount of time.

- **Non-threatening requests**. Make a non-threatening request that the person has a high likelihood of complying with. For example, "Sir/Ma'am, would you take your dog out to the car. There are so many people here that she might get upset. I'll help you as soon as you return, so you won't have to wait any longer." OR "Would you please turn your radio off, it is difficult to hear you through this glass with the music playing."

Support Staff and the Phone
NOTE: Because of the distance between folks, people will often say things on the phone or even worse, by email that they would never say in person. Aside from all the information in the previous sections, what follows is specific to phone contacts.

- **You're NOT required to accept abuse, verbal violence, or obscenity**. Callers should be informed, calmly, of how they're expected to communicate and warned that if they continue their abuse, the call will be terminated. If the abuse continues, hang up the phone. *Document with exact quotations.*
- **NOTE:** If they're the kind who swears for "punctuation," you should ask them to stop, if it offends you. If the verbalizations are abusive, however, terminate the call and notify your supervisor or law enforcement officer. Support staff must be expected to take responsibility to set firm limits with individuals on how they will speak to you.
- **Threats**. If someone makes any sort of threat, get as much information as you can from the suspect; who is the target of the threat, where the bomb is, who's calling (they do sometimes answer that question), etc. Notify an officer and your supervisor. *Document with exact quotations.*
- **Personal information**. Don't reveal personal information. Furthermore, if a caller is flirtatious or otherwise requests personal information, inform his/her LEO. *Document with exact quotations.*
- **Overly personal remarks.** Set firm limits. Inform the caller that you don't accept personal remarks. Terminate the call if they continue. Notify your supervisor, and in many cases, the law enforcement officer whom they were calling. Try to give as much detail as you can whether the remarks were merely inept attempts to flirt by a socially clueless individual or something more predatory. *Document with exact quotations.*
- **Unavailability.** When an officer isn't available, the best thing to say is "He/she is unavailable right now." If you have a good prediction of when he/she WILL be available, give it to the caller. Ensure that calls like this get through to the officer. Things a receptionist shouldn't say:
  a. "He isn't back from lunch." This implies that the officer is taking his sweet old time, and is therefore a selfish person.
  b. "I think she's still having coffee." Don't share personal information.
  c. "He's in the middle of a big problem or a crisis." This implies that the office has problems and this may make the public anxious. It also implies that what the caller is telephoning about isn't as important.
  d. "She went home early." Creates both resentment and envy. They need the officer, but they're unavailable.
  e. "He's not in yet." This is also infuriating. He's late when the caller needs him.

f. If, however, the needed officer isn't going to be available for several days or more, try to either get an idea of the problem and pass the information to another officer or his/her supervisor.

- Putting callers on hold. When you ask to put them on hold, get a response before doing so. If the caller is irate, and attempts to continue to argue with you, state, "I must put you on hold now" and do so. If you're connecting them with another party, be sure to inform that person that the caller is irate. When you reconnect with the person, don't apologize after putting them on hold. Instead, thank them for their patience. You didn't do anything wrong.

- **Close-ended question to end call**. This can be used when the call is relatively straightforward, but the caller still seems unsatisfied. "Is there anything else I can help you with before I hang up?"
  a. Don't use this if the call has become tense or aggressive, as the other party may think you're being sarcastic.
  b. There are some people, however, who will seize any opportunity to continue talking.
  c. If you *have* used one closed-ended question and answered it, it is time to end the call now.

- **Get rid of negative energy before answering the phone again.** Particularly after an intense call, take a break, even thirty seconds. Stand up and stretch or otherwise get rid of some of the tension you may have incurred so that it isn't transferred into your next call.

- **Don't just say, "I don't know."** Tell the caller, "but I know who can answer your question. I'll get them for you right now."

- **Assessing for crisis.** Speaking with people on the phone is only different from speaking face-to-face in the details. The differences are in form, not substance, in that you have to ask for what you can't see. The following are questions that might be relevant in specific situations. Some may not be asked by support staff—in part, this will depend on your agency protocols.
  a. Ask for the caller's name and number, and in some circumstances, other demographic details. "We sometimes have a bad connection, and might get cut off. I want to be sure that I can call you back if that happens." Sometimes this is a marvelously effective way of assisting a panic-stricken or agitated person to calm down. The attention required to give "vital statistics" can assist the individual in ordering their thoughts. Ask for a description of the problem: then ask further questions to understand the context.
  b. If you're at all concerned that there is a risk of suicide or violence, immediately notify officers/dispatch. DON'T rely on putting the caller on hold, or merely try to transfer the call with the push of a couple buttons. Support staff must have a way to access help without leaving the caller alone without a voice, in the event of a crisis.
  c. If there is any sense of chaos, violence or danger, ask if anyone has been hurt. If so, how—get specifics.
  d. Ask who is with the caller. If the caller is circumspect, talking quietly or otherwise not forthcoming, ask them to say "yes" or "no" concerning if they can talk freely. If they can't talk freely, you will have to ask "yes/no" questions to ascertain what is going on. Obtain assistance from someone else in the agency.

APPENDIX D

Concerning Military Personnel,
Both Active Duty and Veterans

There are many reasons to be concerned for our military these days. Many young men and women, and many not so young, have been serving overseas in terribly dangerous conditions. Many are coming home wounded. Some will never return. Many soldiers, either still on active duty or veterans, are suffering from a variety of physical and psychiatric disorders. Of perhaps greatest concern are Post Traumatic Stress Disorder (PTSD) and Traumatic Brain Injury (TBI). Some people suffering from PTSD may be hyper-vigilant, and hair-trigger responsive to anything they perceive, rightly or wrongly, as a threat.

Please remember, too, that many female soldiers and a startlingly high number of male soldiers are suffering from PTSD due not to combat, but due to sexual assault from fellow soldiers. Police officers should be aware that the soldier they stop for a traffic stop, particularly a woman, may interpret your friendly interaction as a threat.

TBI can have a variety of profoundly damaging effects, many of which are permanent. In particular, if the injury is to the pre-frontal cortex, which mediates impulse control, the individual may have a difficult time suppressing rage and even violence.

We have both been to a number of trainings on questions regarding interactions between law enforcement and the military. They raise more questions than answers for both of us. Consider these questions:
- "If they don't tell you, how would you know they have PTSD? Or TBI?"
- One suggested intervention to aggressive soldiers is, "Stand down, soldier." We are sure it works. But in one consultation with a Department of Veterans Affairs Police officer, he stated, "A lot of the guys police officers will have trouble with are people who had trouble in the military. They are often people with authority issues. That kind of military order may be just the thing to blow them up."
- It is often suggested that a police officer with military background, whenever possible, be the one to interact with the soldier/veteran. This *can* be very helpful – sometimes. However, one can, thereby, get in the same dilemma as statements like, "Only female officers should talk to rape victims," or "Males from the Middle East do not like interacting with women officers, so whenever possible, have a male officer give the orders." We adamantly oppose this kind of thinking. All it will encourage is hesitancy: if an officer starts worrying that he or she is not the right person to interact with any citizen, they will surely fail, and may also get hurt when their hesitancy is regarded as weakness. Regarding the first statement in this bullet point, there is nothing wrong

with a police officer who has military experience stepping up to speak with a soldier/veteran, and that fact may prove helpful. But you don't have to be drug addicted to talk to a drug addict, and you don't have to be rich to talk to a corporate thief; similarly, it is not requisite that the police officer who has the lead is ex-military.

Let's go back to basics. First of all, further education on such issues as TBI, PTSD and what our military is going through, positive and negative, will, of course, be a benefit to your work as a law enforcement officer. Beyond that, **DEAL WITH THE BEHAVIOR, NOT THE CAUSE.** If you maintain this perspective, you will never be confused by worries about what diagnosis the person has, what drugs they are on or what history they might have lived.

Appendix D Information Regarding Military Subjects of Police Interest

Many military folks have had disciplinary problems or committed crimes while in the military. A lot of that information may not be present in their civilian records. However, all you need to do is call the Department of Veterans Affairs Police. They have access to nationwide records within the military regarding infractions and violations of the law. Incidents such as aggressive behavior in a military facility such as a hospital may also be recorded. Whenever there is time, always call to get what may prove to be vital information. In fact, armed with that information, you (or, for example, your crisis negotiators) will have a good idea how to communicate with the individual.

APPENDIX E

The Question of Positional and Compression Asphyxia
By Gary M. Vilke, MD, FACEP, FAAEM

Background on Positional Asphyxia

- The concept of "Positional Asphyxia" was originally based on research that had significant methodological flaws (Reay, et al 1988)
- The premise of positional asphyxia was that if you left a patient in a hobble restraint position, he would tire, go into ventilatory failure and then asphyxiate into cardiac arrest.
- The hobble position is defined as prone with hand cuffed behind the back and ankles restrained with a device that is then pulled up and tethered to the handcuffs leaving the knees bent.
- The original research and dozens of papers since have NEVER shown hypoxia (low oxygen levels in the blood) to develop in the hobble position.
- The original research and dozens of papers since have NEVER shown hypercarbia (elevated CO_2 levels in the blood) to develop in the hobble position.
- In fact, the only paper to report that the hobble position results in positional asphyxia, actually demonstrated that oxygen saturation levels IMPROVED in all subjects who were left in a hobble position.
- Subsequent studies evaluating obese subjects also have demonstrated that when left in a hobble position, they will not asphyxiate.(Sloane, et al 2014)
- All of these studies prove that people left on their stomachs in a hobble position will not die from asphyxiation, which includes both thin and obese individuals.

Best practices

When encountered with a patient in a hobble restraint, certain assessments of a patient are critical and the documentation of the findings in the pre-hospital record is essential.

A. Assess the level of consciousness. Is the patient awake or not and is he verbal?
B. Assess perfusion. Is his skin color good and does he have a strong regular pulse?
C. Place on a monitor as soon as feasible and document first rhythm.
D. Place on pulse oximeter as soon as feasible and document O2 sat. If placing on a finger, make sure the hand is getting good perfusion through the handcuff if the O2 sat reading is low.
E. If the patient can be safely transferred to a supine position with approved 4-point restraints secured to the gurney – this is the optimal position as one has full access to the patient's airway and direct visualization of the face and access to the chest.
F. If the patient cannot be safely transferred out of the hobble position, attempt to transfer the patient in a lateral decubitus position on the gurney – preferably with the face and chest facing the EMS personnel to optimize monitoring.

G. Face down on the gurney in the hobble position is the least desirable position as the patient cannot be easily monitored or accessed if the physical status changes. If utilizing this position for transport, care must be taken to assure the airway is clear and not obstructed by sheets or the mattress. ***Despite all of the data supporting the safety of the hobble position, this is the position that will have the most scrutiny in a lawsuit if a patient deteriorates into cardiac arrest.

H. Ongoing monitoring and vigilance is important. The issue of medical concern is not the actual hobble position, as this is deemed physiologically neutral, but rather the concern is the underlying medical condition (drug induced or not) that required the patient to be hobbled in the first place.

I. These recommendations are meant to supplement, not replace, existing EMS protocols (blood glucose assessment, IV fluids, etc)

Background on Compression Asphyxia

- The concept of "Compression Asphyxia" evolved after the theory of positional asphyxia was essentially debunked. (Chan, et al. 1997, Chan et al 1998)

- The premise of compression asphyxia was that a certain amount of weight is often placed on the back of an individual to get a him into custody and handcuffed. Often this weight is multiple officers holding the person down with hands, forearms or knees. During this time period while the weight is being applied, the theory is that the subject would tire, not be able to breathe (ventilate), go into ventilatory failure and then asphyxiate into cardiac arrest.

- Research with up to 225 lbs of weight on the backs of healthy volunteers has not demonstrated physiological changes that would indicate that asphyxiation is likely with these weights. (Michalewicz, et al 2007)

- Studies with weights on the backs of normal subjects has also shown that cardiac output and blood pressure are not impacted.(Savaser, et al 2013)

- If an individual is alive, moving and breathing after the weight has been removed and then subsequently goes into cardiac arrest, the weight did not cause compressive asphyxia. *There is not a delayed asphyxiation*, it either happens while the weight is on or it does not occur.

- Even if the weight on an individual is so great as to restrict adequate ventilation, if the subject is breathing once the weight is removed, the person will breathe out the retained CO_2 and will recover. The effects of the weight are not lasting and a breathing individual will self-correct very quickly.

- It takes a great deal of weight, consistently placed over the ventilatory muscles of the back, for a significant length of time with essentially complete impedance of ventilation without breaks to breathe in order to theoretically cause a death due to compressive asphyxia.

- If a person is vigorously and repeatedly yelling or screaming, he is moving air in and out of his lungs and thus is not meeting the "complete impedance of ventilation" criteria and thus is not in a position at that time to cause asphyxiation.

  NOTE: That being said, other medical emergencies CAN present with the *sensation* that one cannot breathe, when in fact they are ventilating fine but are suffering from a myocardial infarction or ischemia, for instance. These patients should be carefully evaluated.

Best practices

When EMS encounters a patient who had weight placed on him to get him into custody, certain assessments of a patient are critical and the documentation of the findings in the pre-hospital record is essential. Basically the patient will either be spontaneously breathing with a pulse, or not. If he is spontaneously breathing with a pulse, then he did not suffer from compression asphyxia and should be assessed and documentation should follow as per the "Best practices" for positional asphyxia (above).

If the patient is not breathing or does not have a pulse, treatment is basically standard advanced cardiac life support measures. Documentation optimally should reflect the events that led up to the cardiac arrest. Often EMS is present or staged within viewing distance of the event. If so, some of the following observations can be critically useful in evaluating the case for quality review or a subsequent legal action:

- How many officers where physically involved?
- Where were they located on the subject? (i.e. holding legs, holding head, knee on back, hands on shoulder, etc)
- How long was weight on the subject?
- Was the weight moving and shifting (did the subject arch up, roll over or was he just laying flat on his stomach)?
- At what point did the subject stop yelling in relation to the cardiac arrest?
- Was the change in status sudden or gradual over time?
- Was there weight on him at the time of the cardiac arrest and if so, how much?

Pearls

Careful monitoring – you will likely be unable to prevent a patient who is suffering from Excited Delirium Syndrome from going into cardiac arrest. Additionally, rapid recognition and treatment is unlikely to change the ultimate outcome for the patient, but careful charting and documentation is extremely beneficial for subsequent legal actions that are likely to arise.

ETCO2 - If possible, document the earliest possible end tidal CO2 level. Pre-intubation with bag-valve-mask is best if feasible, as this value if low or normal, will support that the individual did not asphyxiate, as CO_2 levels are high in patients who asphyxiated.

Careful accurate documentation with details as clear as possible. These cases in which there is a cardiac arrest often end up in litigation, so clear documentation of what was observed and reported with specific details is incredibly helpful in evaluating the case.

Appendix E CAUTION

Medically evaluate the subject carefully, even if the person is vigorously and repeatedly yelling or screaming. It may be obvious that he is moving air in and out of his lungs and thus is not in a position at that time to cause asphyxiation – however other medical emergencies, like myocardial infarctions or ischemia can present with the sensation of difficulty breathing and should be considered during the assessment.

References

Chan TC, Vilke GM, Neuman T, Clausen JL: Restraint position and positional asphyxia. Ann Emerg Med 1997;30(5):578-586.

Chan TC, Vilke GM, Neuman T: Reexamination of custody restraint position and positional asphyxia. Am J Forensic Med Pathol 1998;19(3):201-205.

Michalewicz BA, Chan TC, Vilke GM, Levy SS, Neuman TS, Kolkhorst FW. Ventilatory and metabolic demands during aggressive physical restraint in healthy adults. J Forensic Sci 2007;52(1):171-175.

Reay DT, Howard JD, Fligner CL, Ward RJ. Effects of positional restraint on oxygen saturation and heart rate following exercise. Am J Forensic Med Pathol. 1988 Mar;9(1):16-8.

Savaser DJ, Campbell C, Castillo EM, Vilke GM, Sloane C, Neuman T, Hansen AV, Shah S, Chan TC. The effect of the prone maximal restrained position with and without weight force on cardiac output and other hemodynamic measures. J Forens Leg Med. 2013 Nov;20(8):991-5. Epub 2013 Aug 30.

Sloane C, Chan TC, Kolkhorst F, Neuman T, Castillo EM, Vilke GM. Evaluation of the Ventilatory Effects of the Prone Maximum Restraint Position (PMR) on Obese Human Subjects. Forens Sci Int 2014;237:86-9. Epub 2014;46(6):865-72. Epub 2014 Feb 14.

APPENDIX F

Suggested Response Protocol for Police Concerning Suspected Excited Delirium Incidents
By Lieutenant Michael Paulus

> **Appendix F Excited Delirium is a Chaotic Rage State**
>
> As discussed in detail in Chapter 59, Excited Delirium is a medical syndrome that is included within a general category: Chaotic Rage. It should not be incumbent upon either eyewitnesses or first responders to distinguish between excited delirium and other similar, equally dangerous forms of chaotic rage. The authors, therefore, recommend that protocols in your jurisdiction be coded for chaotic rage, with a clear understanding that this term encompasses excited delirium and other similar states, whatever the cause.

When considering a response to suspected Excited Delirium incidents, it is important to understand what the law enforcement officer is facing. Dr. Deborah Mash of the University of Miami Brain Endowment Center has called Excited Delirium, "a medical emergency that presents itself as a law enforcement problem."

Keeping this in mind, we in law enforcement find ourselves presented with a dilemma comparable to dispatching the fire department to a bank robbery. They do not have the appropriate equipment or training to handle the high-risk nature of a bank robbery. By the same token, EMS personnel are not dispatched to intervene in domestic disputes.

Why, then, is law enforcement sent to a medical emergency that requires a minimum of an advanced life support ambulance crew to address? There is nothing on the officer's duty belt, in their squad car, or in their facility that will address hyperthermia, acidosis, cardiovascular collapse, or other life-threatening issues that are common in an Excited Delirium incident.

At least one West Coast medical examiner has said that in an Excited Delirium incident, the police just get in the way and can do nothing for the subject. This points out that, in a very important sense, law enforcement does not have the primary role in these incidents, but a critical backup role. It just so happens that this "back-up" comes first. Unless the individual is under complete physical control, medical assistance cannot be rendered.

It is crucial to develop a multi-disciplinary approach to adequately respond to individuals in excited delirium states. Some of the most common stakeholders in such a plan include: law enforcement, corrections, EMS personnel, fire personnel, 9-1-1 dispatch, emergency room physicians/nurses, coroners, medical examiners, mental health professionals/consumers, risk managers and the appropriate State/ District attorney. Your jurisdiction may have different stakeholders, maybe more or maybe less, but the critical issue is to identify those that are, or should be, part of a best practices response to these, all too often, fatal incidents.

What is proposed here has been a successful multi-jurisdictional response since July 1, 2008 in Champaign County, Illinois.[35] It is offered for use as a template to help establish a protocol that works for your community within the confines of the resources you have available.

The effectiveness of this protocol relies upon law enforcement officers understanding what they are dealing with and calling for additional backup early on in the response. In addition, the dispatcher/call taker must have the knowledge and ability to reasonably identify incidents that require sending additional resources to the scene as early as possible.

The number of personnel sent to the scene will be dependant on what resources are available, but four to six (4-6) law enforcement personnel should be dispatched to the scene, if possible. CIT (Crisis Intervention Team) officers should be sent, if available, as well as a supervisor. Interagency agreements are common to allow various departments to share resources in times of emergencies such as these.

EMS should be sent at the same time as law enforcement personnel, thereby saving precious time in getting the medical personnel and equipment to the scene as quickly as possible. Some communities have a combined EMS/Fire Department. Those that don't will then need to consider if sending a Fire Rescue truck is a possibility, along with EMS. Some jurisdictions have, as part of their City Ordinance that any "medical emergency" requires a Fire Rescue truck be sent. If this is the case, expect the EMS crew as well as the Fire Rescue personnel to be dispatched to the scene. The Fire Rescue's role will be discussed shortly.

One of the toughest decisions a first responder will make could be containing the situation until the medical personnel arrive instead of physically contacting the subject. Whenever possible, law enforcement should wait until EMS/Fire Rescue has arrived before making physical contact with the subject. Of course, this is contingent on how immediately dangerous the subject is to himself/herself, the law enforcement personnel, other first responders, and bystanders. This is where the role of the officer trained as a CIT officer *may* help the subject. There is no guarantee that the subject in the midst of an Excited Delirium incident will be able to be talked down. The benefit of having an officer trained to recognize a person in crisis and then attempt to use the verbal de-escalation techniques to reach an "island of sanity", as the authors of the text call it, is worth the effort.

There are two situations when officers should not wait for EMS arrival: imminent risk of serious injury to either a first responder or to the subject. First responder safety is of primary importance as it is the first responder who is responsible for resolving this situation. Furthermore, standing by until EMS arrives, while the subject starts to or continues to injure themselves runs counter to the goal of getting them to the hospital as safely as possible. However, whenever there is NOT imminent risk, it should be considered by first responders to wait until EMS is on scene before making contact with a person suspected of being in a state of Excited Delirium.

One way to help officers understand the dangers that individuals in excited delirium states present to themselves is the concept of "capture myopathy," a term from the veterinary sciences that deals with the issues related to capturing animals and the physical stressors that accompany their capture. Capture myopathy is a physical condition that may result in death. Relating this to the capture of the suspected Excited Delirium subject is an easy one considering that the longer the struggle goes on with first responders the greater the risk for the subject. Thus, whenever it is possible to have EMS on scene before going hands on with the subject it lessens the potential for making the current condition of the subject worse.

The EMS unit should stage closer to the subject than is usual in many other situations; however, this is not to say they should put themselves in needless jeopardy. Given that EMS personnel have the training and resources to deal with the medical emergency, it is critical that they be in a position to see the subject as soon as possible. If there is a field sedation protocol in place, it will be important for them to observe the subject to estimate the amount of medication needed, or at the very least, to call in to the Emergency Room to get orders from the attending physician. It is, of course, incumbent upon the law enforcement personnel to keep the EMS personnel safe, as they do not have the means to protect themselves from serious injury should the subject attack.

It might be a good time to briefly discuss the types of medications that your EMS Medical Director could consider using in these situations. To be clear, I am not making any recommendations on medication here; that is the provenance of medical personnel. Nonetheless, it is essential that all stakeholders understand something about the medications that are used for field sedation, so that they can put in place restraint procedures best suited to facilitate their administration. One common sedative that most ambulances carry currently is midazolam, which also goes by the trade name, Versed®. A drug that my EMS Medical Director is currently using on the ambulance rigs is Ketamine. This is a dissociative anesthetic that has been used for a long time, mainly in the Emergency Room, not in the field. This has started to change and is being considered and used in more than just my area of East-Central Illinois. [36] Whatever your EMS crews carry, it is incumbent on law enforcement to know the best way for the Paramedics to deliver the drug to the subject and what law enforcement will need to do to facilitate that delivery.

The role of the Fire Rescue personnel is to support the EMS personnel with the treatment of the subject. This can be through driving the ambulance from the scene to the hospital, or by helping with the treatment of the subject in the back of the ambulance. If EMS and Fire are separate, it is important to note that the rescue truck does not have to have a code response. It is also important to make sure they don't park too close, which might make it hard for other emergency vehicles to enter or exit the scene.

I have adapted a method of control originally developed by Mr. Chris Lawrence, of the Ontario Police College in Ontario, Canada. I refer to it as Multiple Officer Control Tactic (MOCT – see step-by-step illustrations at the end of this section). As the first responding officers arrive on the scene, it is important to assess what is actually happening. This will minimize the potential for missing important information, such as dangerous environmental conditions or other people with injuries that are not recognized because your attention is too focused on the subject.

As soon as reasonably possible, officers along with EMS/Fire personnel should develop a plan on addressing the incident. This will mean officers will need to know if the EMS paramedic will sedate the subject. This decision is the sole discretion of the paramedic and not law enforcement personnel. Law enforcement should have someone designated to be in charge of the incident, a quarterback, if you will, to assign personnel and keep track of what is going on. This does not have to be the highest-ranking person at the scene, just someone who is running the operation.

The quarterback will assign what limb each officer will be responsible for as well as the less lethal weapon officer, if one is available. Advising the capture officers of the EMS decision on whether or not there will be a sedative given, will let the officers know what steps will be taken once control is gained of the subject.

Now that there is a plan for capturing the subject that includes EMS, it is important to consider which less lethal weapon options are available to the officers.
- OC spray may temporarily blind the subject, but it can not be counted on to incapacitate a subject in this extremely agitated state.
- Electronic Control Devices (ECDs) (i.e. Tasers®) provide a means to knock the subject down from a distance as opposed to tackling the subject. It must be understood that voluntary compliance is unlikely when a person is in this state, so the number of deployments should focus only on getting the person to the ground, and allowing the officers to get into a position to control the limbs. If an agency equips their officers with ECDs, the subject can best be put under control and restraint through "cuffing under power." This tactic has been taught as a part of the ECD usage and works well when dealing with resistive arrest subjects and may prove effective with the Excited Delirium subject as well. A clear distinction must be made between this procedure and any attempt to use an ECD device to *elicit* compliance. This will NOT happen with a subject in an excited delirium state.
- Some agencies have less lethal impact rounds known as bean bag rounds, as well as plastic impact rounds. These could also be used as knock down options, provided they are available at the scene, or close by.

- The last option would be for a physical takedown of the subject. There are studies that have shown that going "hands on", physically grabbing, wrestling, or fighting a subject, has the greatest potential for injury to both the subject as well as the officers involved. We must get physical control of the subject that requires hands on control, but the takedown should be viewed as a last resort in lieu of other less lethal means.

After capturing the subject, they are placed face down with arms out to their sides and feet spread apart. This position makes it the hardest for the subject to resist or attack the officers. This position is also consistent with the arrest and control tactics used most often by law enforcement. In other words, it is NOT necessary to learn a completely new arrest tactic for an incident that may happen infrequently.

I have adapted a method of control originally developed by Mr. Chris Lawrence, of the Ontario Police College in Ontario, Canada. I refer to it as Multiple Officer Control Tactic (MOCT). The tactic isolates the shoulders of the subject by placing the armpits of the officer on the back of the subject's shoulders, raising the subject's wrists, turning their palms to the sky, placing the officers legs in a position so it is the legs that are keeping the subject's arms raised, and finally moving the arms above the shoulder line to completely isolate the shoulders. This makes the shoulder a weak joint and does not allow the subject to bring their arms under their body, which continues the struggle.

The legs are controlled by separating them and having the officers put their chests on top of the subject's legs just above the ankle. Whether the officers are back to back, or in between the subject's legs, the subject will not be able to keep moving forward, something that could enable them to continue the struggle. If there is a fifth officer available, this person should be up at the subject's head, pushing down on the shoulder blades. This would be the best position for the quarterback, since this person has the best view of the entire control process.

One of the advantages of this MOCT is that there is no one lying on the subject's back or lower abdomen. Concerns about restricting the subject's breathing from too much weight on their back are alleviated because it is based on mechanical control of each limb in such a way that prevents the subject from moving, not weight on the subject's back. **Another benefit of the MOCT is that it is gross motor skills based. Since these subjects are often sweating profusely, possibly covered in blood, the fine motor arrest tactics often taught in academies, are not very effective. The gross motor tactics of the MOCT allow officers to control the arms and legs of these subjects effectively in the sometimes cramped conditions that they face.**

This MOCT position can be accomplished with four officers, and as few as three officers. Fewer than that, and there is no reasonable way to prevent the subject from continuing to struggle. The MOCT can be performed by EMS and Fire personnel along with law enforcement. As long as personnel understand the mechanics of how to isolate the different limbs, the subject can be controlled. In communities where there are only one or two officers available, two well-trained EMS personnel and/or Fire personnel could give you enough people to capture and control the subject.

Once the subject's limbs are controlled by the personnel on the scene, this is the point that the sedation can occur, if EMS has a sedation protocol in place. The type of sedative used will dictate the best position of the subject to administer the sedative. If there is to be an injection of the sedative, the buttocks and the thigh are positioned as to make this possible. If a nasal-atomized sedative is used, it is better for the subject to be mechanically restrained prior to placing the subject on their back in order to deliver the sedative. As stated previously, the decision to sedate or not sedate is solely the Paramedic's, not the law enforcement officer.

There are going to be incidents where either there are not enough officers present or EMS has advised that sedation is not going to take place which will mean the process may have to be adapted to the situation at hand.

It is important to understand that whatever means officers, EMS, and/or Fire personnel use to capture the Excited Delirium subject there must be frequent training that involves all of the participants. This develops the common understanding of what each of the responders will do or can do to assist in getting the subject controlled.

It has been documented in numerous incidents that the subject in this state will continue to struggle with the very people that are capable of helping them. Please understand, however, that field sedation is not a panacea. Sedation allows the EMS personnel to begin to treat the subject's underlying life-threatening medical issues as quickly as possible.

Once the sedation has been given, or if there is no sedation protocol in place, or the Paramedic does not choose to sedate the person, the subject will need to be restrained in such a way as to allow the EMS personnel to treat the subject safely. This is accomplished by using multiple sets of handcuffs so as to allow the subject to be placed on their back with their arms down by their sides. This gives the EMS personnel access to the subject's veins in the arms to get IVs started. Remember, that the hands must be cuffed with chain link handcuffs, not the hinged handcuffs, as hinged cuffs will torque the wrists when the subject is lying on their back. Once the arms are secured with enough handcuffs, a minimum of three in a daisy chain configuration, then the legs are restrained with a hobble restraint.

There are various types of hobble restraints, but a simple nylon web restraint with a couple of cam buckles allows the legs to be secured quickly together and then tied to the backboard. This will prevent the subject from kicking the EMS personnel in the squad, as well as the ER staff at the hospital. It is also easily removed at the hospital by either law enforcement or nursing staff.

After the arms and legs are secured, the subject should be placed in the "recovery position", on their left side, pending placement of the subject on a backboard. This position is recognized by EMS personnel as beneficial for the subject's heart, as well as preventing the subject from aspirating their own vomit, should that occur. If the EMS crew is already on hand, the subject will be placed directly on a backboard, and loaded into the ambulance.

The subject should be secured onto the backboard, in the supine (face up) position, with whatever standard restraints are used by your local EMS crews. Some will use larger nylon straps with buckles, or they may use "spider straps" to keep the subject secure on the backboard. Once they are secured on the backboard, they are loaded onto the gurney and then placed in the ambulance, where at least one officer will ride with the ambulance crew. The quarterback will need to make this assignment to ensure someone rides with the subject. The officer's role is to advise the EMS staff of what occurred with the subject before the ambulance arrived. The officer is also on hand to be able to release the subject from the handcuffs should this be needed by the EMS personnel. The officer should take note the actions of the EMS personnel with the subject, while en route to the hospital for future documentation.

Upon arrival at the hospital, the officer should advise the ER staff of the subject's actions before they arrived on the scene as well as actions taken with the subject after their arrival. This will give the ER staff a better idea on what has happened to the subject since law enforcement and EMS arrived to treat the subject. **The request for a core body temperature should be made as soon as possible.** Subjects with very high body temperatures are consistent with people in this state. Unfortunately, if the core body temperature is not taken, a valuable piece of evidence is missing, which could help to explain the dire state the subject was in, at the time of law enforcement involvement.

There are several other tests, in addition to the core body temperature, that the ER physician can order that will help them identify the medical state the subject is in and what direction the treatment will take. This can be a "work up" of several tests that include:

- Initial vital signs
- Arterial Blood Gas
- Serum Lactate (acid level)
- CBC (red and white blood cells) and Complete Metabolic Panel
- Total CK and CKMB, Troponin (for heart attack)
- ETOH (alcohol)
- TSH (thyroid)
- 10 drug urine (drugs of abuse), urine HCG (females only)
- EKG, CXR
- Head CT without contrast

This is not a complete list, but one that will help the ER physician get an idea on the current status of the subject. These tests are for the physician to help treat the subject, but if the subject dies, they then become critical evidence of the dire medical condition the subject was in when law enforcement made contact.

If the subject dies, there most certainly will be a thorough investigation. However, if the subject does not die, the opportunity is usually missed for further investigation. The incident may be memorialized in the station house story of the "naked guy out in the snow bank". This loses a valuable opportunity to document what Dr. Mash has called "flicker events" in which a person gets into this excited state and then works their way out of it. These flicker events could be predictors of future incidents that portend a dire ending.

One consideration, made in conjunction with your coroner and your medical examiner, should be to harvest the brain sections of the subject who has just expired. This must be done, generally, within 12 hours and the samples sent to Dr. Deborah Mash from the University of Miami's Brain Endowment Center for analysis.[37] Dr. Mash is able to test for heat shock proteins and cocaine levels in the brain of the subject that can help investigators, coroners, and medical examiners in identifying the incident as an Excited Delirium incident. Specimen kits are available from Dr. Mash and should be kept available in the event that a sudden in-custody death has occurred and it has the signs and behaviors that are consistent with a suspected Excited Delirium case.

The focus of this investigation should be on recreating at least the last 24 hours before the incident, but preferably longer. This will create a complete picture of the various factors that led to the involvement of law enforcement and EMS. The force used to gain control of the subject will be reviewed for reasonableness, but the investigation should not remain at that level.

There are numerous incidents where the subject was demonstrating superhuman strength, seemingly unlimited endurance, and incredible pain tolerance. These behaviors are what have led law enforcement and corrections to use force that is needed to get the subject under control and to the hospital. If the subject dies then the investigation tends to focus just on the force and not what might have caused the behavior in the first place.

Investigators should attempt to collect as much medical information as possible about the subject. This may indicate the serious medical condition the subject was in at the time that law enforcement and EMS were contacted. If the medical tests were done, as previously stated, for medical purposes, then the results will be available for investigative purposes. The goal is to completely explain what happened, and what actions were taken in order to give the subject the best *possibility* of survival.

Investigators should attempt to collect information from the subject's criminal, medical, psychiatric, social worker, hospitalization, and jail/prison histories. This could give the investigator clues to other underlying causes for the subject's behavior. Evidence regarding the subject's prescribed medications as well as if the subject was compliant or non-compliant with those prescriptions should be located.

Witnesses and responders should be interviewed as soon as possible for their observations of the subject and the timeline of those observations. This will help the investigator understand the progress of the subject's behavior leading to their involvement with law enforcement personnel. The longer witnesses go without being interviewed, the greater the potential for failed or distorted recollections.

Since the officer was only concerned with the recognition that the subject needed to receive medical attention, and not with what caused the subject's behavior, it is now the investigator's task to seek to identify the cause of the incident. Primary emphasis should be on stimulant drug abuse and then possible psychiatric causes. The investigator will face a difficult task if the medical testing mentioned previously was not done.

The investigator and administrator should understand that it is usually *after* the subject has already reached an out-of-control state that the call goes out for assistance. Because of this, law enforcement is already behind the curve on this subject's condition. The process of sudden, unexpected, in-custody death has been likened to a "freight train to death". If law enforcement is called and arrives on scene with a subject who is already "pulling into the station"; as they may have reached the tipping point in which their physical condition is irreversible. The officers are then left in a state of bewilderment, wondering what could have been done differently.

If the investigation focuses on just what the officers did and not the condition of the subject, the potential for inaccurate conclusions is possible. This will not help the family of the subject, the officers involved, the agency, or the community to understand the incident.

SUMMARY

To summarize, dispatch personnel should gain as much information from the caller, on the condition of the subject, as possible. It is important to understand this could be a *medical emergency* that requires the appropriate number of officers, correctional personnel, EMS, and Advanced Life Support (ALS) to be dispatched to the scene.

If the officers observe the subject acting in an agitated chaotic manner *before* the call comes in from dispatch, they should assume that this is likely a *medical emergency*, and call for additional backup and EMS as soon as possible. The officer should assess the situation and determine the need to make contact with the subject, dependent upon the circumstances. It is preferable wait to make contact until EMS is on scene, unless the previously described exceptions are present.

A plan, in conjunction with EMS, should be made as quickly as possible in order to capture the subject. Once the subject is face down on the ground, consider using the MOCT (Multiple Officer Control Tactic) to quickly overcome the subject's resistance. If sedation has been decided upon by EMS personnel, it is then necessary to control the subject until that is accomplished. Restraining the subject with enough handcuffs to keep the subject's hands to down by their sides as well as restraining their feet, to keep them from kicking first responders needs to be done in an organized manner. Remember the use of chain link handcuffs on the subject's wrists instead of hinged handcuffs to prevent possible injury to the subject's nerves.

The subject should then be secured to a backboard, face up, and loaded onto a gurney. Law enforcement or corrections should assist EMS in loading the subject into the ambulance. At least one officer should accompany EMS personnel to the hospital. It is necessary for the officer to articulate the subject's actions prior to the arrival of EMS, and any and all actions taken by law enforcement and EMS on the scene prior to arriving at the hospital.

Careful documentation of each incident, especially those that survive, can paint a clear picture of the tense, uncertain, and rapidly evolving situation faced by the first responders.

This guide may be used as a template to develop your own multi-disciplinary response to this multi-faceted problem based on the resources available in your community.

If you have questions about this protocol, please contact Michael Paulus at
michael@michaelpaulustraining.com

Multiple Officer Control Tactic (MOCT) – An Illustrated Guide

Figure#1- (Pin#1) Patient's arms are above the shoulder line with the officer's armpit on top of the shoulder. Patient's arms are controlled by officers by use of "figure four" along with a chain-link handcuff. Patient's arms are raised by using the officer's outside leg. Weight is kept off the patient's back to isolate the patient's shoulder.

Figure#2- (Pin#2) Patient's legs are moved out from the centerline of the body to limit their power. Officers wrap the patient's leg with their arms and tuck the heel under the armpit on the outside of their body. Weight is kept low towards the patient's ankles.

Figure#3- (Pin#3) Skeletal isolation is maintained by having two officers on the arms, two officers on the legs and then one officer at the patient's head. The officer at the patient's head is pushing down on the patient's trapezius muscles and monitoring the patient's status. This can be achieved by as few as three officers.

Figure#4- (Sedation#1) - EMS IM injection is achieved after the "quarterback" has confirmed that the arms and legs are controlled enough to allow EMS to approach the patient. EMS will move in from the sides which allow better access to buttocks or upper thigh of the patient.

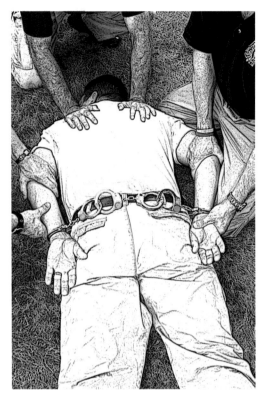

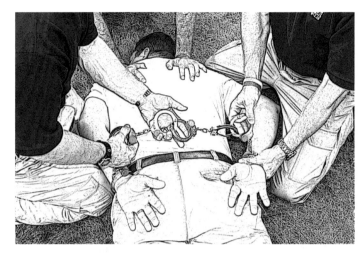

Figure#6- (Cuffing#2) - If the subject is larger, then four or more sets of handcuffs should be applied so that the patient can be placed in the supine position.

Figure#5- (Cuffing#1) - Once sedation has been given, officers will bring one arm behind the back at a time and apply at least three sets of handcuffs in a daisy chain configuration to allow the patient to be turned to a supine position. This will allow EMS to access the arm to establish an IV if warranted.

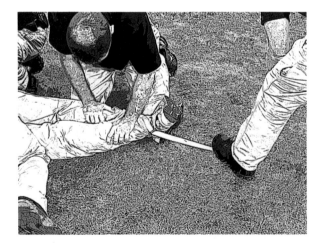

Figure#7- (Cuffing#3) - The patient's legs are brought together, ankles crossed if possible, then the nylon hobble is applied and pulled away from the patient. The other officer holds the patient's legs to keep them secured.

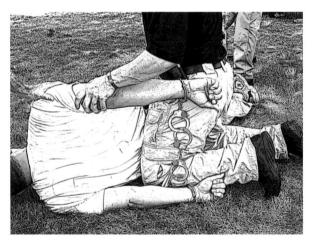

Figure#8- (Recovery#1) - If EMS is not on scene when the patient is captured, the officers are advised to place the patient in the left recovery position until EMS arrives on scene. Sedation can still be administered in this position.

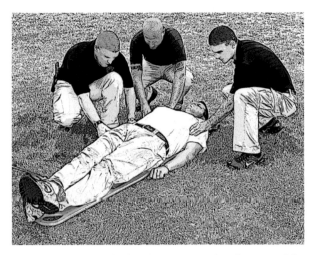

Figure#9- (Backboard#1) - The patient is placed on top of the backboard with the series of handcuffs under their back. This starts to limit the patient's ability to resist.

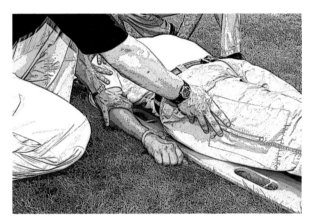

Figure#10- (Backboard#2) - Close-up showing patient on top of handcuffs while on top of the backboard.

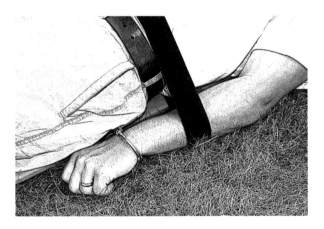

Figure#11- (Backboard#3) - Close-up of patient's arms while handcuffs are under the body and spider straps are applied. Notice that an IV could be started while in this position.

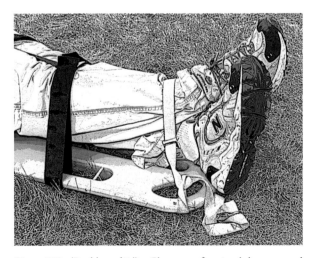

Figure#12- (Backboard#4) - Close-up of patient's legs secured to the backboard using the spider straps and the nylon hobble tied to the end of the backboard.

Endnotes

1   This book doesn't cover physical defensive tactics. We will not discuss techniques of evasion, breaking free of holds, restraint, or combat. Those tactics need to be learned first-hand and can't be addressed in a text. The only route to skill in force-on-force defensive tactics is pattern drills and pressure-testing: a type of training where you can, within circumscribed limits, go all out.

2   See Appendix A.

3   See Rhodes, Richard. (1999). *Why they kill: The discoveries of a maverick criminologist.* New York: Vintage, on the work of sociologist Lonnie Atkins, who coined the phrase "violentization," to describe the process in which a victim of violence becomes a perpetrator. Atkins focused on the family, but violentization can also occur later in life.

4   Rhodes, Ibid.

5   See Ekman, Paul. (2003). *Emotions revealed.* New York: Times Books, Henry Holt and Company.

6   One of the authors first learned this method from Ken Good of http://www .strategosintl.com/

7   You will sometimes see the same thing with people for whom English isn't a first language.

8   One of the best books on manipulation is: Allen, B. & Bosta, D. (1981-2002). *Games Criminals Play: How you can profit by knowing them.* Berkeley: Rae John Publishers. (ISBN: 0-9605226-0-3).

9   See: Hare, R. (1999). *Without conscience: The disturbing world of the psychopaths among us.* New York: Guilford Press.

10 Another term you may be familiar with is anti-social personality disorder. This diagnosis adequately describes the "criminal wing" of the psychopathic personality, and is a legitimate diagnosis in its own right. However, it doesn't adequately address the psychopath's "narcissistic wing," the qualities of callousness, sadism, grandiosity, etc. which complete the picture. In fact, some psychopaths never indulge in overtly criminal acts, at least not violent ones. They manipulate stock markets, run businesses, and become politicians instead.

11 We are grateful to the late Dan Kelleher, former professor of Antioch University, for the image of the "undamaged self."

12 Arieti, Silvano. (1974). *Interpretation of schizophrenia.* 2nd ed. New York: Basic Books.

13 Other major categories of stalkers are:

    a. **Relational stalkers** often an extension of a controlling or violent relationship, the stalker either keeps tabs on his or her partner, or pursues them once they have left.

    b. **Obsessive stalkers** a hyper-focus on the victim, not necessarily to kill or even harm, but always to control. This stalker can be well-aware that the victim does not desire contact, and may be afraid of or hate him. But just as the germ-obsessed person MUST wash his hands 50 times, despite *knowing* that they are clean, the obsessive stalker has to have the attention of his victim.

    c. **Psychopathic stalker** such an individual may certainly have been in a relationship or be obsessed with his victim. There is also considerable "ego" involved; this stalker's psychological energy focuses on himself rather than the victim. A true predator, he is doing something he enjoys. Why? Because he can (for amusement), or because the victim, in some way, offended him (for revenge).

14 Our thanks to Aaron Fields of the Seattle Fire Department for that example.

15 An actual incident. The engineer was killed trying to jump clear when the manic person wrecked the train.

16 Researchers note that a mixture of alcohol and cocaine is particularly dangerous, as the body synthesizes them together into a new substance, cocaethylene. See: http://jpet.aspetjournals .org /content/274/1/215.abstract

17 According to New Jersey Lawman website (http://www.njlawman.com/2002_ line_of_duty_deaths.htm), there were 120 line-of-duty deaths in 2009. This included homicide, vehicle accidents, line-of-duty illness, and accidental weapons discharge. According to a police suicide prevention website (http://www.policesuicideprevention.com/), there were 143 police officer suicides in 2009. Our thanks to Dr. Sherwin Cotler for drawing our attention to the availability of these statistics.

18 Sherwin Cotler, Ph.D., Personal Communication

[19] Kris Mohandie, Ph.D.; J. Reid Meloy, Ph.D., A.B.P.P.; and Peter I. Collins, M.C.A., M.D., F.R.C.P.(C). (2008). "Suicide by cop among officer-involved shooting cases." Other studies show different percentages of suicide by cop. Captain Rick Walls (see footnote 20 below) notes that in Los Angeles, the rate is about 10%, attributing this lower number to the high rate of officer-involved shootings involving non-suicidal gang members attempting to "shoot it out" with the police.

[20] The authors are extremely indebted to Captain Rick Walls of the Los Angeles Police Department for vital information on suicide by cop, which he presented at the Institute for the Prevention of In-Custody Death's 2010 Convention. Much of the information in this chapter, particularly in regards to the "preplanned event" is based on Captain Walls' information. He has kindly given permission for us to use his work here. Captain Walls in currently engaged in research regarding veterans, PTSD, traumatic brain injuries, suicide and suicide by cop. In addition to the information we have cited in the text, Captain Walls can provide essential information on investigation of suicide by cop, and help for officers, their family members and surviving family members of the suicidal person. He can be contacted at rick@rwallsassociates.com.

[21] The authors are aware of one case where a surgeon was making cuts on her wrists. Given her skill, it was clear that she was *not* putting herself at risk. She cut perfectly and called punctually for help. She was informed that she would be arrested for the next incident and she discontinued the behavior.

[22] Levinas, E. (1985). *Ethics and infinity: Conversations with Philip Nemo.* translated by Richard Cohen, Pgh, PA: Duquesne University Press. See also, Grossman, D. (1996). *On Killing: The psychological cost of learning to kill in war and society.* Santa Ana, CA: Back Bay Books.

[23] De Becker. G. (1997). *The gift of fear: Survival signals that protect us from violence.* United States and Canada: Little Brown and Company.

[24] Consider the so-called "21 foot rule" regarding bladed weapons. A person can cut you from considerable distance before you can deploy your weapon. That rule, however, is too simplistic. As one defensive tactics expert, Chris LeBlanc, stated to one of the authors: "That is being re-visited on a few levels. Dennis Tueller, the originator of the drill, actually apologized for it (tongue in cheek) at some firearms thing that our range-master went to. He meant it to just be an illustration of reaction times, but the *Surviving Edged Weapons* video sort of made it law. Compounding the problem is that the original presentation concerned an officer standing there with a *holstered* weapon. The range is different if your weapon is drawn and aimed at the knife-wielder. Some officers seem to think that if a guy with a knife is within 21 feet, he is automatically "shootable," and somehow, if he's beyond 21 feet, they are safe. Most officers will get it if it's placed in context. So, if he's twenty-five feet away, he's not a threat? Really. Or, How about if he's ten feet away, but there's a barrier between you that he will have to climb over to get at you. Do you need to shoot him because he's within 21 feet? On the other hand, even assuming you are weapon-up and firing, even if you get hits, you often will not stop the attacker, even with center mass shots, at least not before he can be on you and doing damage. When that is considered, one considers putting the distance out further, to 30 feet, to put more (telling) rounds on. What is being looked at now is simply that, as in so many cases 'situation dictates.' The problem with that is that it highlights the needs of realistic force-on-force training at regular intervals. How can one read situations that one hasn't ever experienced, even in drills?"

[25] We first heard this method presented by David Grossman. See above reference for his book, *On Killing* (endnote 22).

[26] See the work of Dr. John Gottman of the University of Washington for a detailed discussion of contemptuous silence and stonewalling.

[27] We owe the image of the hands as a fence to Geoff Thompson, who has authored a number of books on his career as a doorman in violent British pubs, as well as exemplary books on self-defense.

[28] We are indebted to John Holttum, MD, Child Psychiatrist from Tacoma, Washington. One of the authors attended a presentation given by Dr. Holttum which influenced us greatly in terms of how to "subdivide" the presenting behaviors of youth and how best to intervene with them. We must underscore that any intervention recommendations are ours, and may be at variance to those Dr. Holttum might offer.

[29] Louv, Richard. (2005). *Last child in the woods: Saving our children from nature-deficit disorder.* Chapel Hill, NC: Algonquin Books. And Sax, Leonard. (2007). *Boys adrift: The five factors driving the growing epidemic of unmotivated boys and underachieving young men.* Philadelphia: Basic Books.

[30] The authors owe a debt for some of the basic information in this section to a form of training called Professional Assault Response Training (PART), thanks to a workshop one of us attended approximately 20 years ago. We have made major changes in their basic 4-part schema, as well as adding a significant amount of new data. Therefore, our approach is, in many aspects, quite different, and it shouldn't be confused with PART's procedures.

[31] Dr. Sherwin Cotler, Ph.D. Written communication.

[32] Salter, Anna, author of *Predators: Pedophiles, rapists and other sex offenders. Who they are, how they operate and how we can protect ourselves and our children.* New York: Basic Books. Our gratitude for the formulation of overwhelming force/respect that she presented in a great story during a seminar.

[33] de Becker, Gavin. (1997). *The gift of fear: Survival signals that protect us from violence.* United States and Canada: Little Brown and (1999) *Protecting the gift: Keeping children and teenagers safe (and parents sane).* New York: Random House.

[34]   This is a brief discussion of a much more complicated issue. It is beyond the scope of this text to go into such planning in detail as this involves a lot of players beyond law enforcement, and gets into a lot of "political" issues on how one responds to the distress of mentally ill or emotionally disturbed people. Inquiries on such case planning should be directed to Ellis Amdur (www.edgework.info)

[35]   The American College of Emergency Physicians (ACEP) put out a white paper in September of 2009 that expressed the ideas that were already in place in Champaign County almost a year prior.

[36]   Note articles regarding the use of Versed and Ketamine that would be of interest to your local EMS Medical Director. American Journal of Emergency Medicine (2007) 25, 977-980; European Journal of Emergency Medicine (2007), Vol 14 No 5, 265-269; Emergency Medicine Journal (2004) 21, 351-354

[37]   Dr. Deborah C. Mash, http://www.exciteddelirium.org/, (305)243-6219, University of Miami, Department of Neurology.

ABOUT THE AUTHORS

Ellis Amdur

Edgework founder Ellis Amdur received his B.A. in psychology from Yale University in 1974 and his M.A. in psychology from Seattle University in 1990. He is both a National Certified Counselor and a State Certified Child Mental Health Specialist. He has written a number of books concerning communication with mentally ill and emotionally disturbed individuals and the de-escalation of aggression, all of which can be secured through his website, www.edgework.info

Since the late 1960s, Amdur has trained in various martial arts systems, spending thirteen of these years studying in Japan. He is a recognized expert in classical and modern Japanese martial traditions and has authored three iconoclastic books on the subject, as well as one instructional DVD.

Since his return to America in 1988, Ellis Amdur has worked in the field of crisis intervention. He has developed a range of training and consultation services, as well as a unique style of assessment and psychotherapy. These are based on a combination of phenomenological psychology and the underlying philosophical premises of classical Japanese martial traditions. Amdur's professional philosophy can best be summed up in this idea: the development of an individual's integrity and dignity is the paramount virtue. This can only occur when people live courageously, regardless of the circumstances, and take responsibility for their roles in making the changes they desire.

Ellis Amdur is a dynamic public speaker and trainer who presents his work throughout the United States and internationally. He is noted for his sometimes outrageous humor as well as his profound breadth of knowledge. His vivid descriptions of aggressive and mentally ill people and his true-to-life role-playing of the behaviors in question give participants an almost first-hand experience of facing the real individuals in question. For further information please see Amdur's website: www.edgework.info

John Hutchings

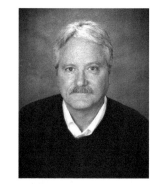

John Hutchings is the Chief of Police for the Tenino Police Department in Washington State. He began his law enforcement career with the City of Orange, California, where he grew up. He, his wife, and two children moved to Olympia in 1985. He served 27 years with the Olympia Police Department before taking over as Chief of Police in Tenino.

Hutchings has worked in every capacity police work has to offer, giving him a very broad base of experience. He completed his B.A. at The Evergreen State College (Olympia) in 2000. He completed his M.A. in Organizational Leadership from Chapman University (Orange, California) in 2004. Besides his M.A., he obtained graduate certificates in Organizational Development and Human Resources.

Chief Hutchings is a Fulbright Scholar (2007/08). He lived in England for three months while conducting a multi-country research project studying the effects of critical incident stress debriefings on police officers. The results of his research are pending publication.

John collaborated with NAMI (National Advocates for the Mentally Ill), and a host of local professionals from the mental health field to create Olympia's CIT program. He is eternally grateful for their work, mentorship, and friendship.

Hutchings has presented at numerous mental health conferences around the State of Washington. He presented on CIT in Sydney, Australia (2003) for the International Congress on Law and Mental Health. John worked closely with a Sergeant from Newcastle, England on the development and assessment of the U.K.'s first Mental Health Awareness pilot course. On behalf of England's National Health Service, John has presented numerous times in North Yorkshire, England on crisis intervention and officer involved shootings. His audiences include the officer on the beat, police command staff, psychologists, and psychiatrists, both experienced and those in training.

Chief John Hutchings is an engaging and entertaining presenter drawing on his years of firsthand police experience dealings with the mentally ill, and involvement with critical incidents.

For additional information, contact Chief Hutchings at jfhutch@ci.tenino.wa.us or 360.742.2529.